"**Captured!** fills in many of the inevitable gaps in our knowledge of the famous Betty and Barney Hill case, and is therefore a must for anyone interested in the remarkable gestation period of UFO abduction research. It is touching but not surprising to read that the brave and prescient investigators who took the Hills' experience seriously assumed that it was a unique, momentous, and isolated event, and never suspected that, instead, it was only the first of thousands of similar covert encounters from the '40s, '50s, and '60s to receive wide public attention. **Captured!** abundantly demonstrates that the most important aspect of the Hills' 1961 abduction lies in their personal courage and integrity in permitting their frightening experience and its later investigation to become public. Tens of thousands of abductees have benefitted from the Hills' extraordinary role in opening doors to the serious study of the UFO abduction phenomenon, thus making possible new therapeutic strategies to help treat their traumas. In the pages of **Captured!**, Betty and Barney Hill emerge, not as victims, but as true, undaunted modern heroes."

> —Budd Hopkins
> World-renowned UFO abduction researcher,
> author of *Witnessed* and *Missing Time*

"Many books have been written about people being abducted by aliens, but *Captured!* tops them all. It is powerful, detailed, and personal. Drawing on the actual diaries written by Betty Hill, this book exposes the shocking events that took place during and after she and her husband Barney were abducted by aliens in the White Mountains of New Hampshire. Further, it documents their many hours of hypnotherapy with Dr. Benjamin Simon and their close ties with military personnel at Pease Air Force Base. Capped by official government records of UFO activity at the time, a replication of the Star Map seen by Betty, and an analysis of the clothing she was wearing at the time of the abduction, all mundane explanations for the event have been eradicated. It really happened."

> —John F. Schuessler
> Mutual UFO Network, Inc.,
> International Director, Emeritus

"With **Captured!,** internationally known UFO investigator/nuclear physicist/lecturer Stanton Friedman, and Betty and Barney Hill's niece, Kathleen Marden, take the historically significant UFO event of the Hills' double abduction and educate the reader with meaningful, typically never mentioned, rich in too-many-to-list details that show the Hills to be blood and flesh, neighbors-next-door-type individuals—not merely footnotes in a UFO double abduction case. The revelations of previously little known personal details of their abduction experience trauma impressed me—a hypnotherapist dealing with abduction trauma—with the similarity of Betty's and Barney's encounters to my own subjects."

—Yvonne Smith, C.Ht.
Director, Close Encounters Resource Organization

Praise for **Top Secret/Majic**

"The most explosive book yet on UFOs."
—*Star Magazine*

"Friedman operates mostly as a scientist, carefully weighing all evidence before coming to a conclusion."
—*Library Journal*

"This book will delight those who can't get enough of crashed saucers and government cover-ups."
—*Booklist*

"Friedman has been involved in UFO research for more than a quarter century. During that time, he has struggled tirelessly against a vast amount of resistance on almost every level. He has uncovered hoaxes, discovered hidden truths, and has fought arrogant bureaucrats and fallacy-happy UFO debunkers, not to mention other researchers eagar to discredit him for their own ends. He is one of the few truly professional UFO researchers."
—Whitley Strieber
New York Times best-selling author of *Communion*

THE TRUE STORY
OF THE WORLD'S
FIRST DOCUMENTED
ALIEN ABDUCTION

CAPTURED!

*The Betty and Barney Hill
UFO Experience*

STANTON T. FRIEDMAN, MSc.
AND KATHLEEN MARDEN

NEW PAGE BOOKS
A division of The Career Press, Inc.
Franklin Lakes, NJ

CAPTURED! THE BETTY AND BARNEY HILL UFO EXPERIENCE
EDITED BY KARA REYNOLDS
TYPESET BY EILEEN DOW MUNSON
Cover design by Howard Grossman/1 2e Design
Printed in the U.S.A. by Book-mart Press

To order this title, please call toll-free 1-800-CAREER-1 (NJ and Canada: 201-848-0310) to order using VISA or MasterCard, or for further information on books from Career Press.

The Career Press, Inc., 3 Tice Road, PO Box 687,
Franklin Lakes, NJ 07417
www.careerpress.com
www.newpagebooks.com

Library of Congress Cataloging-in-Publication Data

Marden, Kathleen.
    Captured! : the Betty and Barney Hill UFO experience : the true story of the world's first documented alien abduction / by Kathleen Marden and Stanton Friedman.
        p. cm.
    Includes bibliographical references and index.
    ISBN-10: 156414-971-4
    1. Alien abduction. 2. Hill, Betty (Eunice) 3. Hill, Barney. I. Friedman, Stanton T. II. Title.

BF2050.M353 2007
001.942--dc22

                                                            2007011941

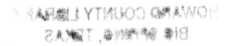

Stanton and Kathy wish to thank the following people:

Jerry Baker, for permission to publish her late husband David's watercolor paintings;

Phyllis Budinger, for her expert opinion on the chemical analyses;

Thomas Elliott, for his generous contribution;

Marjorie Fish, for her curiosity, patience, and perseverance;

Picture Perfect, for the photo donation;

Patrick Richard, for permission to publish his paintings;

Ben Swett, for his sworn statement and guidance;

Walter Webb, for his investigation, guidance, and generous contributions;

Bruce Maccabee, for reviewing the manuscript and writing the foreword;

Linda Moulton Howe, John Schuessler, and Yvonne Smith, for reviewing the manuscript and writing an endorsement;

All of the anonymous individuals for their behind the scenes assistance;

and John White, our literary agent, for seeing this through.

Additionally we want to acknowledge the splendid effort by the people at Career Press/New Page Books to expedite publication. We truly appreciate your efforts.

Special thanks to Kathy Marden's husband,
Charles,
and Stanton Friedman's wife,
Marilyn,
for their unremitting support and understanding; and
Barbara Stavropoulos,
for her daily injection of humor.

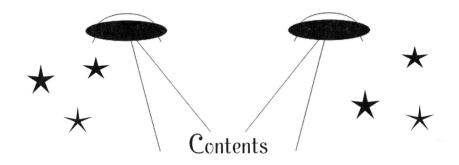

Contents

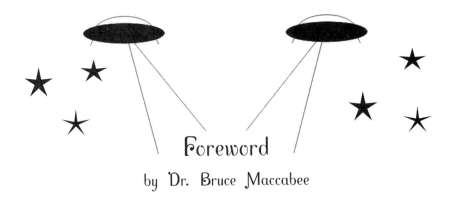

Foreword

by Dr. Bruce Maccabee

After all these years since I first read their story, I still find it somewhat amazing that the aliens didn't know how to operate a zipper and would have ripped Betty's dress off her if she hadn't shown them how to operate it. (Perhaps they had forgotten because it was so long ago in their cultural history, or perhaps they had bypassed the zipper period of development and jumped directly to the Velcro period.) And after all these years I am still surprised that *they* were surprised that Barney's teeth could be removed, but Betty's couldn't. Did they also bypass the false teeth era? Or perhaps the aliens don't have teeth. So now we know that way back then they didn't know everything. But they *did* demonstrate their technical superiority by performing on Betty what appears to have been an amniocentesis several years before that procedure was common in Earth hospitals. Well, it seemed to be an amniocentesis, but maybe it was something else far more advanced. Will we ever know?

And my mind still boggles over the way Betty allowed all that pink dusty stuff to just blow away in the wind. It was chemical evidence of the abduction! And then there were the shiny spots on the car with the rotating magnetic fields that were ignored by investigator Walter Webb. What? Did you say rotating magnetic fields in the metal of a car? That's *impossible*!

Reading this book I felt that "it's deja vu all over again," except this time I was learning the answers to questions I had when I first read about Betty and Barney Hill almost 40 years ago. Furthermore, I now had the benefit of 40 years of UFO history and my own investigations into numerous sightings. Way back then, in that ufologically more innocent era, when flying saucers seen in the sky and perhaps on the ground were essentially the whole story, I could not have known that numerous other cases of abduction would be reported over the ensuing decades.

To more fully understand the historical importance of the Betty and Barney Hill case, one must turn back the clock to the 1960s, when the only public reports of direct interactions with "space beings" were the sightings reported by the so-called contactees (George Adamski being the most famous). These contactees reported enlightening and delightful experiences aboard highly advanced flying craft. They reported having conversations with friendly aliens who were protecting the world from evil on a cosmic scale and who advised humanity to stop building atomic bombs. The contactees told fantastic stories that attracted thousands of people to their numerous lectures. They enjoyed their cosmic interactions. They had a following.

Then along came Betty and Barney. They told family members, a few close friends, and some UFO investigators (including the Air Force) what they consciously remembered of a *traumatic experience* which had been *imposed upon them* (they had not asked to be abducted), and they explicitly requested that their story *not* be widely publicized. They wanted to live their lives as if the sighting events had not happened. (Their story became public several years later when this confidence was broken by a reporter who, against the Hills' wishes, published a major article in the *Boston Traveler*.)

This reluctance to publicize their story was unlike the publicity-seeking contactees. What I realized many years later was that their sighting report was the beginning of a paradigm shift that became apparent after the publication of Budd Hopkins's book *Missing Time* in 1981. By the early 1980s it was obvious that the people who told the stories of involuntary capture by aliens were not just a new form of contactees. Instead, they were involuntary *abductees*. The difference between the contactees and the abductees could be expressed in the following simple phrase: Contactees have a good time, *abductees don't*! (In the last 10 years or so there have been some people who would claim they were taken against their will, but then found that they appreciated the experience. I suppose in the future some people will consider it an honor to have been abducted and some people will actually look forward to abduction.)

I was one of the many who did not accept their story as true when I first read it in 1966 or 1967 in *The Interrupted Journey* (John Fuller, 1966).

I did not have the good fortune, as did Stanton Friedman, to meet the Hills many times through the years, and of course, I was not privy to any family discussions with the Hills, such as reported by Betty's niece, Kathy Marden. The information that was available in Fuller's book and published in numerous articles over the years did not give a complete account of the sighting events or the impact on the lives of the Hills, and left wiggle room for the skeptics to propose earthly explanations. This book, unlike Fuller's, contains more than just a history of the Hills' abduction. It also contains numerous refutations of the explanations offered by the skeptics in the years since Fuller's book. Information that was left out during the original telling of the story, but available in the hypnosis transcripts and other documents, is now brought forth to confront the proposed explanations. Coauthor Marden is clearly thoroughly familiar with the skeptical arguments as well as with the Hill abduction information, and she brings forth the refuting information each time she reaches an event that has been "explained." For example, one of the first explanations was by the Air Force Project Blue Book investigator who suggested that the "light" they saw was only a powerful anti-aircraft searchlight on clouds, such as is sometimes used in cities for advertising purposes. This was ridiculous on the face of it, because they were in a rural area where there would be no use for a powerful spotlight. But also, there were hardly any clouds to shine the beam on. And, of course, they would have recognized it as a searchlight because they could have seen the glowing line made by the light beam going up to the clouds. Furthermore, a searchlight on clouds couldn't explain any of the numerous motions and other things the Hills described about the "light" they saw.

Another proposed explanation was that the Hills failed to identify a planet that appeared near the moon, and for some reason this caused them to panic and turn off the main road. This silly explanation is completely contradicted by the dynamics of the object in the sighting: It repeatedly moved back and forth, up and down, with large changes in sighting direction, and even crossed the face of the moon. Barney reported that through binoculars, while standing beside the car (before the abduction), he could see "people" inside the "light," and at one time these people seemed to be looking out through windows at him. It is well known that, *even with binoculars*, a planet does not appear to be windows with people looking out!

Much of the detailed descriptions of the events during the abduction were obtained during hypnosis sessions conducted by Dr. Benjamin Simon.

The skeptics have given Simon high marks for proposing a "logical" explanation for the abduction story: The various events during the abduction were all nightmares that Betty vocalized while sleeping, and Barney picked up on them and took them in as real events that had happened to him. (Simon was less certain about explaining the initial and final portions of the event that were consciously recalled in the days, weeks, and months *before* the hypnosis sessions began.) Of course, this does not explain how Barney's story could diverge considerably from Betty's, as it does in many places. Nevertheless, the skeptics did not criticize Simon when he tried to *lead the witnesses* into believing that his explanation was correct. He repeatedly tried to convince Betty and Barney that the abduction, with its strange windowed craft and crew of strange humanoids, were all results of dreams. They could not be led; they refused to accept his explanation.

The skeptics' willingness to accept Simon's attempt to lead the witnesses is in complete contrast to the criticisms that skeptics have leveled against other UFO investigators who have used hypnosis to retrieve abduction stories (for example, Budd Hopkins, David Jacobs, and John Mack). These investigators have been uniformly criticized for "leading the witness" to provide stories that the hypnotists want to hear. This is, however, a false criticism. Instead, these UFO investigators have been very careful to *avoid* leading the witnesses. They have even done experiments to find out if witnesses can be led away from their main story, so occasionally they have intentionally attempted to lead the witness away from a logical next step in a story or suggested something that contradicts some part of the story. When they do this they find out, *as did Dr. Simon*, that the witnesses are difficult or impossible to lead! The skeptics should reverse their opinion and compliment the investigators for discovering that the witnesses stick to their stories, even under hypnosis. (Incidentally, the alien "leader" told Betty that she probably would not remember much of the abduction and Barney wouldn't remember anything. Apparently the aliens did not understand the workings of the human brain as well as they thought they did.)

There is some physical evidence to confirm the Hills' story, aside from the possible radar confirmation that is described herein. There is, of course, the star map constructed by Marjorie Fish, which seems to provide an identification of the source of the alien craft (Zeta 1 or 2 of the constellation Reticulum). Then there is the chemical analysis, first reported in detail here, of the stains on Betty's dress, torn during the abduction. The important fact to be noted is that the stain cannot be explained as something normal. Then there are Betty's and Barney's watches, which had stopped and could not be restarted.

Finally, there are the shiny spots on the trunk of the car where a compass rotated rapidly. According to Betty, a physicist had suggested that she walk around the car with a compass and note where it pointed. (This physicist was probably aware of the numerous stories of magnetic effects of UFOs. For example, Fred Johnson, a prospector, was near Mt. Adams in the state of Washington in June, 1947, when saucer-like objects passed nearly overhead at high speed. He noted that his compass rotated as they passed by [see *brumac.8k.com/ KARNOLD/KARNOLD.html*]. So she got a compass and walked around the car holding the compass near it. She apparently saw nothing unusual, until she noticed the shiny spots that had not been there before their trip. When she held the compass over the shiny spots, the needle rotated. Thinking it might be because of hand vibration, she set the compass on a spot and took her hand away. The needle still rotated. Barney repeated her experiment, and a day later several other family members witnessed this strange effect, so there is no doubt that it occurred. The question is, what could have happened to a small area of the car to make a compass rotate? One can do a simple experiment: Place a compass on the flat, level surface of a car and see what happens. When I did it, nothing happened. Oh yes, the compass pointed in some direction, but it stayed there. I found that various locations on a car are magnetized in different directions (they make the compass point in different directions), so that if you *move* a compass along the surface of the car you may find that the direction of the needle changes, perhaps even rotates. But with the compass in a fixed position relative to the car, the needle stays in a fixed position. Only a rotating magnetic field could make the compass rotate. But how could there be a rotating magnetic field associated with the thin steel of the car body? It seems impossible! But apparently it was true. Were circulating currents within these spots causing a rotating field in the metal? (I don't know how currents could exist in the metal, and if they did, I don't know how they could make the field rotate.) Could rotating fields be left over from some bizarre thing like a magnetic "tractor beam" that made the beeping noises that seemed to come from the trunk of the car before and after the abduction? There have been numerous reports of cars stopping and other bizarre effects attributed to possibly magnetic effects of UFOs *when the UFOs were nearby*. But the spots on the trunk presented a presumably electromagnetic effect when the UFO (presumably) was *not* nearby. I know of only one other clear case of a strange electromagnetic effect that was present long after a UFO had departed from the scene (see *www.brumac.8k.com/MagneticUFO/MagneticUFO.html*).

With the publication of this book, the skeptics' wiggle room has shrunk to zero. No longer can they get away with ignoring or minimizing the importance of various details in order to claim they merely saw a light that "could be anything," or that they "misidentified a planet," or that they simply confabulated the whole story based on Betty's dreams. Instead, the Hills' story still stands as a strong reminder that we can't explain everything that happens—UFOwise or otherwise—in this universe, and we'd better be prepared for further surprises.

Dr. Bruce Maccabee
Author, *Abduction In My Life*

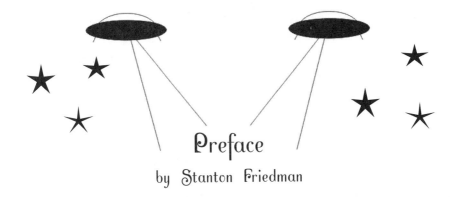

Preface

by Stanton Friedman

I had read John Fuller's *The Interrupted Journey* soon after it came out, as well as Fuller's article "Aboard a Flying Saucer" in the October 4 and October 18 issues of *Look Magazine*, 1996. The story was quite fascinating, but I didn't see any way to really validate it, so it was firmly in my "gray basket": not enough data. Certainly the basic concept of alien beings connected with flying saucers didn't bother me. It seemed reasonable that if there were alien spacecraft flying around our atmosphere, there would be beings inside some of the craft. Even allowing for remote-controlled devices, some intelligent being had to be running the controls. (It is interesting that in recent years many Western nations have developed unmanned aerial vehicles for reconnaissance and sometimes for attack purposes.)

I also wasn't particularly bothered by the humanoid appearance of the aliens. Space pioneer Willy Ley had long ago written an interesting analysis of how an advanced being should look—pretty much humanoid, with the head at the top (so as to spot the approach of enemies more quickly), two eyes to get 3-D imaging, two ears for binaural location skills, limbs for grasping, and so on. It seemed obvious, from looking at creatures on Earth, that there are favored arrangements. For example, few life forms seem to have three eyes, or three legs, or three ears.

What moved me into the acceptance column was the opportunity to have dinner with Betty and Barney in Pittsburgh, Pennsylvania, in November of 1968. I was working as a nuclear physicist on the NERVA nuclear rocket program at Westinghouse Astronuclear Laboratory in the small town of Large, just outside of Pittsburgh. We had an active UFO Research Institute that had started as the Pittsburgh Area

Subcommittee of the National Investigations Committee on Aerial Phenomena (NICAP) run by Major Donald Keyhoe. Our group had a lot of professional people, and we had separated from NICAP because we didn't want them controlling what we said in public. I was doing quite a bit of radio and TV work, having begun my public speaking as a the result of an appearance on the *Contact* talk show on KDKA radio. It was one of the oldest stations in the United States, and broadcast at a power level of 50,000 watts, clear channel. So, especially in the evening, there was a very large audience. A coworker at Westinghouse had heard my first show with host Mike Levine. His producer on *Contact* had called me at 6:30 one evening to see if I could do a 7 p.m. show. I suspect that he had called other people and had been turned down. Because I lived fairly close to the station, I agreed to do the show. Indianapolis broadcaster Frank Edwards had originally suggested to me that I get in touch with *Contact* in response to my query about to how to start going public about UFOs. I had met Frank in Indianapolis while working for the Allison Division of General Motors on the Military Compact Reactor Program. Frank sent me a copy of his book *Flying Saucers: Serious Business,* which became a best seller. Initially when I called the station, I was told, "don't call us, we will call you." Then, to my surprise, they did.

I had done a number of subsequent "CONTACT" shows, when people at KDKA called to ask if I was aware that Betty and Barney Hill would be in town to do a KDKA-TV program. I said I would very much like to meet them and was told, because the KDKA people trusted me, where they were staying. I called the Hills and we agreed to meet for dinner. I was impressed with Betty and Barney during the three hours we were together. It turned out that KDKA people were also impressed. The Hills were obviously intelligent, had a sense of humor, and never seemed to enlarge on what was in the book. In short, I bought the story. I was indeed fortunate to spend time with them both, because Barney died just three months later.

In the decades following Barney's death, I saw Betty many times at her home, at conferences, and during interviews for my documentary, *UFOs Are Real.* We appeared together on TV programs such as David Susskind's, and the *Tomorrow Show* with Tom Snyder.

Not too long thereafter, I received a call from Coral Lorenzen, cofounder (with her husband, Jim) of the Aerial Phenomena Research Organization in Tucson, Arizona. Coral told me that a woman named Marjorie Fish in Ohio was trying to make sense out of the star map that appeared in *The Interrupted Journey.* Although she was originally skeptical, a visit with Betty had inspired her to continue building three-dimensional models of our local galactic neighborhood. She was a member of Mensa (as I was at that time) and wanted to talk to a scientist to have her work checked. I was living in California by then and was traveling a lot. I talked to Marjorie, and during one of my trips, was able to visit her at her home in Ohio. At the time, she was employed as a 3rd-grade school teacher.

I discuss the Hill case and Fish's work at almost all my college lectures ("Flying Saucers ARE Real"), and use a slide of one of her largest models, an approximately 3-foot cube that contains 246 stars.

I helped explain Fish's work after a paper she gave at an annual symposium of the Mutual UFO Network in Akron, Ohio, in 1973. She was quite shy and was more at ease talking to astronomers than to the general public. I visited Fish, who was by this time in Oak Ridge, Tennessee, where she was now working as a technician for the Oak Ridge National Laboratory, when filming my documentary in 1978. I was co-script writer, technical advisor, arranged all the interviews, and was on location for all of them.

I shared my early information with Bobbie Ann Slate Gironda, a writer in Southern California with whom I worked on several UFO articles. The first-ever article about Fish's work appeared in *Saga* magazine for July, 1973, by Bobbie and myself. I instigated *Astronomy Magazine*'s article about Fish's work as well. Certainly that work gave me a whole new viewpoint on Earth's place in the scheme of things.

I was especially pleased that Kathy Marden invited me to help out some on this book. Frankly, I consider the Hill case one of the most important UFO cases ever investigated. The Hills were very active in their community, were well respected, and were certainly not seeking publicity when the story broke. Dr. Simon had an extraordinary professional background with regard to helping people through difficulties caused by apparently traumatic experiences. No, he didn't know much about UFOs, which means his own biases didn't push the story toward reality. This was the first abduction story that received such in-depth investigation in terms of the number of good people involved over a long period of time. It certainly opened the door for many other respectable people to be willing to risk telling their abduction stories. The intensive and careful star map research by Marjorie Fish gave a whole new perspective as to where alien visitors might originate and how different the colonization and space travel situations would be for intelligent beings just down the galactic street.

In the course of my lecturing on the subject in all 50 states, nine Canadian provinces, and 16 other countries throughout the past 39 years, I have often been asked what difference it makes if aliens are indeed visiting. Their visits should give us an entirely different perspective on how we look at ourselves. It takes us down from the top of the heap when we recognize how much more advanced, at least technologically, our visitors are than are we. It forces us to try to see how we must look to them. Clearly we Earthlings don't have our act together. Are we not a primitive society whose major activity is tribal warfare? As a nuclear guy I am much more aware than most of the dangers of nuclear proliferation. The best hope I see to avoid a nuclear holocaust is for us to begin, as Earthlings to recognize that the majority of problems on this planet are *planetary* problems requiring *planetary* solutions. Obviously, they include global warming, degradation of the environment, and inadequate use of our resources to feed, house, and educate our society. We need more understanding of our superficial differences, such as religion, skin color, gender, and nationalistic identity. These can't be effectively solved without cooperation. The easiest way for us to recognize that we all have something in common is to see ourselves as the aliens must see us. A review of the history of the abduction of Betty and Barney Hill is a major step in moving forward. Perhaps we can understand what our visitors want and why they haven't enslaved us as we Earthlings have so often enslaved the "others." My audiences react just as favorably to the story of Betty and Barney Hill now as they did decades ago when I first started telling it.

Introduction

by Kathleen Marden

In the early 1990s, when I embarked upon a historical journey through the life of my late aunt, the world-famous UFO abductee, Betty Hill, I could not have imagined that it would culminate in a book. Although family ties had assigned me a front-row seat to the UFO encounter's aftermath upon my aunt and her husband, Barney Hill, I devoted my adult life to other academic endeavors. I was aware of the lambasting that Betty had taken as a result of her claims of multiple UFO sightings, and I, as were her critics, was skeptical. I had also been indoctrinated by her claims about the unique characteristics of the hypnotic techniques of Dr. Benjamin Simon, who played such a large role in their lives pertaining to their UFO encounter. She insisted that, unlike other hypnosis inductions, Simon's enabled a pathway to the truth, without false memory formation. My background in education and social work and a wholesome dose of curiosity sent me spinning down a 15-year path to seeking the truth. I explored the work of the 20th-century hypnosis experts and immersed myself in the research currently being carried out in universities throughout America. I transcribed the Hills' hypnosis tapes and conducted a point-by-point comparative analysis of their regressions. Then I read Dr. Simon's scholarly work about his type of hypnosis and scrutinized his hypnotic suggestions to Betty and Barney. Along the way, I encountered the concept of false memory formation and the reasons why perfectly normal people come to believe fantastic, improbable personal information. Without prejudice, I pitted this information against the Hills' conscious, continuous memories of a UFO encounter and hypnotically recovered memories of an abduction.

From my position as a UFO investigator and the director of field investigator training for the Mutual UFO Network, the largest nonprofit public membership organization dedicated to the scientific investigation of UFOs, I plunged into the quagmire of UFO abductions. More specifically, I took aim at Betty. A natural debater, she reveled in the opportunity to set me straight when I played devil's advocate, which I most often did during hours of taped interviews. I witnessed her fiery denigration of other self-identified abductees and abduction investigators, and her defense of her own case. I read everything I could put my hands on, both pro and con, and interviewed the surviving individuals involved in her case, both military and civilian. It took me through many twists and turns, through the ambivalence of skepticism and reluctant belief. Along the way I encountered an abundance of inaccurate and misleading information. But I also found an abundance of solid, accurate, scientific research. I personally researched the Hills' personal, medical, and employment histories, and assessed their social and psychological makeup. To complete my research, I studied the chronological collection of correspondence spanning 40 years, to and from individuals who investigated the Hill UFO encounter.

There has been much speculation regarding Betty and Barney Hill's alleged UFO abduction on September 19, 1961. John Fuller's *The Interrupted Journey* introduced the general public to the initial investigation, the details of the events that the Hills consciously remembered, and the hypnosis. However, some of his facts were inaccurate, and the hypnosis transcripts were incomplete. This led to speculation that cast doubt upon the Hills' story. As is often the case, Betty's memory of the events became inconsistent as time passed, which further contributed to an inaccurate mythology. Debunkers tirelessly attempted to puncture the Hills' story, and when the facts were not enough, they resorted to the omission of significant information and the addition of misinformation. Once stated, this misinformation was repeated over and over again by most of the skeptical scientists who wrote about the story. Many of the true facts have been suppressed, and disinformation has been added to cloud the issue.

My intimate knowledge of the case has given me a unique perspective that only a close confidant could acquire. It was through my genetic link to Betty and our trusting relationship that she revealed to me her inner thoughts. My mother, Janet, was her younger sister, and when I was a small child we lived next door to Betty in Portsmouth, New Hampshire. Later, when my parents built a home in nearby Kingston across the street from my grandparents' farm, Betty was a frequent visitor. At least once a week she traveled the 19 miles from Portsmouth to Kingston and always brought friends to meet the family. In 1956 she introduced us to Barney Hill, who would later become her husband. On September 20, 1961, she phoned my mother to confide the details of their UFO sighting the previous night in New Hampshire's White Mountains. At the time, I was a 13-year-old adolescent who listened to their conversation in wonder and disbelief. As the weeks and years passed and the aftermath unfolded, I gained a firsthand observer's perspective on this life-changing event. I was a primary witness to the highly polished spots on the trunk of their car, the severed binocular strap, the inoperable watches, and the deep scrapes on the tops of Barney's shoes. This circumstantial evidence immediately raised suspicion that something more than a sighting had occurred. I witnessed Betty's and Barney's anguish over their apparent amnesia and a period of missing time following a close encounter with an unconventional craft and its occupants. I accompanied the Hills to Dr. Simon's house near Boston when astronomer J. Allen Hynek interviewed them in the presence of John Fuller. I was with them when they discovered the alleged abduction site. I was there on the weekend of their famous 1967 Sky Watch and have the photos to prove it. I accompanied Betty to her "landing site" and scanned the skies for the alleged squadrons of UFOs that were reported flying nightly in New Hampshire's skies. Later in Betty's life, I lectured about her experience and appeared with her on several television programs.

This book would not be complete without an objective evaluation from both the social science and physical science perspectives. Therefore, Stanton Friedman, the world-renowned UFO researcher, lecturer, and author has joined me to search for the truth, no matter where it might lead us. He has spearheaded the investigation of the major personalities who became part of the aftermath. In conjunction with Marjorie Fish, he launched a scientific investigation and peer review of her star map work. He interviewed Betty and Barney and conducted his own investigation into their claims. And he has scrutinized 40 years of investigative files, correspondence, and literary works—pro and con—pertaining to the Hill case.

This exhaustive investigation will lead the reader through the Hills' adult lives from sociological and biographical perspectives. The events leading up to the UFO encounter and the alleged abduction will be explored with a critical eye. Barney's psychosomatic illness, precipitated by the UFO encounter, will be scrutinized. The formal UFO investigation and the major players in the research, including their personalities and ideas, will come to light for the first time. Additionally, a comparative analysis of the Hills' hypnosis transcripts will be conducted to identify areas of consistency and inconsistency in their individual recall of the events of September 19–20, 1961. We will pit recent research findings on the characteristics of hypnosis and false memory formation against the Hills' hypnosis transcripts. Further, we will compare the frightening nightmares that Betty experienced only days after the UFO encounter with a point-by-point analysis of her hypnotic recall. We will explore the events that precipitated the betrayal of trust that led to the public disclosure of the Hills' UFO experience. The scientific investigation of Betty's star map, the analysis of the anomalous substance that destroyed the dress she wore on the night of the UFO encounter, and her cooperation in scientific experiments will be revealed. The skeptics' and debunkers' critical arguments will be reviewed and the facts will come to light. For the first time, we will expose the secret information regarding the physical and social characteristics of the alien abductors. And finally, we will follow Betty through the ramifications of Barney's untimely death, her multiple UFO sightings, her investigation of self-proclaimed abductees, and her move toward skepticism.

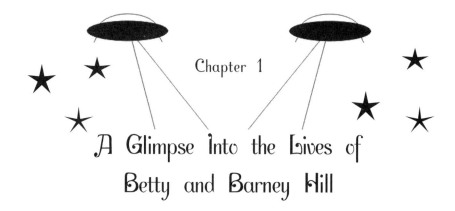

Chapter 1

A Glimpse Into the Lives of Betty and Barney Hill

When Betty and Barney Hill planned their impromptu "honeymoon" trip to Niagara Falls in mid-September, 1961, they were fulfilling the final stage of their marriage commitment and seeking a relaxing and intimate, albeit short, vacation. Although they had married on May 12, almost 16 months earlier, time and distance had obstructed their mutual goal to spend time together. Betty, with a chuckle, once told me that she had never intended to marry Barney. It had nothing to do with the fact that he was black. In all probability he proposed to her because he'd grown tired of the drive from Philadelphia to Portsmouth. They had planned to "just be friends." But as they spent more and more time together, they began to change their minds. What had been a friendship developed into a strong, loving bond, and they were married in Camden, New Jersey, on May 12, 1960. However, job commitments forced them to remain apart for the next 10 months. Betty, a social worker for the State of New Hampshire, made her home in Portsmouth, while Barney, a city carrier for the U.S. Post Office, resided in Philadelphia. The long-awaited job transfer from Philadelphia to a location closer to Betty had come through on March 17 of that year. The job offer was in Boston, a 60-mile commute each way, and Barney would be required to work the graveyard shift—a huge sacrifice and major adjustment. However, his desire to be with his wife, if only for a few hours a day, spurred Barney on, and he decided to accept the new position.

The couple had met five years earlier in the summer of 1956, when Barney, his then wife, and their two children vacationed at the home of mutual friends. Formerly from Philadelphia, their friends ran a boarding house where Betty had rented a room while her own home was being moved and remodeled into apartments. For many years, New Hampshire's beaches had enticed the Hill family to flee from the sweltering summer city heat to the warm sands and brisk breezes along Hampton Beach.

Betty and waitresses of Rudy's Farm Kitchen in Hampton, summer of 1938. Courtesy of Kathleen Marden.

Although their encounter was brief and formal, the Hills exchanged addresses with Betty and they occasionally corresponded.

As a precursor to her return to college for a degree in social work at the University of New Hampshire, Betty was working as a cashier and hostess at a favorite beach lunch spot. Her summer employment would help to cover her college tuition and purchase her books. She told the coauthor, Kathy, that she enjoyed the Hills but had little time to spend with them because she was working from 11 a.m. until 8 p.m. seven days a week. The Hills expressed an interest in renting a room at her home on a later vacation, if one was available on a short-term basis.

Early the following year, when Barney and his wife separated, he contacted Betty, and soon their friendship developed into a romantic relationship. They spent long weekends and vacation time in each other's company, sharing common interests, a keen intellectual bond, and a sense of adventure. One weekend, Betty's parents invited her to dinner, and she took Barney along to meet the family. Soon, she introduced him to her extended family, and all but a couple of racially prejudiced individuals took an immediate liking to him. From Kathy's perspective, as a young adolescent, it seemed that assimilation into her family was an easy process for Barney. He was kind, gregarious, genteel, and well-informed about the social and political issues of the day. The Barrett family was politically involved, and they enjoyed others who shared their common interest. This made for many hours of interesting conversation, spirited debate, and cheerful commiseration.

Betty, also a divorcée, had struck out on her own after 14 years of marriage. She had met her first husband during the summer after her sophomore year at UNH, when a prolonged bout with an abdominal infection had prevented her from returning to college. After a period of recuperation, she worked as a waitress at Rudy's Farm Kitchen, a restaurant in Hampton, N.H. Full-course dinners were served for the price of $1. That is where she met Bob, a young, divorced chef to whose warm personality she was immediately attracted. In a taped interview with Kathy she stated, "Bob Stewart seemed like the best thing on the horizon, so I grabbed him. Either you went to college or you got married, so I got married. I thought he was a pretty good guy, frankly, and it took me years to find out different. These were the days when most people didn't even have jobs. We were coming out of the depression. He was hard-working, and anything that I wanted he got for me." They were married on June 7, 1941, in a small ceremony at the town hall in Alton, N.H. Betty's parents gave them their blessings and stood up for them.

Shortly after she married her first husband, his three biological children were put in her custodial care, a completely unforeseen event. Betty and Bob had intended to support them and to see them during weekend visitations, but a turn of events necessitated a change. Their biological mother had remarried and just given birth to twins. Betty said that "when she found out that Bob had remarried she picked up the three kids and dumped them at Bob's mother's house." Bob's mother found that she was incapable of caring for three children under the age of 8. So Betty and Bob took them in, and three years later, Betty legally adopted them. Bob transferred to a higher-paying job as a machinist at the Portsmouth Naval Shipyard, and Betty started a full-time job as a mother and homemaker. She said that she found the job extremely challenging, but she adjusted to her new circumstance and made the best of it. She nurtured them through their formative years, and as they gained their independence, she followed suit. Tired of Bob's philandering, she decided he would be happier with his girlfriend, and she would be better off alone.

She purchased her new home with the settlement from her divorce and worked for a time at the W.T. Grant Company, a local department store. Then the Gulf Oil Company approached Betty with an offer for the sale of her house. At a meeting at a downtown restaurant with her real estate agent, Charlie Gray, and the oil company representative, Betty struck a heavily negotiated deal for a good sum of money—at least double the initial offer. Later, when she inquired about the fate of her house, the company informed her that they planned to demolish it. In turn, she offered them a dollar for it on the condition that she would move it to a different lot. When they accepted her offer, she had to find land close to the original location. With the help of her real estate agent she purchased a large vacant lot on a nearby corner. But before she could move the house to it, a new foundation and utilities had to be installed, and she had to find a temporary dwelling. This is when she moved into the boarding house where she met Barney. The profit from the sale of her land made it financially possible for Betty to return to college to finish her baccalaureate degree.

In the summer of 1957, just prior to her senior year in college, she completed fieldwork at a home for delinquent girls, The Leighton Farm School near Philadelphia, where she worked as a counselor. She and Barney had already begun a romantic relationship, and this position made it possible for them to be together. She finished near the top of her class in her social service major and was inducted into the Alpha Kappa Delta Sociology Honor Society. After graduating, Betty found employment with the New Hampshire Division of Welfare, a job that she absolutely loved. She decided to remain in New Hampshire because she owned a house in Portsmouth and wanted to be near her family, with whom she had a close, mutually supportive relationship.

Little is known about Barney's early adult life. His records reveal that he dropped out of high school and served as a store clerk in Philadelphia before he enlisted in the U.S. Army during a peacetime draft. He was 18 years old on May 10, 1941, his conscription date, just seven months prior to America's entry into World War II. He served in the Army for nearly three years, where he qualified as a marksman and truck driver. During his tenure in the service he married his first wife, Ruby, and fathered a son. An accident with a grenade caused Barney to lose his teeth, necessitating dentures, and he was discharged in fair condition from the Aberdeen Proving Ground on May 8, 1944. His enlisted record gives him a character reference as "excellent." In July 1944, after his discharge, Barney secured a position with the U.S. Post Office as a city carrier. Four years later, his second son was born. By all accounts he was a devoted and involved father. We have not been able to locate records concerning his early level of community involvement, with the exception of his participation in the Boy Scouts of America. In 1957, he served as a committeeman for Troop 133 in Philadelphia.

Barney was a nurturing uncle who was involved in the education and socialization of his nieces and nephews. He and Betty were frequent visitors to Kathy's childhood home and were always cheerleaders for their personal and academic success. They joined immediate family members on educational excursions to museums and involved young family members in their own social and political activities. From an adult perspective, Kathy thinks that Barney's participation in youthful family activities helped to ease the pain that he experienced due to his physical separation from his sons in Philadelphia. He saw them as often as he could, but their school schedule limited the time that they could spend in New Hampshire. The summer weeks that his sons spent in New Hampshire were some of Barney's happiest times.

Betty and Barney Hill in the late 1950s. Courtesy of Kathleen Marden.

When he relocated to New Hampshire, Barney had to leave family, friends, and the city way of life behind. Except for the small communities that had sprung up along the Massachusetts border, New Hampshire was a sparsely populated agrarian state with an economic base in lumbering, dairy and poultry farming, textile and leather manufacturing, stone quarrying, and tourism. Portsmouth was an exception to the rule, but could not compare to Philadelphia. Pease Air Force Base had assumed control of a 4,365-acre parcel of land in the greater Portsmouth region in 1951 and completed base construction in 1956. In 1961 it housed the 100th and 509th Bombardment Wing Units. The Air Force Base and the Portsmouth Naval Shipyard boosted Portsmouth's economy and added a heterogeneous, multicultural flair to the area. Portsmouth was, at that time, a small city with a strong military influence.

Additionally, the proximity of the state's largest university had a positive impact on the social, cultural, and intellectual environment of Portsmouth.[1]

Barney's warm, gregarious personality, combined with the gift of humor, quickly endeared him to a large group of friends. He and Betty had developed an excellent relationship with their tenants, Dot and Henry and their three children, who lived in one apartment. Jean, Bill, and their two children lived in the second. Both were airmen, stationed at Pease Air Force Base, and both were from the Deep South. A familial atmosphere filled the tenement house as the couples gathered in the evenings to exchange thoughts on the events of the day. Their children played together while the adults drank coffee and snacked on whatever the wives had baked. Friendly cooperation filled the building and all enjoyed each other's companionship. Betty said that the most difficult task for Barney was to curtail their social activity when he had to prepare to leave for his job in Boston.[2]

But this fellowship did not temper the longing that Barney had for his two sons. His daily four-hour commute to Boston and back and his difficulty adjusting to an upside-down sleep schedule compounded the stress of his move. Additionally, racial prejudice was no stranger to New Hampshire. It may not have been overt, but it boiled slowly beneath the surface. Needless stops by small-town police officers and whispers of racial prejudice in housing and employment rattled this proud, Virginia-born African-American. As can be expected in anyone who undergoes major life changes in conjunction with approaching middle age, Barney's many adjustments were beginning to increase his level of anxiety. Because Betty had a weeklong vacation from her job as a child welfare worker, Barney decided that he would like to join her for a chance to rest and enjoy her company.

On his drive to the South Boston Postal Annex on Friday evening, September 15, 1961, Barney decided to request a few days off from his new job as a distribution clerk in order to surprise Betty with a trip to Niagara Falls and Montreal. His request was granted, so on Saturday morning, while Barney rested, Betty prepared for their trip. The banks were closed on weekends and these were the days before credit cards, so the Hills pooled their funds of less than $70. They decided that if they were frugal, not eating in many restaurants or staying at fancy hotels, they could afford to leave on Sunday morning. Betty borrowed a cooler from her friend Lei, shopped for provisions, and prepared the car for their trip. That afternoon, Barney packed his suitcase and asked his tenants Dot and Henry to "look after things" while they were gone. Their tenant Bill had gone to Pennsylvania, and his wife, Dot, was staying with friends for a few days.

On Sunday, September 17, Betty and Barney cheerfully packed their remaining belongings into their car. For protection, in the event that they were forced to sleep in their car, Barney slipped Betty's pistol under the floor mat of the trunk. Betty put their dog, Delsey, into the back seat, and they left for their holiday. First they traveled across Vermont to Niagara Falls and Toronto, then to the Thousand Islands area, and finally to Montreal. On Tuesday, September 19, they planned to book a hotel and take in the nightlife in the bustling city. However, Barney took a wrong turn, and after failing in his attempt to interpret directions given in French, he decided to drive to the outskirts of the city, hoping to locate a motel that would accept Delsey. When he realized that he was too far away from Montreal's downtown area, he continued to drive east. When the radio announced that tropical storm Esther was whirling its way up the east coast toward New Hampshire, he and Betty decided to head for home. Esther's winds had reached 130 miles per hour as she boiled off the Virginia coast, and her projected path would have landed her full impact on Cape Cod. The Hills felt an urgency to return to Portsmouth before it, too, became engulfed in wind and rain. Although they would be required to travel into the early morning hours, it seemed necessary. They agreed that if they grew tired, they would stop for the night in New Hampshire's White Mountains.

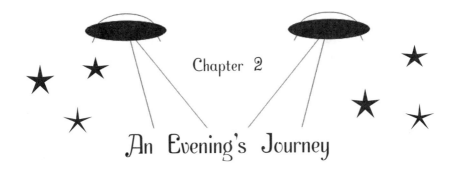

Chapter 2

An Evening's Journey

On the evening of September 19, 1961, the skies over New Hampshire's western slope did not foretell the rain and winds that tropical storm Esther would deliver on southern New Hampshire's seacoast region only two days later. It was a warm, starry, moonlit night, and Betty and Barney were taking in the familiar scenic views that they had grown to love. The Hills were relaxed and enjoying the view during the last leg of their journey home. As Betty sat in the passenger seat of her 1957 Chevy, Barney maneuvered south along the state's major north–south route, connecting New Hampshire's wilderness region to U.S. Interstate Highway 93 in Ashland.

Betty's interest was aroused by what she at first thought was a falling star, until it suddenly came to a stop in the southwestern sky. As it inched its way upward, she thought she was taking in her first observation of a satellite (her father was excited about the space program, frequently venturing outside at night to search the sky for satellites, but Betty had not joined him in that activity). When it left its even course, ascended toward the moon, and stopped, Betty's curiosity piqued. This unique craft so sparked her curiosity that she insisted that Barney stop at the side of the road in order to look at it himself. She was dumbfounded as she observed it take on an unconventional, erratic flight pattern and travel across the face of the moon. By the time she handed the binoculars to Barney, the object had again changed course, and seemed to be rapidly descending in their direction.

Barney, a conservative, pragmatic thinker, planned to explain away Betty's interest by assuring her that she had spied a conventional airliner en route to Canada. Yet when he viewed the craft through binoculars, he too observed its unconventional flight and lighting patterns. As he drove south on Route 3, Betty and Barney were awestruck by the perplexing object. It rapidly changed direction, ascended and descended vertically, and hovered motionless in the sky. This enigmatic phenomenon both piqued Barney's interest and confounded his sensibility. His intelligent, no-nonsense attitude left no room for the nonsensical belief in flying saucers. However, although he remained cool for Betty's sake, he was quietly ruminating about the remarkable sight. He entertained the idea of ending their dilemma by stopping at a cabin for the night. However, he continued to motor his way along Route 3, stopping briefly from time to time to take in the game of cat and mouse that the ever-descending, silent craft seemed to be playing with them.

Then, as they motored around a slight curve near Indian Head, a natural granite rock formation resembling a Native American profile just south of the narrow valley through Franconia Notch, they entered a wide expanse. Almost directly in their path, the couple encountered the flattened, circular disc, hovering silently an estimated 80 to 100 feet above their vehicle. Barney rapidly brought the car to a halt in the middle of the road and grabbed his binoculars for a closer look, opening the car door for a less encumbered view. Quickly, in an arcing movement, it shifted from its location directly ahead and rested above the treetops in an adjacent field. Barney pocketed Betty's handgun and walked toward it. The silent, enigmatic craft was huge—maybe 60 to 80 feet in diameter—with a double row of rectangular windows extending across its rim. As he approached it, two red lights at the end of fin-like structures parted from the sides of the craft, and it tilted toward Barney. Lifting his binoculars to his eyes, he spied a group of humanoid figures moving about with the precision of German officers. As the craft tilted downward and began to descend toward him, one of the strange creatures that remained at the window communicated a frightening message. Barney had the immediate impression that he was in danger of being plucked from the field. Overcome with fear, and with all of the courage that he could muster, he tore the binoculars from his face and raced back to the car. Breathless, trembling, and in near hysterics, he told Betty that they needed to get out of there or they were going to be captured.

As Barney rapidly accelerated down the highway in an attempt to escape from the craft, it shifted directly overhead. Suddenly, rhythmic "buzzing" tones seemed to bounce off the trunk of their vehicle, and they sensed a penetrating vibration. They drove on without speaking until, somewhere down the road, they heard a second series of buzzing sounds. Vague memories of encountering a roadblock, of seeing a huge, fiery red-orange orb resting upon the ground, and feeling a desire for human contact preoccupied their thoughts. They looked for an open restaurant to no avail, so they drove on through Concord, picked up Route 4, and made a beeline to Portsmouth, expecting to arrive at approximately 3 a.m. The Hills were surprised to notice that, as they crossed into Portsmouth, the dawn was streaking the sky in the east.[1]

Betty, a prolific writer, chronicled much of her adult life in daily diaries and typewritten accounts. After her death, more than 43 years later, Kathy found an excerpt in which she wrote, "We entered our home, turned on the lights, and went over to the window and looked skyward. We stood there for several minutes. Then, Barney said, 'This is the most amazing thing that has ever happened to me.' We both wondered if 'they' would come back." She recorded Barney's comment that their arrival time (shortly after 5 a.m.) was later than expected. "We felt very calm, peaceful, relaxed. We sat at the kitchen table, looked at each other, shook our heads in puzzlement, and asked each other, 'Do you believe what happened?' We agreed that it was unbelievable, but it had really happened. We would return to the windows and look skyward."

Barney said that he felt "clammy," so he took a shower. Then, while Betty showered, Barney retrieved their personal articles from the car. She called out to him to leave them on the porch, and he agreed that it was a good suggestion. Moments later, they retired in an attempt to get some restorative sleep.

When they awoke, Barney offered two suggestions: First, they would enter separate rooms and attempt to draw the object that they had observed. After they completed their drawings they noted the uncanny similarity between them. They were remarkably alike in detail. Second, he suggested that they should refrain from ever telling anyone, anticipating that because their experience was so fantastic, they would never be believed. Betty, a strong-willed, independent woman, promptly disagreed.

Betty wrote, "When we woke up in the afternoon, Barney asked me if I had the feeling they were still around. I agreed with him and we watched the skies, going to the windows and looking up; going out on the back porch. Looking, looking, and seeing nothing. It was beginning to rain so Barney brought our belongings into the back hall."

Later that day, from her Kingston, New Hampshire home, Kathy overheard Betty's telephone conversation with her sister, Janet Miller.

She was beginning to lose her feeling of "peace and calm, and was start-ing to feel an uneasiness." She felt that her sister, who observed an un-conventional craft in the mid-1950s, might be "the one person to whom she could tell [her story] without prejudice." Janet listened carefully, asking Betty questions throughout the conversation. Then she announced that she would "check around" and return her call in a few minutes. Excitement boiled through the Miller house as the word began to spread.

Curious, Kathy prodded her mother for the details of the conversa-tion. As she recounted it to those present in the room, she added that she had once witnessed an unconventional craft. She was returning home from a shopping trip when she observed a silent, blimp-shaped craft hov-ering over an adjacent field. In amazement, she and the residents of a neighboring house watched as several smaller, disk-shaped objects ap-proached the craft from several directions, and entered it. Then, almost instantaneously, the mother ship ascended vertically and disappeared from sight. This conversation was Kathy's introduction to the topic of flying saucers.

Artist's recreation of Barney in the field in Lincoln, N.H.
Courtesy of Kathleen Marden.

Janet phoned a neighbor whose husband was a physicist, seeking professional advice to convey to Betty. Coincidentally, a family friend, the former chief of police in neighboring Newton, New Hampshire, arrived on the scene. He advised Janet that all UFO sightings should be reported to Pease Air Force Base. Moments later, Janet repeated to Betty the directions that she had received both from the family friend and from the physicist via his wife. He suggested that she conduct a simple experiment with the aid of a compass. She was to place the instrument near the car's metallic surface in several locations as she circled around it and report her findings back to Janet.

In her diary, Betty described what happened next:

I took the compass and went out to the car. Barney refused to go, saying that he was trying to forget what happened. It was still raining but I could see my car clearly under the street light in front of my home. I walked around it, holding the compass and not knowing what I was looking for. When I came to the trunk area, I saw many highly polished spots, about the size of a half-dollar or silver dollar. The car was wet from the rain but these spots were clearly showing. I wondered what they were. I placed the compass over them, and it began spinning and spinning. I thought it must be the way I was balancing the compass, so I placed it on the car and took my hand away. The compass was really spinning and continued to do this. As I was watching this I was filled with an unexplained feeling of absolute terror. I was standing there in the rain, under the street light, and telling myself, "Don't scream, keep calm, and don't be afraid, everything is all right."

Moments later, a reluctant Barney and his upstairs neighbors all experimented with the compass and observed the strange markings on the trunk of the car while Betty phoned the Miller household, 19 miles away in Kingston, to report what she had found. She agreed to phone Pease Air Force Base, and the Miller family made plans to visit her.

By Thursday, September 21, 1961, tropical storm Esther boiled off Maine's rocky coast, lashing New Hampshire's seacoast with gusty, gale-force winds that downed tree limbs and caused power disruptions. The Miller family was preparing to join the Hills in their Portsmouth home as soon as the storm subsided. Kathy and her two younger brothers always looked forward to their visits with Betty and Barney with excited anticipation. They respected Betty for her intelligence, achievements, and leadership skills, and enjoyed listening to her pearls of wisdom and sage advice. But Barney made them laugh. He always had a good-natured joke or a magic trick that elicited a multitude of cheerful giggles and kept them coming back for more. He played games of chess or checkers with his nephews and listened contentedly as the group talked with him about school, friends, activities, and interests. But, on the day in question, Barney's mood had changed. He was quiet and contemplative.

Don Miller joined his brother-in-law in the living room while Betty, compass in hand, led Janet, with children in tow, in the direction of her blue and white Chevy Bel Air. Kathy and her brother Glenn peered curiously at the several highly polished, half-dollar-sized circles while they took turns lifting their youngest brother, Tom, high enough to see them. Betty held the compass against the side of the car, along the wheels, and finally up to the trunk. The group watched in amazement as the needle spun wildly over the spots. Janet spied her older children futilely attempting to rub the spots away and cautioned them not to touch them. Suddenly she became apprehensive about the spots, thinking that they might be radioactive, and quickly shuffled her charges back into the house.

Once inside, Betty passed her watch around the living room urging each family member to attempt to fix it. When she and Barney checked the time on their wind-up watches on the morning of September 20, they discovered that both had stopped ticking. However, they placed no particular significance upon the apparent coincidence, because wind-up watches frequently stopped if they were not wound on a daily basis. They simply reset and wound their watches, expecting them to function normally. Both were amazed to discover that their watches were broken. We will never know if they were destroyed at exactly the same time, because both thought that their watches merely needed to be rewound. But one fact is irrefutable: Both watches sustained irreparable damage on the night of September 19–20, 1961.

Curiously, on the morning of September 20, Barney's pant legs were speckled with "pickers" and plant matter, and the tops of his good dress shoes were badly scraped. The plant debris could have deposited upon his pant legs when he entered the field to view the UFO at close range. However, there was no reasonable explanation for the ruined shoes. Somehow he had broken the leather strap that fastened his binoculars around his neck, and his upper back was sore. Additionally, Betty's new blue dress was torn....

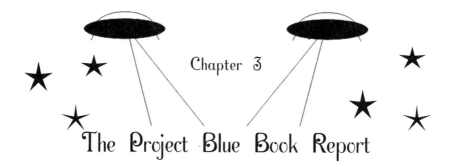

Chapter 3

The Project Blue Book Report

Betty phoned the 100th Bomb Wing at Pease Air Force Base in neighboring Newington, New Hampshire, to report an unidentified flying object on September 21, 1961, the day after the sighting. She and Barney gave the interviewing officer a general description of the craft they had observed. Barney omitted his observation of the humanoid figures that communicated with him through a double row of windows, fearing that he might be thought a "crackpot." Later that day, Major Paul W. Henderson phoned the Hills and questioned both of them extensively. According to Betty, he seemed very interested in the wing-like structures that telescoped out from each side of the pancake-shaped craft, and the red lights on their tips. Betty wrote, "Major Henderson asked to speak with Barney, who was hesitating about taking the phone. But, once he was on the phone, he was giving more information than I had. Later, Barney said he had done this, for Major Henderson did not seem to express any surprise or disbelief. Later, Major Henderson called back and asked if we would be willing to be put through to somewhere else, and have our call monitored. We agreed to this. One call was transferred to another place and today we do not know with whom we were talking."[1] The next day, Major Henderson phoned to inform the Hills that he had been up all night working on their report and that he needed a few more details. It was Betty's contention that he took their report very seriously, making it quite clear that the Air Force was aware of the existence of unidentified flying objects.

Major Henderson, on Air Force Form 112, No. 100-1-61, officially reported to Project Blue Book that "on the night of 19–20 Sept between 20/0001 and 20/0100 Mr. and Mrs. Hill were traveling south on Route 3 near Lincoln, New Hampshire, when they observed, through the windshield of their car, a strange object in the sky. They noticed it because of its shape and the intensity of its lighting as compared to the stars in the sky. The weather and the sky were clear at the time."

In a supplement to Form 112, Major Henderson transcribed the following information:

A. Description of Object

1. Continuous band of lights—cigar-shaped at all times despite change in direction.

2. Size: When first observed it appeared to be about the size of a nickel at arm's length. Later when it seemed to be a matter of hundreds of feet above the automobile it would be about the size of a dinner plate held at arm's length.

3. Color: Only color evident was that of the band of light, which was comparable to the intensity and color of a filament of an incandescent lamp. (See reference to "wing tip" lights.)

4. Number: One

5. Formation: None

6. Feature or details: See 1 above. During periods of observation wings seemed to appear from the main body. Described as V-shaped with red lights on tips. Later, wings appeared to extend further.

7. Tail, trail or exhaust: None observed.

8. Sound: None except as described in item E.

B. Description of Course of Object

1. First observed through windshield of car. Size and brightness of object compared to visible stars attracted observers' attention.

2. Angle of elevation, first observed: About 45 degrees.

3. Angle of elevation at disappearance: Not determinable because of inability to observe its departure from the auto.

4. Flight path and maneuvers: See item E.

5. How the object disappeared: See item E.

6. Length of observation: Approx. 30 mins.

C. Manner of Observation

1. Ground-visual.

2. Binoculars used at times.

3. Sighting made from inside auto while moving and stopped. Observed from within and outside auto.

[D is missing]

E. Location and Details

On the night of 19–20 September between 20/0001 and 20/0100 the observers were traveling by car in a southerly direction on Route 3 south of Lincoln, N.H., when they noticed a brightly lighted object ahead of their car at an angle of elevation of approximately 45 degrees. It appeared strange to them because of its shape and the intensity of its lights compared to the stars in the sky. Weather and sky were clear. They continued to observe the moving object from their moving car for a few minutes, then stopped. After stopping the car they used binoculars at times.

They report that the object was traveling north very fast. They report it changed directions rather abruptly and then headed south. Shortly thereafter, it stopped and hovered in the air. There was no sound evident up to this time. Both observers used the binoculars at this point. While hovering, objects began to appear from the body of the "object," which they describe as looking like wings, which made a V-shape when extended. The "wings" had red lights on the tips. At this point they observed it to appear to swoop down in the general direction of their auto. The object continued to descend until it appeared to be only a matter of "hundreds of feet" above their car.

At this point they decided to get out of that area, and fast. Mr. Hill was driving, and Mrs. Hill watched the object by sticking her head out the window. It departed in a generally northwesterly direction, but Mrs. Hill was prevented from observing its full departure by her position in the car.

They report that while the object was above them after it had "swooped down" they heard a series of short, loud "buzzes," which they described as sounding like someone had dropped a tuning fork. They report that they could feel these buzzing sounds in their auto. No further visual observation was made of this object. They continued on their trip and when they arrived in the vicinity of Ashland, N.H., about 30 miles from Lincoln, they again heard the "buzzing" sound of the "object"; however, they did not see it at this time.

Mrs. Hill reported the flight pattern of the "object" to be erratic; [it] changed directions rapidly, [and] during its flight it ascended and descended numerous times very rapidly. Its flight was described as jerky and not smooth.

Mr. Hill is a civil service employee in the Boston Post Office and doesn't possess any technical or scientific training. Neither does his wife.

During a later conversation with Mr. Hill, he volunteered the observation that he did not originally intend to report the incident but in as much as he and his wife did in fact see this occurrence he decided to report it. He says that on looking back he feels that the whole thing is incredible and he feels somewhat foolish—he just cannot believe that such a thing could or did happen. He says, on the other hand, that they both saw what they reported, and this fact gives it some degree of reality.

Information contained herein was collected by means of telephone conversation between the observers and the preparing individual. The reliability of the observer cannot be judged, and while his apparent honesty and seriousness appears to be valid, it cannot be judged at this time.

As an "additional item," Major Henderson included the following information on the front page of his intelligence report:

During a casual conversation on 22 Sept 61 between Major Gardiner D. Reynolds, 100th BW DCOI and Captain Robert O. Daughaday, Commander 1917-2 AACS DIT, Pease AFB, NH it was revealed that a strange incident occurred at 0214 local on 20 Sept. No importance was attached to the incident at that time. Subsequent interrogation failed to bring out any information in addition to the extract of the "Daily Report of the Controller."

It is not possible to determine any relationship between these two observations, as the radar observation provides no description. *Time and distance between the events could hint of a possible relationship.* [Note: emphasis by author.]

Signed Paul W. Henderson

Major USAF

Chief Combat Intelligence

The Project Blue Book 10073 Project Record Card regarding the New Hampshire sighting reads as follows:

1. Date: 20 Sep 61

2. Location: Lincoln, NH

3. Date-Time Group: Local 0001-0100 GMT: 20 0401-05002

4. Type of Observation: Ground-visual, Air-Intercept radar

5. Photos: No

6. Source: Civilian

7. Length of Observation: 30 min.

8. No. of Objects: 1

9. Course: N

10. Brief Summary of Sighting: Continuous band of lights. Cigar-shaped at all times despite changes of direction. Wings seemed to appear from main body. Described as V-shaped and red lights on tips; later wings appeared to extend further. Appeared about 45 degrees. Varied direction abruptly and disappeared to the north.

11. Comments: Both radar and visual sightings are probably due to conditions resulting from strong inversion which prevailed in area on morning of sighting. Actual source of light viewed is not known but it has all the characteristics of an advertising searchlight. Radar probably was looking at some ground target due to strong inversion. No evidence indicating objects were due to other than natural causes.

12. Conclusions: Optical condition. [Later changed to "Inversion." Later changed to "insufficient data." All crossed out and written in longhand on the original card.] Aircraft, Balloons, Airships, etc. [blank]

13. Other: Observation due to unusual optical condition resulting from atmospheric conditions. [Written in longhand on card.]

14. Evaluation of Source Reliability: Probably good.

15. Analysis and Conclusions: Both the radar and visual sightings are probably due to conditions resulting from the strong inversion which prevailed in the Lincoln, N.H. area on the morning of the sighting. The actual source of light viewed by the witnesses who reported the visual sighting is not known but it has all of the characteristics of an advertising search light. The radar probably was looking at some ground target due to the strong inversion. There is not evidence which would indicate that the objects in these sightings were due to other than natural causes. [Written in longhand.]

The original Project 10073 Record Card for the sighting lists the "Type of Observation" as Ground-Visual and Air-Intercept Radar—not Ground-Radar as later reported (see Appendix). However, this page was removed from later reports. Betty has always contended that she was told that jet interceptors were scrambled to chase the unidentified flying object. This page seems to give supporting evidence that Betty was indeed accurate in her statement.

An aerial view of the capture site.
Courtesy of Kathleen Marden.

It is interesting to note that Project Blue Book commented that the object that the Hills observed had the characteristics of an advertising searchlight. Advertising searchlights are used to attract attention to all types of events, including grand openings and movie premiers. The searchlight is generally mounted on a ground mobile unit and it sends spikes of light miles into the air to attract crowds. An advertising searchlight at 11 p.m. during the off-season in a sparsely populated area? Hardly. This is incongruent with the Hills' description of a brightly lighted, structured object only hundreds of feet above their car, that projected V-shaped wings with red lights on their tips and an unconventional lighting pattern. Section 11 seems to ignore the information contained within Section 10.

A form titled "The True Extract of 'Daily Report of the Controller,' ACS [Air Communications Service] Form 96 for the Date of 20 September 1961" outlines the actual ground-visual report. It informs us that the Air Force personnel observed an unidentified aircraft on precision approach radar 4 miles out from the control tower. It continued its approach and pulled up at half a mile. Shortly thereafter, radar picked up a weak target downwind, and then radar contact was lost. The tower was advised of the aircraft's presence when it was on final approach, and also when it made a low approach. However, the tower was not able to see any aircraft at any time. The Air Intelligence Information Report failed to mention an Air-Intercept Radar observation at any time, although that box is checked off on the form, suggesting that there may have been one. The "Daily Report of the Controller" reads as follows:

> 0614Z (0214 a.m.) OBSERVED UNIDENTIFIED A/C [aircraft] COME ON PAR [precision approach radar] 4 MILES OUT. A/C MADE APPROACH AND PULLED UP AT 1/2 MILE. SHORTLY AFTER OBSERVED WEAK TARGET ON DOWNWIND, THEN WHEN IT MADE LOW APPROACH, TWR [tower] UNABLE TO SEE ANY A/C AT ANY TIME...JC CERTIFIED TRUE.
>
> Signed
> ROBERT O. DAUGHADAY
> Captain, USAF
> Commander

The Headquarters of the 817th Air Division at Pease Air Force Base did not transmit the Hills' UFO sighting to the Air Technical Intelligence Center (ATIC), Wright-Patterson Air Force Base, until September 29, 1961—eight days after the report was transcribed. It stated, "Non-availability of observers for early interrogation precluded electrical transmission of the report." It was sent by E.B. Lobato, CWO W2, USAF. This delay was not consistent with Air Force procedure. Also, because the Hills were readily available for early interrogation, reporting the UFO the day after they returned home from their trip, one must ask, who were the other observers who *weren't* available? This Air Force statement suggests that either a cover-up was already in progress, or there were additional witnesses. In 1965, when reporter John Luttrell was doing research for his *Boston Traveler* articles, he located additional witnesses. Unfortunately, when he left his job as a reporter, he handed over all of his files to his editor. Those files have never been located and were probably destroyed.

Project Blue Book received a ground-radar sighting report of another unidentified flying object from the North Concord, Vermont, Air Force Station on September 22, 1961. This ground-radar sighting occurred on September 19, 1961, at 5:22 p.m., eastern standard time, less than six hours prior to Betty's first observation of the UFO. The Project Blue Book 10073 Card regarding the Vermont sighting reads as follows (transcribed from Brummett/Zuick Air Command and Staff College Research Study):

1. Date: 19 Sept. 61

2. Location: N. Concord AFS, Vermont

3. Date: Time Group-GMT 19 2122Z September 19 at 5:22 PM

4. Type of Observation: Ground-Radar

5. Photos: No

6. Source: Military

7. Length of Observation: 18 min.

8. Number of Objects: 1

9. Course: S

10. Brief summary of sighting: Return on H/F [height-finder] radar size of a/c appearing as normal target at 62,000 appeared 196 deg. At 84 mi, lost on contact 199 deg. At 80 mi, going NW then S and gradually S on scope 18 min. [The original TWX on file at Project Blue Book describes the UFO as a "large aircraft."]

11. Comments: Relative low speed and high altitude coupled with erratic course including weather balloon.

12. Conclusion: Probably balloon.

On September 25, 1961, Project Blue Book's Director Major Friend sent an information request regarding the North Concord, Vermont Air Force Station radar sighting report to the USAF's Foreign Technology Division (FTD). On September 28, 1961, Colonel Paul J. Slocum, chief of electronics at the FTD, replied in the following memo (also transcribed from Brummett/Zuick Air Command and Staff College Research Study):

1. The relatively low speed and high altitude of the subject UFO, coupled with erratic course (including hovering), appear to rule out a normal aircraft target and favor some target as a weather balloon.

2. It is suggested that if it is desired to pursue the investigation further, a check might be made of the activities in the area responsible for launching and tracking weather balloons.

On November 22, 1961, Captain Pallas L. Tye, Jr. of the USAF's Climatic Center in Ashville, North Carolina supplied the following report to the USAF's Foreign Technology Division:

ATTN OF: CCDPD

SUBJECT: Copy of Selected Rawinsonde Observations

TO: Air Force Technical Intelligence Center

Foreign Technology Division, TD-E

Wright-Patterson Air Force Base, Ohio

1. Reference: Your telephone call at 1415 EST 15 Nov 1961.

2. We are sending copies of Rawinsonde observations (WBAN 31 ABC) from Portland, Maine, for 17 through 22 Sep 1961.

3. Lincoln, New Hampshire does not take Rawinsonde observations, and Portland, Maine, is the closest station.

FOR THE DIRECTOR
Signed
Pallas L. Tye, Jr.
Captain, USAF
Administrative Officer
Atch: Photocopies of Rawinsonde Obs.

According to U.S. government fact sheets, 6-foot-wide helium- or hydrogen-filled weather balloons carry a small rawinsonde instrument package, suspended below. The instruments transmit information regarding wind speed and direction, temperature, air pressure, and humidity. A weather balloon rises at about 1,000 feet per minute and bursts at approximately 100,000 feet when it has expanded beyond its elastic limit (about 20 feet in diameter).

It is interesting to note that North Concord, Vermont, is only 17 miles west of Lancaster, New Hampshire, the area where Betty first sighted the anomalous craft. The radar target was about 80 miles to the south/southwest of the Air Force base.

Major Brummett and Captain Ernest R. Zuick, Jr., in an Air Command and College research study, noted that the Concord, Vermont, original TWX on file with original Blue Book material described the radar target as "a large aircraft."[2] Obviously, even if it flattened out at high altitudes, a 20-foot-wide weather balloon is not a large aircraft. Additionally, the balloon has a very small radar cross section, so only the instrument package shows up on radar. The one in question was tracked going northwest, then south for a period of 18 minutes. If it were spotted at 62,000 feet, by the time the Air Force station lost contact with it, its altitude would have been approximately 80,000 feet, assuming that it continued to ascend at the rate of 1,000 feet per minute. When a weather balloon enters the stratosphere it should travel in a west-to-east direction with the flow of the jet stream. However, the object in question traveled *against* the strong horizontal upper atmospheric wind currents. This raises concern that the object on the radar target may not have been a weather balloon.

According to Major Brummett and Captain Zuick, there is no indication that additional requests were made for the Vermont radar sighting, and photocopies of the rawinsonde weather balloon observations were never found by researchers. Although no correlating data can be located, the time and location of the radar target in relation to the Hill sighting is an interesting coincidence. It is unfortunate that Project Blue Book failed to investigate the North Concord, Vermont, Air Force Station report, the Pease Air Force Base radar report, or the Hill UFO sighting report. Instead, it ignored the significance of these reports and assigned easy, prosaic explanations to them.

Although on September 21 and 22, 1961, Pease Air Force Base seemed extremely interested in the Hills' UFO encounter, by November of 1961, the cover-up was complete. The official Air Force release regarding its assessment of the Hill report, shown in the following list, requires a sentence-by-sentence analysis:

Information on Barney Hill sighting, 20 September 1961, Lincoln, New Hampshire

1. The Barney Hill sighting was investigated by officials from Pease AFB. The case was carried as insufficient data in the Air Force Files.
   [Previously it had been listed as "weather inversion," an atmospheric condition in which a layer of warm air overlies a cooler air mass and can cause an uncorrelated radar target or an optical mirage; "Jupiter"; and "optical condition."]

2. No direction (azimuth) was reported and there are inconsistencies in the report.
   [The Hills reported that they were traveling south when they noticed the object at an angle of elevation of approximately 45 degrees. It was south of them and then headed north very fast. Then, it changed direction and headed south. There were no inconsistencies in the report.]

3. The sighting occurred about midnight and the object was observed for at least one hour.
   [The Hills' preliminary report states that the craft was observed for at least 30 minutes.]

4. No specific details on maneuverability were given.
   [It changed direction abruptly, it hovered, and it ascended and descended numerous times very rapidly. Its flight was described as jerky, not smooth.]

5. The planet Jupiter was in the southwest at about 20 degrees elevation and would have set at the approximate time the object disappeared. Without positional data the case could not be evaluated as Jupiter.
   [It departed in a generally northwesterly direction, according to Barney. Betty couldn't see it when she stuck her head out of the window.]

6. There was a strong inversion in the area.
   [This is a favorite Blue Book explanation. The Mount Washington Observatory reported, "It is possible a weak inversion set up in the valleys overnight, as the valley locations are more prone to the diurnal effects of the sun, but I think that the cloud cover would have prevented any radiational cooling in the valleys. The fact that warmer air was moving in on a steady west wind would lead me to believe that most all locations, valleys, and summits would have had similar warming trends."[3]]

7. The actual light source is not known. As no lateral or vertical movement was noted, the object was in all probability Jupiter.
   [The Hills reported lateral and vertical movement by a cigar-shaped continuous band of lights that, at closest approach, was the size of a dinner plate at arm's length. As it hovered, V-shaped "wings" began to extend with red lights on the tips.]

8. No evidence was presented to indicate that the object was due to other than natural causes.
   [It is incomprehensible that an objective analysis of the Hills' report could have yielded this conclusion.]

It is evident that The U.S. Air Force's Project Blue Book's conclusions were inconsistent—not Betty and Barney Hill's description of the object. They were an average couple who carried out their obligation as United States citizens to report an anomalous craft in New Hampshire's skies. The Air Force did not conduct a real investigation. As it so often did, Blue Book ignored the unconventional aspects of the case and assigned it to one conventional category after another. When none fit, they assigned it to the category of "insufficient data."

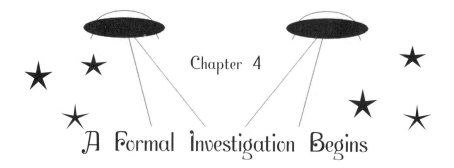

Chapter 4

A Formal Investigation Begins

A profound sense of curiosity about the UFO encounter in New Hampshire's White Mountains prompted Betty to visit the Portsmouth Public Library on September 23, 1961, where she checked out *The Flying Saucer Conspiracy* by Major Donald Keyhoe. Keyhoe, the director of the National Investigations Committee on Aerial Phenomena, a nonprofit corporation founded in 1956, argued that the government was conspiring to suppress information about unidentified flying objects. The book would be the Hills' formal introduction to information about flying saucers. It also informed them that others had witnessed similar objects, and this knowledge gave the Hills some consolation. Betty wrote in her unpublished memoirs, "In this book was an address where one could write if one had a sighting. At the time, NICAP (National Investigations Committee on Aerial Phenomena) was an organization unknown to us. I wrote a letter to them explaining the experience and the fact that Barney had seen figures in the windows."

Within a few days, Betty began to experience a series of disturbing nightmares about the event. Immediately before waking in the morning, she seemed to experience flashbacks of horrifying memories of being captured and taken aboard the craft. To Betty, the most perplexing aspect of the nightmares was that they included real, consciously recalled events about the sighting and the two series of beeping sounds upon the rear of their car. These real events seemed to flow into a continuous memory of abduction. They were so distressing that she decided to jot them down on notepaper to "try to relieve some of the pressure." Betty wrote, "At first, I didn't tell anyone about them, they were so weird." She said she hid them and tried to forget about them. But in November, she retrieved the notepaper, and although she had not dreamed the events in sequence, she pieced them together to develop a logical, sequential story line. Although she did not record the exact dates of her dreams, she decided that they had begun 10 days after her UFO sighting.

Four weeks after their UFO encounter, Betty and Barney informed their family that scientists were investigating their sighting. In a letter dated October 17, 1961, NICAP Secretary Richard Hall responded to Betty's letter:

> Major [Donald] Keyhoe will be writing to you at greater length but he wanted me to send you this interim reply to your letter of September 26. We were greatly impressed by your report and we are making preparations for an investigation. Our Boston subcommittee [investigative unit] will probably contact you in the near future. The chairman is Walter Webb, but any of our subcommittee investigators will be carrying identification cards signed by Major Keyhoe. Mr. Webb is a close friend and an adviser to NICAP and you can trust him completely.

Four days later, on October 21, 1961, Walter Webb initiated his preliminary investigation at the Hills' home, interviewing them individually and together for a six-hour period. He did not take a tape recorder, but wrote extensive notes during the interviews.

Webb was employed as chief lecturer at the Charles Hayden Planetarium in Boston, Massachusetts. He graduated from Mount Union College in 1956 with a Bachelor of Science degree in biology before pursuing a career in astronomy. Early in his career he had worked for Dr. J. Allen Hynek, Project Blue Book's astronomical consultant, at the Smithsonian Astrophysical Observatory in Cambridge, Massachusetts, where he served the Satellite Tracking Program as a general assistant. After Sputnik II was launched, Webb served as a satellite camera operator atop Mount Haleakala in Maui, Hawaii. Although Webb had been investigating UFO reports since 1952, it was through his association with Hynek that he developed an intense curiosity about the scientific analysis of the data that Hynek had access to. This led to Webb's association with NICAP and a close friendship with Assistant and Acting Director Richard Hall.[1] Later, Webb served as assistant director at Boston's Charles Hayden Planetarium and an astronomy consultant for NICAP, APRO, and later, the Mutual UFO Network. In 1994, the Center for UFO Studies appointed him as their senior research associate. He spent 32 years at the Charles Hayden Planetarium at Boston's Museum of Science.

On October 26, 1961, Webb wrote the following excerpt in a confidential report to NICAP, titled, "A Dramatic UFO Encounter in the White Mountains of New Hampshire—September 19–20, 1961":

The UFO came around in front of the car and stopped in midair to the right of the highway "8 to 10 stories" [80 to 100 feet] above the ground. The height given was a rough guess and the distance was even more difficult to estimate, but the object probably was not much more than 100 feet away, which meant that the Hills had to look up at a 45-degree angle to see the UFO. The lighted edge of the object, a row of windows through which a cold, bluish-white fluorescent glow shown, was visible, and a red light on each side of the object could be seen. The UFO was no longer spinning.

NICAP investigator Walter Webb. Courtesy of Walter Webb.

Mr. Hill braked the car to a halt, but left the headlights on and the engine running. His wife handed him the binoculars and he tried to look through the windshield with them. Then he opened the door on his side and stepped out onto the highway for a better look. At that moment the UFO shifted position from right to left in front of the car and hovered again in midair. Barney still believed that what he was seeing had a rational explanation—a military helicopter perhaps having some fun with them. What amazed him though was the ease with which this craft seemed to move and stop, and the absolute lack of any sound at this close range.

Looking through the binoculars, he watched in fascination as the object, tilted downward slightly, began descending slowly in his direction. He could see eight to 11 separate figures watching him at the windows. They seemed to be standing in a corridor that encircled a central section. Suddenly there was a "burst of activity"—the figures scurried about, turned their backs, and acted as if they were pulling levers on the wall. One figure remained at the window. At that instant the red lights began moving away from the object, and Mr. Hill could see that the lights were on the tips of two pointed, fin-like structures sliding outward from the sides of the "ship."

The figures, according to Barney Hill, were of human form dressed in shiny black uniforms and black caps with peaks or bills on them (which could be seen when the figures turned their heads). The uniforms were like glossy leather. When they were standing at the windows he could see down to their waists. When they moved backward to the wall, their legs were partially visible. The figures reminded the observer of the cold precision of German officers; they moved smoothly and efficiently and showed no emotion except for one fellow operating a lever who, Mr. Hill claims, looked over his shoulder and smiled.

The approaching UFO finally filled up the entire field of the binoculars. The "leader" at the window held a special attraction for the witness and frightened him terribly. The witness said he could almost feel this figure's intense concentration to do something, to carry out a plan. Mr. Hill believed he was going to be captured "like a bug in a net." That is when he knew it was no conventional aircraft he was observing but something alien and unearthly containing beings of a superior type, beings that were somehow not human.

"I don't believe it!" he said as he put down the binoculars. He could see the figures in the object with the naked eye (an inch long at arm's length, but this is highly uncertain in my opinion). The UFO was now an estimated "5 to 8 stories" [50 to 80 feet] up and possibly between 50 and 100 feet away (hard to judge or to recall). The Hills remember that no light from the thing fell on the ground and there was no sound.

In recent years, skeptics have portrayed Barney as a highly suggestible individual who imagined a close encounter only after he had read Keyhoe's book and absorbed the content of Betty's frightening dreams. They suggest that he saw only a distant, star-like object that seemed to be following his vehicle. To further their argument, they imply that his vivid imagination caused him to become frightened and to leave the main highway, wandering off course on tiny secondary roads. He is characterized as having vague memories of lights in the sky, hazy visions, paranoia, and fatigue. To test this hypothesis, Kathy interrogated the family members who possessed knowledge of Barney's memories immediately following his sighting. They all testified that Barney verbalized a clear, consistent memory of the events that occurred on September 19–20, 1961. He observed an unconventional craft and its bizarre humanoid occupants at close range. The craft interacted with the Hills' vehicle and left highly polished, magnetized spots on its surface as evidence. This was not a confabulation that developed days later, after he read *The Flying Saucer Conspiracy*. It did not come to light later when he overheard Betty discussing her dreams. It was a conscious, continuous memory of a real, awe-inspiring event. Within hours of his sighting, he told his tenants, his family, and later, NICAP Investigator Walter Webb, about it.

Webb's investigation report, "A Dramatic UFO Encounter in the White Mountains, NH," came to the attention of two IBM employees, Robert Hohmann and C.D. Jackson, when they joined Major Donald Keyhoe for lunch at the XII International Aeronautical Congress in Washington, D.C., on October 4–5, 1961. On November 3, 1961, Hohmann wrote a letter of introduction to the Hills on behalf of himself and Jackson, requesting an interview. He stated that their principle interest was to attempt to verify the origin of "these vehicles" according to existing scientific theory proposed by Professor Hermann Oberth of Germany (the father of rocket science). Additionally, he wanted to gain insight into the meaning of the whole phenomenon.

Robert Hohmann, born December 24, 1918, was educated at Miami University where he studied English and history. Fluent in German, he left college to serve in the U.S. Army in Europe during World War II as a driver of VIPs and an interrogator of prisoners of war. He served in Europe for three and a half years, according to his widow, and had a high security clearance, but never talked about specifics. After the war, he completed his education at Notre Dame University, where he earned a Master's degree. He then joined IBM and remained in their employ in the Hyde Park, New York, area for 25 years. He traveled extensively as part of his job, taught classes on technical writing, worked closely with scientists and engineers, and arranged presentations for IBM executives.[2] C.D. Jackson was a senior electrical engineer for the same company. In the 1960s, he was employed in New York, Virginia, and Alabama. Extensive research efforts have failed to uncover additional information about C.D. Jackson.

When Hohmann and Jackson visited the Hills on November 25, 1961, Betty and Barney thought that they might finally get some answers to their myriad questions concerning UFOs. The Hills incorrectly assumed that the men were government scientists, visiting in an official capacity. However, Hohmann and Jackson's inquiry seems to have resulted in more questions than answers. Betty wrote in her unpublished diary, "They were questioning us in specific areas. How many miles was it from Colebrook to Portsmouth? How long did the trip take? Why did we average 25 to 30 miles per hour on a clear night with no traffic on highways with fast speed limits? What happened between the two series of beeping sounds? Were any of our belongings missing? How did Delsey, the dog, react? Had we had any strange events since that time? Did we have any nitrates in the car? They stimulated our thinking and we were able to pinpoint specific areas at certain times."

Barney and Mr. C.D. Jackson, 6/10/67.
Courtesy of Kathleen Marden.

Betty and Barney began to ruminate more than ever about the unanswered questions pertaining to their UFO sighting—more specifically, about the apparent missing time. On the morning of September 20, 1961, they noticed that their arrival time was later than they anticipated, but placed no particular significance upon the time differential. After

Hohmann's and Jackson's visit, they realized for the first time that, allowing for their observation stops and a period of slow driving, they arrived home at least two hours later than they should have. The exact moment when they became aware of a period of missing time has often been misquoted and used by skeptics to imply that it was Robert Hohmann and C.D. Jackson who planted the previously unrecognized discrepancy in the Hills' minds. To be accurate, the Hills became aware of the two- to three-hour span of missing time during this November 1961 meeting, *not the element of missing time itself*. They had always had a conscious, continuous memory of arriving home later than they had anticipated. Betty reported to Kathy that Hohmann's and Jackson's questions stimulated Barney's and her thinking. They began to remember some of the events that transpired between the two sets of beeping sounds when the craft interacted with their vehicle. They recalled that Barney, without explanation, made a rapid left-hand turn onto a secondary road, and all communication ceased. Betty later explained that she assumed Barney had taken one of his many shortcuts, and that if they became lost, they would find their way with no problem. They speculated about Barney's behavior, when he put his arm across his eyes, uttering, "Oh no, not again." Immediately after making the turn, he spotted a large, fiery orb by the side of the road, silhouetted against a stand of trees. The missing time and their apparent period of amnesia played repeatedly in their minds.

Shortly after the UFO encounter, the Hills' dachshund, Delsey, developed an epidermal fungus infection, which was treated by a veterinarian; then she was stricken with respiratory maladies. The Hills had adopted Delsey from a Newton, New Hampshire, couple only six weeks prior to their trip and did not have copies of her veterinary history. At the time, they placed no unusual significance upon Delsey's medical problems. But within weeks, Betty realized that Delsey had not been bathed following her exposure to the craft. Additionally, she expressed concern that Delsey had suddenly begun to whimper, shake, and move her legs, as if running in her sleep, following their September trip. Although most dogs exhibit this type of behavior from time to time, it was intense and persistent in Delsey.

Hohmann's query about nitrates was actually directed to Barney. He deliberately asked some extraneous questions designed to put the Hills on the defensive. This was one that was asked merely as a diversionary tactic. He asked Barney if he or anyone in his family had any association with the nitrates industry. The unexpected, out-of-context question elicited a response of mild annoyance in Betty. Then she realized she *did* have nitrates in the trunk of her car—a bag of fertilizer. She enjoyed tending to a large vegetable garden every summer at her parents' farm in Kingston. At the end of the season, she had placed her remaining fertilizer in her vehicle, but had not transferred it to her shed prior to their trip. Hohmann and Jackson did not explain their interest in the purpose of nitrates or nitrogen. Betty wondered why the occupants of an extraterrestrial craft would be drawn to nitrates. During her lifetime this question was never satisfactorily answered.

Also present for the five-hour meeting was Barney's friend, Major James MacDonald, a retired Air Force intelligence officer at Pease Air Force Base, then working as a USAF consultant. In a confidential letter discovered in Betty's archival materials, she wrote, "It might be well to leave out that Jim MacDonald was formerly with the CIA. I think this is something that he was not supposed to reveal. Since he is a friend, we would not want to cause him any difficulties." A retired U.S. Air Force colonel informed Kathy that if MacDonald were *actively* employed by the CIA, he would have been undercover as an Air Force officer, and it would be a serious violation if he told anyone. However, MacDonald had indeed retired when he informed the Hills about his former CIA position, negating the problem.

His tie to the intelligence community has led to speculation among researchers that his presence at the meeting was more than social, but Betty has consistently rejected this idea. MacDonald's role at the meeting seemed to be to ask the questions that Betty desired answers to, while Betty's primary focus seemed to be on the questions asked by Hohmann and Jackson. The substance of MacDonald's questions revolved around Hohmann's and Jackson's knowledge of UFO abduction—specifically, had they ever encountered a case identical to the Hills'? If so, had that person been able to initiate a second contact if they so desired?

One thing is clear about MacDonald's role at the meeting: It was he, not Hohmann, who first suggested that the Hills might consider hypnosis as a means of discovering what transpired during the two hours of missing time. Hohmann agreed that it would be advisable.

Major MacDonald was one of many of the Hills' friends who were officers at Pease Air Force Base. They enjoyed social gatherings together on Saturday nights at the base officer's club. Several also attended Betty's and Barney's church, where they were active in its couples group. Major MacDonald dated and later married one of Betty's best friends, and Barney served as the best man at the wedding.

Dr. James Harder and Dr. J. Allen Hynek. Taken in Tucson.
Courtesy of Kathleen Marden.

At the suggestion of Hohmann, Jackson, and MacDonald, Betty and Barney embarked on repetitive weekend journeys to the White Mountains in a concerted effort to jog their memories. They attempted to find the location of a steel construction, railroad-type bridge they had crossed when they left Route 3. At that time, there were three, whereas today only one remains. The other two have been dismantled and replaced by modern bridges. Where did they encounter the roadblock that weighed so heavily on their minds? They were certain that they had encountered a roadblock, but could not pinpoint where it occurred. What was the frightening message that the being in the flying saucer communicated to Barney? Why did it take them so long to arrive at their home in Portsmouth? Allowing ample time for their observational stops, they still should have arrived at home much earlier than they did.

According to Betty, shortly after Hohmann's and Jackson's visit, a bizarre, unsettling event occurred at her home. Betty stated that, upon returning to their Portsmouth home after a full day's exploratory journey to the White Mountains, she and Barney unlocked their door and entered their kitchen. To their amazement, they discovered a pile of dried brown leaves in the center of their table. They checked their doors and windows, and they seemed secure, but somehow, someone had been able to enter their home. They returned to the table and began to discard them. But as the leaves parted, Betty and Barney gasped in astonishment, as they discovered Betty's blue earrings. These were the earrings that she had taken on their trip to Canada, the ones that matched her blue dress, the ones she was wearing on the night of their encounter. She hadn't realized that they were missing. She hadn't even thought about them since she slipped them onto her earlobes on the morning of September 19. In an undated diary entry, she wrote, "My eyes filled with tears [that] ran down my cheeks. I did not want Barney to see my reaction, so I picked up my earrings and went into the bedroom, and put them into my jewelry box where they still remain. I have never worn them again." Why had they been placed upon her table in this bizarre manner? Could someone have entered their home without a key? Did it offer a clue to what occurred during the period of missing time? Betty suspected that it did.

At the time, Betty and Barney reported the earring incident in strictest confidence to only her closest family members. Kathy remembers their visit to her childhood home and the feelings of distress they exhibited when they discovered that their house had been illegally entered. They felt a sense of violation and vulnerability. The adults in the room expressed concern about Betty's and Barney's privacy and safety, and they devised a plan to install deadbolt locks to thwart additional unlawful entries.

Kathy's inquiries have revealed that the Hills did not report this occurrence to any investigator at the time of its occurrence. The earliest publication of this incident seems to have been initiated by Dr. Berthold Eric Schwarz, in the August 1977 *Flying Saucer Review*. On June 20, 1974, Dr. Schwarz, a psychiatrist and neurologist from Montclair, New Jersey, with an interest in the paranormal, penned his first letter to Betty. He had attended a lecture given by her and had also read what he referred to as a "surefire" article she had written. He wrote, "To my mind, what you hinted at, plus other things that have happened to you since your unique experience, are of the utmost significance, and if they could be written up for *FSR*, which is distributed as you know, to many of the leading libraries, universities, and medical schools in the world, there might be many worthwhile effects." He became Betty's confidant and friend, and they corresponded on a regular basis for the next 30 years.

The Hills lived alone and no one had a key to their apartment, so family members and friends could not have been playing tricks on them. They began to think that some agency, perhaps the Air Force or the CIA, didn't want their UFO encounter to be investigated. Once, when Betty picked up the phone receiver, she simultaneously heard a second party answer, "Base Intelligence." This incident caused her to suspect that her phone line was tapped. In order not to appear paranoid, the Hills decided to keep the intrusions secret. They forged ahead, undeterred by these events, and continued to search for answers.

Betty and Barney also began to experience anxiety about driving in unpopulated areas at night, especially when they encountered a situation that brought back memories of their UFO encounter. In the early morning hours of January 17, 1962, Barney and approximately 25 clerks at the South Postal Annex in Boston saw a large, red, rounded object, low in the western sky. It turned sideways, showing a narrow edge, and disappeared. According to Betty, Barney wondered if this was the same object he had witnessed in the White Mountains the previous fall. One night, Barney encountered a roadblock on his way to work that brought forth such paralyzing fear that he returned home. Later, during an evening drive, Betty and Barney spotted a car surrounded by teenagers, stopped at the side of the road. Suddenly, Betty became overwhelmed with a feeling of panic and grabbed the door handle in an inexplicable attempt to flee. For no apparent reason, seemingly mundane events were inducing feelings of terror in Betty and Barney. This marked a significant change in their psyches. They did their best to maintain normality, to follow through with their everyday routines, and to be good family and community members, but the events of September 19–20, 1961, would forever change their routine, ordinary lives. More than ever, they needed answers.

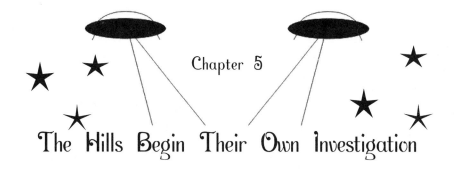

Chapter 5

The Hills Begin Their Own Investigation

On March 12, 1962, Betty and Barney wrote to Dr. Patrick Quirk, a psychiatrist from Georgetown, Massachusetts, to request a Saturday morning appointment, explaining that they were both employed weekdays. They enclosed NICAP's "UFO Investigator," a bulletin that briefly described their September 19–20 experience, and informed Dr. Quirk that they had been interviewed by Walter Webb and two "electronic engineers," Mr. Robert Hohmann and Mr. C.D. Jackson, from Hyde Park, New York. They continued, "Many puzzling aspects remain, so it is felt that hypnotism could clarify these. We have handled this experience with confidentiality, with the exception of NICAP and a very few close friends. Our motive is to obtain information that could be helpful in a scientific way." An appointment was arranged, but Dr. Quirk did not attempt hypnosis. He recommended that the Hills should wait to see if more conscious memories of the experience would emerge. Betty and Barney were beginning to remember information that they had previously forgotten, and Dr. Quirk explained that, in time, they would remember more without the use of hypnosis.

Then, in November, Betty and Barney received a package from Robert Hohmann and C.D. Jackson, the two investigators who had interviewed them the previous November. It contained a report that the two had been working on, titled "A Historic Report on Life in Space: Tesla, Marconi, Todd." They presented it to the American Rocket Society's 17th Annual Meeting and Space Flight Symposium on November 13–18, 1962. The purpose of the paper was to examine the original data of Tesla, Marconi, and Todd to determine whether or not current science was duplicating the effort made by these men to detect radio frequency communication from extraterrestrial life forms on some distant planet. They explored Tesla's experiments in high frequency (1892–1907) involving possible interplanetary communication. Tesla stated, "The nature of my experiments precluded the possibility of the changes being produced by atmospheric disturbances....Although I could not decipher their meaning, it is impossible for me to think of them as having been entirely accidental...a purpose was behind these signals. They are the results of an attempt by some human beings, not of this world; to speak to us by signals...I am absolutely certain that they are not caused by anything terrestrial."[1]

Hohmann and Jackson then discussed Marconi and Todd's observations and experimentation (1899–1924), including Marconi's wireless transmission experiment across the English Channel in 1899. In September 1921, Marconi was in the Mediterranean Sea aboard his 220-foot yacht when he detected the phenomenon that he described as interplanetary communication. He expressed the belief that the signal had originated in outer space, and he spoke of a listening experiment conducted by Amherst College astronomy professor David Todd. He, in cooperation with the United States government, used a radio-photo message device to attempt to detect signals from the planet Mars as it made a close approach on August 22, 1924.

Hohmann and Jackson, who were assembling all data regarding these signals into a historical model, examined the hypothesis of Dr. Frank D. Drake that older civilizations that were searching for life would detect the transmissions of a young civilization that had just discovered radio. If this were followed to its logical end, Tesla's 1899 experiments would have transmitted radio signals to some of our nearer planets. Hohmann and Jackson cited research by Su-Shu-Huang of the Institute for Advanced Study at Princeton that suggests that stars nearly identical to the sun are most likely to have developed life. They believed that scientific investigation must follow even strange paths. As we shall see in Chapter 19, their work with the Hills attempted to launch the beginning of such a path and to remove some of the strangeness pertaining to interplanetary communication.

Carl Sagan, who held a doctorate in astronomy and astrophysics from the University of Chicago, also spoke at the American Rocket Society Conference. Betty and Barney read an article about his address in the *Boston Globe*, and in a letter dated November 25, 1962, reported the following to NICAP investigator Walter Webb:

> Dr. Sagan, assistant professor of astronomy at Harvard, has worked out an equation as his way of expressing the mathematical

probability that intelligent beings from outer space have visited the Earth. As expressed in numbers, the formula means that at least one million of the hundred million stars in our Milky Way galaxy have planets which have developed civilizations capable of travel between the stars. This means that every star, such as our sun, would be visited at least once every million years. If life is found, visits would be more frequent, possibly every few thousand years. The next step would be the maintenance of some kind of base within the solar system to provide continuity for successive expeditions. He believes the moon would be a reasonable place for this.

The Hills stated that they found their ever-increasing knowledge of the science of extraterrestrial communication to be both interesting and exciting. They also had recently taken part in an interesting meeting at the home of their minister. It involved both a discussion about hypnosis and a discussion about UFOs with Air Force officers from Pease Air Force Base. In a letter to NICAP Investigator Walter Webb dated November 27, 1962, they wrote:

Dear Walter,

Last Friday night we met with a small group of people to discuss our sighting. This was not a planned meeting, as far as we know. Present were: colonel in intelligence, research engineer, pilot, navigator, hypnotist, minister, and us. Actually, the minister whom we have known for some time invited us to visit at his home and casually mentioned that a few of his friends would be there. The hypnotist discussed this art and read some poetry which he had published and was being released that day.

Most of the people left, leaving the above-mentioned group. We found out that the colonel has known of our sighting for some time. Also, we were made aware that the Air Force does know of the existence of UFOs, but that they publicly deny this, because they are swamped with fictitious reports that waste their time, money, and effort in disproving these. They need to be free to concentrate on the valid reports.

The group seemed to reach the following conclusions (theories): The red lights on the wing tips were not running lights to guard against collision as our planes have, but were probably some type of equipment which might have been used in "beeping" us.

The beeping sounds, maybe a sonar type, were to test our reactions, or a means of establishing communication with us, or some type of listening device, or a way of attempting to control us.

This beeping device left a neutralizing effect on the trunk of the car, resulting in the clean, clear spots on the metal where no dirt or dust accumulated for a few days, and this agent deteriorated.

We talked with the hypnotist for a long time, and he appeared at first to be interested in hypnotizing us. Of course, we are still puzzling over the length of time our return trip took; also Betty's dreams of being captured, fantastic as they are.

Coincidentally, Ben, the hypnotist, asked about the same questions that the psychiatrist whom we consulted last spring asked. He came to the same conclusions, although he did make us aware of the reasons for his questions. To summarize, both said that there was a very good possibility that we had been captured and made to forget this by the use of hypnotism. Both felt that hypnotism was too dangerous to use at this time, but to concentrate on this and we may remember by the natural process of recall.

Ben questioned both of us closely about our feelings the first–second days after the sighting, and decided that our reactions were typical of a post-hypnotic state and some suggestion: our intent to forget all about this at first and then later deciding against this; our feelings of being "suspended," not of shock, or fear, or curiosity—these came later.

Ben said that many times if hypnotic amnesia is used, the person will recall in dreams, particularly if one tries to block the amnesia, such as Betty dreamed she tried to do. If one does not try to block, then that person will not recall, or will need a long time to do this.

Ben reached the decision that in his opinion, we were captured. The use of hypnotism to bring this back was too dangerous; the possibility of shock, convulsions, or—if the experience was too terrorizing—amnesia for a while. Secondly, he did not know where hypnotic blocks had been set up to control us, and this could be "messy." Our impulse might be to run, so we would need to be restrained to prevent us from running through a window or into a wall. This would add to our fear.

He did cheer us up a bit; he said that undoubtedly somewhere there is a scientist writing his thesis on prehistoric Earth people and we have contributed to his study.

This whole situation is unbelievable, fantastic, and weird, but we felt that you might like to know about this; also confidential.

We were wondering if this meeting Friday night could be some type of Air Force investigation being done on a very quiet basis, or just a group of men interested in UFOs on a personal basis.

So many unanswered questions! We wonder if we will ever know fully what happened that night.

It was a pleasure seeing you, and whenever you are in this area, visit us.

Very truly yours,

Betty and Barney

The hypnotist at the meeting was Captain Ben Swett, a B-47 navigator for the 509th Bombardment Wing of the Strategic Air Command at Pease Air Force Base.

In retired Colonel Swett's sworn testimony, dated December 29, 2006, he recollected that he read some of his poems from a book of poetry he had recently published to a group at the Unitarian Church Rectory in Portsmouth. After the poetry reading, the minister said he had heard that Swett was studying hypnosis, and that those present would like to hear about it. So he was invited to read poetry, and then he was questioned about hypnosis. He wrote, "I wasn't a member of the church and didn't know anyone

> Swett's career in the Air Force spanned from 1955 to 1985, when he retired as a full colonel. He served in several Air Force bases in the United States, in Vietnam (1970), and in the Office of the Secretary of Defense at the Pentagon. His last assignment was as the director of engineering and standardization for the Defense Industry Supply Center in Philadelphia.

there except the pastor. After my poetry reading, he said he had heard I was studying hypnosis, and they would like to hear about it. Those who came for the poetry left, and a few remained. I gave them a brief overview of hypnosis, including some of its uses and abuses. As I was about to leave, two people came up to me, introduced themselves as Betty and

1963 photo of Air Force officer Ben Swett.
Retired as a full colonel.
Courtesy of Ben H. Swett.

Barney Hill, and asked me if hypnosis could be used to recover lost periods of memory. I said, 'Yes, that's one of the classical uses of clinical hypnosis.'"[2]

In the same sworn statement, retired Colonel Swett wrote the following:

They started telling me about something that happened to them as they were driving home from Canada on the night of 19–20 September 1961— a light in the sky that seemed to follow them and then circled them, and being stopped on the road, and how they later realized they had a three-hour gap in their memories. As they told the story, Barney's face kept twitching spasmodically on one side. I didn't like the looks of that. They said some of their friends thought the light that followed them was a UFO and asked me what I thought about UFOs. I said, "There are a lot of reports by credible people." Then they asked me if I would hypnotize them to recover the gap in their memories. My first thought was, "I don't want to wade into whatever is making his face twitch like that. I'm not a psychiatrist." Then I thought, "UFOs…I'm an Air Force officer…hypnosis…I have no credentials." So I said, "No, I'm not qualified to do that." There was some discussion of UFOs. Three of the men obviously knew a lot about Air Force UFO reporting—more than I did—but I didn't know them.

Betty and Barney walked outside with me, and we talked for rather a long time. I was skeptical of their story, but responded as best I could. They said several people had suggested they try hypnosis, and since I had studied it and recommended it for recovering memories, they thought they would go ahead with it. I said that recovering those memories might reveal a lot of trauma, and cautioned them against going to an amateur hypnotist, such as myself, or a half-baked hypnotherapist. I said they needed to find a reputable psychologist or psychiatrist who used hypnotherapy.

As the ensuing months passed, the many changes in Barney's life's circumstances increasingly caused anxiety and exhaustion. The long daily commute to his job in Boston, the necessity of sleeping during daylight hours, his physical separation from his sons, his civil rights and church activities, and the UFO investigation all began to have a negative impact on his health. It is easy to understand why Barney's 160-minute-a-day commute contributed to his diagnosis of high blood pressure, headaches, and insomnia, and eventually an ulcer that failed to respond to conventional medical treatment. The unanswered questions regarding the period of amnesia following his close encounter with a UFO placed additional stress upon Barney.

By June 1963, Barney's physician suspected that his physical maladies were psychogenic when his symptoms had failed to respond to traditional medical treatment. He referred Barney to Dr. Duncan Stevens, a psychiatrist whose office was in the same building.

Barney felt comfortable in the care of Dr. Stevens, and his conventional psychotherapy seemed to be progressing well. However, Barney's ulcers had failed to retract, and this tenacious medical condition remained perplexing.

Then, on September 7, 1963, Captain Ben Swett presented a formal lecture on hypnosis to one of the adult study groups at the Unitarian church in Portsmouth. The Hills attended the lecture and approached him after his talk. They informed him that they had not yet been hypnotized but that Barney was seeing a psychiatrist he liked and trusted. Swett's sworn testimony reveals, "He had mentioned the UFO incident, and the psychiatrist

Dr. Stevens received his medical degree at Wayne State University in Detroit, Michigan. He practiced medicine in Michigan before entering the Navy in 1942, where he served in the rank of commander in the Medical Corps in the Pacific Theater on Hospital Ship LST 464. Following his naval service he practiced psychiatry in Connecticut before moving his practice to Exeter, New Hampshire. He was the psychiatry advisor to Phillips Exeter Academy and a partner at the Exeter Clinic.[3]

wasn't astonished, but they were not working on that." At this point, Captain Swett strongly encouraged Barney to ask his psychiatrist about the use of hypnosis to recover the gap in their memories.

Several weeks later, unannounced visitors rang Betty and Barney's doorbell. They were two pleasant, middle-aged women from Massachusetts: Lauri D'Allessandro and Merlyn Sheehan. They had read about the Hills' UFO encounter in NICAP's bulletin and asked if they could talk with them about it. They also mentioned that they had previously witnessed a UFO, so Betty and Barney hoped that they might be able to gain some understanding of the perplexing phenomenon through a discussion with them. Lauri invited the Hills to attend a UFO meeting in Quincy, Massachusetts, on Sunday November 3, 1963, at 2 p.m. The agenda for the meeting included new eyewitness UFO sightings, slides, a report by the group's president (NICAP's "UFO Evidence Report"), and tape recordings of a talk by the Harvard astronomer and debunker, Donald Menzel. After they mulled over Lauri's invitation, they did attend in an effort to learn more.[4]

But instead, the Hills found themselves giving their first public presentation to the group of 200 members and guests. Howard Roy chronicled their remarks to the group in "The Off Beat," a two-and-one-quarter-page typed report written shortly after the meeting. (John Fuller's 1962 date on page 284 of *The Interrupted Journey* is incorrect.) He wrote, "Barney Hill is a quiet, well-spoken fellow with a strange tale to tell and a couple of question marks where a memory ought to be. All he wants from anyone is a couple of answers and a line on a couple of hours he lost a while back in the New Hampshire hill country...and maybe someone to reassure him that he is not a fugitive from *The Twilight Zone*." (This was a TV program that Barney had never seen.) The Quincy meeting of the Two State Unidentified Flying Object Study Group of Massachusetts and Rhode Island attracted more than 200 members from Mahomet, Hyannis, Sandwich, and New Bedford, Massachusetts.

Roy's report chronicled the Hills' journey through New Hampshire's White Mountain region, emphasizing Barney's former skepticism and firm disbelief in unidentified flying objects. Barney recalled the Air Force investigator's particular interest in red, lighted tips on the bat-wing extensions that telescoped from the sides of the craft. Next, he recounted Barney's close encounter in the field south of Indian Head and the bizarre events that followed, including Barney's statement that the craft hovered over his vehicle and slowed to a speed that kept it directly over his car.

Through binoculars he could clearly observe the craft at a height of approximately a 10-story building above his car. He described the saucer-shaped UFO, it's occupants, and the stubby, wing-like fins that moved outward from the body of the craft, adding that the Air Force investigators expressed a particular interest in them.

Roy reported that Barney told the group that he returned to his car, laughing a little hysterically, and started to drive off, but the craft remained overhead. Suddenly the entire car vibrated, and there were about two dozen "beeping" sounds that felt as if something had hit the trunk of the car.

Then, Barney reportedly stated, 20 to 30 miles farther along Route 3, he and Betty reached a point near Ashland, New Hampshire, when they were confronted with a brilliant orange moon in the roadway. He then recalled taking a left turn off the highway while saying, "Oh God, not again." That was the last Barney remembered until he reached his home in Portsmouth.

Roy's report included the following interesting tidbit of information regarding the condition of Barney's car when he inspected it after arriving home: Barney allegedly stated that the trunk was unlocked and covered with "shiny spots," each about the size of a silver dollar, which caused a compass to gyrate erratically when placed near them.

The statement that the car's trunk was unlocked has brought much speculation from researchers. Could Barney have forgotten to close it? Did the craft's magnetic force unlock it? Could the Hills have driven for two hours with an open trunk and failed to notice it? At what time of day did Barney notice it was unlocked? Was Barney mistaken, or did Howard Roy misunderstand his statement? Betty insisted that it was not unlocked—only that it appeared to have been opened and its contents ransacked. This piece of the puzzle remains a mystery.

When Barney had completed his presentation to the Two State UFO Study Group, Betty faced the room of 200 spectators. Although she hadn't planned to reveal the content of the nightmares she experienced in late September 1961, she wrote in her diary, "We spoke briefly about our experience. Then, I found myself telling the group about the nightmares that I had, hoping that someone, somewhere could give us information so that we could have some understanding of what had happened to us. No one could."

Howard Roy reported the following excerpted material:

The car makes a sharp left turn and suddenly the motor dies. There are possibly eight to 11 men standing in the road. They approach the car as the couple sits motionless. The men open the doors and they direct the couple to get out.

They were taken to the space craft they observed earlier, taken to separate rooms and questioned at length. The men were "human in form," Mrs. Hill recalled, but somewhat shorter than the average human, with larger chest cavities and somewhat larger noses. Their hair and eyes were black and their skin had a grayish hue.

She was told that she would not remember anything of the experience and, if somehow she did manage to, her husband's recollections would be different—hence, nobody would believe their story.

In addition to a brief synopsis of her dream material, Betty mentioned the unexplained fact that Delsey, who had never been sick before, suddenly developed a severe fungus condition and internal disorder after returning home from the UFO encounter. For this, she was treated by a veterinarian.

On November 10, 1963, Jeanne Weller, the secretary/treasurer of the study group, formally thanked the Hills for "an excellent dissertation on their remarkable experience." She added, "I have received many calls from members and guests complimenting you both on the tremendous recounting of your experiences and your charming personalities. I had hoped to see you after the meeting at the D'Allessandros' but there was a last-minute change of plans." Then she presented the Hills with an honorary membership to the Two State UFO Study Group.

If Betty and Barney were looking for answers, they didn't find them at the UFO Study Group. Instead, they overrode their previous decision to maintain some semblance of confidentiality about their encounter and unwittingly created an information trail that would lead to writer John Luttrell. Two years later, Luttrell would use a tape recording of the Hills' statements made at this meeting as a foundation for his sensational articles in the *Boston Traveler* newspaper. Although it was alleged that Steve Putnam, the president of the Two State UFO Study Group, supplied a tape recording of this meeting to Luttrell, in a recent conversation with Walter Webb, Kathy learned that this was not the case. The tape recording may have been made by Luttrell himself, or another individual who attended the meeting. It is clear, however, that Betty went to her grave believing that it was he.[5]

This was done without permission and with protests from the Hills. Additionally, Barney, the skeptic, was forced to listen to Betty's rendition of nightmares—nightmares that he irritably rejected as nothing more than dreams. Betty seemed to be seeking confirmation that her dreams reflected subconscious recall of a UFO abduction. In contrast, Barney, who wanted to concentrate primarily on community affairs and the civil rights movement, was being dragged into uncomfortable territory. The significance of their UFO encounter was beginning to take on a life of its own that would overshadow their civic involvement. Further, this impromptu admission before the UFO study group of 200 would not remain confidential. If confidentiality was what they desired, they had just made a huge error.

Shortly thereafter, Barney's health declined and he developed a physically debilitating condition that forced him take a three-month leave of absence from his job at the U.S. Post Office. His traditional medical treatment continued to be augmented by psychotherapy, but his health did not improve.

It is important to note that in the late fall of 1963, Barney experienced a breakthrough memory of the roadblock that preceded the abduction. This significant flashback occurred prior to the Hills' first appointment with Dr. Benjamin Simon. Barney was making a concerted effort to hyper-focus on the unexplained roadblock that has always been a part of his conscious, continuous memory. He reasoned that, by penetrating his amnesia, he would know the truth, and it would relieve his anxiety. He and Betty were already beginning to experience a spontaneous lifting of repressed memories pertaining to the event. Family members were attempting to support Barney by stimulating his memory during this period. Kathy and her parents were counseling Barney by mentally walking him through a moment-by-moment recollection of his journey immediately after he heard the beeping sounds to when he turned off from Route 3. Suddenly, in a great eruption of intense emotion, he shrieked to us the details of his retrieved memory in what seemed to be a classic abreaction. He described men in the road who signaled him to stop by swinging their arms in a pendulum motion. His motor died and the men began to approach his car with a strange, nonhuman, side-to-side, swaying gait.

The release of emotion seemed to have a cathartic effect upon him, but Kathy and her parents were so disturbed by this amazing revelation that they all remember it to this day.

At his next therapy session, Barney mentioned his continuing anxiety over his apparent amnesia and Betty's nightmares, and requested a referral to a competent psychiatrist who used hypnosis. His psychotherapist, Dr. Stevens, agreed to set up an appointment.

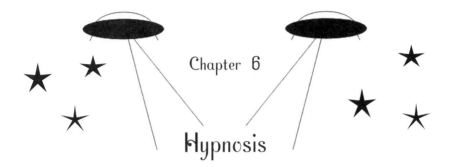

Chapter 6

Hypnosis

The complex events that precipitated Barney's psychiatric symptoms commanded expert intervention. With this in mind, Dr. Stevens sought out the best hypnotherapist he could find within commuting distance of the Hills' Portsmouth, New Hampshire, home. He made a referral to Dr. Benjamin Simon.

Benjamin Simon was a Russian immigrant who came to the United States with his parents when he was a boy. He completed his baccalaureate degree at Stanford in 1925, and received a master of science degree in chemistry from the same institution in 1927. Four years later, he was awarded a doctor of medicine degree from the Washington University School of Medicine. He had developed an interest in hypnosis when, in 1922 as an undergraduate, he served as a hypnotic subject for an experiment in the psychology department at Johns Hopkins University. In 1934, during his psychiatric residency, he used hypnosis as a therapeutic procedure for the first time. Then, in 1942, he found a more extensive use for hypnosis while he was a consultant in neuropsychiatry at the General Dispensary in New York. It is there that he received training in the medical use of hypnosis.

During World War II, he served as a lieutenant colonel in the Army and was awarded the Army Commendation Medal, the American Campaign Medal, and the Victory Medal.[1] Dr. Simon set up the Psychiatric Center at the Mason General Hospital in Long Island, New York, the Army's chief psychiatric center in WWII. At its peak, the hospital was a 3,000-bed psychiatric facility with an average one-month turnover. However, once acute symptoms ameliorated, psychotherapy would continue in a clinical setting, ensuring that symptoms did not recur. It is during this time frame that hypnosis came to the forefront in the treatment of amnesia and conversion hysteria. There, through the use of hypnosis, Dr. Simon treated soldiers returning from combat who exhibited symptoms of combat neurosis or what we now refer to as post-traumatic stress disorder. He was skilled in the use of deep trance hypnotherapy, sometimes as an adjunct to narcosynthesis (analysis that is conducted while the patient is in a drug-induced—typically by "truth serums" such as sodium pentothal or other barbituates—drowsy state, which makes the patient recall repressed memories), to resolve psychosomatic issues related to traumatic amnesia.

His success rate was so high that his work was celebrated in the documentary movie *Let There be Light* by John Huston. Dr. Simon, who served as the movie's technical advisor, demonstrated the effective use of hypnosis in the treatment of hysterical neurosis, including paralysis, stuttering, blindness, and amnesia. Hospital personnel assisted a steady stream of patients who were unable to enter the examining room under their own volition, into Dr. Simon's office. Next, he hypnotically induced each patient to the deepest trance level that he could individually attain, sometimes with the aid of narcosynthesis. Then, Dr. Simon skillfully facilitated the recall of the specific traumatic events that precipitated their psychiatric symptoms. When

he was satisfied that he had uncovered the source of each soldier's trauma, Simon commanded the removal of the hysterical symptom. A soldier blinded by his best friend's gruesome combat-related death suddenly regained his vision. Another, who was psychogenically crippled on the battlefield, obeyed Dr. Simon's command to arise and walk. The audience, again and again, witnessed the patient's powerful abreaction followed by the purging, cathartic effect of the release of repressed emotions. Over the next several weeks, patients participated in group psychotherapy, physical therapy, occupational therapy, educational therapy, and recreational therapy. As the documentary closed, the camera panned to a cheerful game of baseball. The viewer quickly recognized the formerly debilitated soldiers, who were now engaged in running bases, pitching, and catching—activities they were too handicapped to perform prior to their hypnotherapy.

After he left the military, Dr. Simon entered private practice in neuropsychiatry and also taught at Harvard and Yale. At one time he owned the Ring Sanitarium in Arlington, Massachusetts, and worked at the Westborough State Hospital and the Worcester State Hospital. When the Hills were referred to him, he maintained an office in the Back Bay district of Boston.[2]

On Saturday morning, December 14, 1963, the Hills had an initial consultation with Dr. Simon. He was skeptical about the existence of UFOs as extraterrestrial craft, but agreed to work with the Hills to resolve Barney's health issues. He was also aware of the fact that Betty was seeking answers to the question of the underlying source of her bizarre nightmares, so he quickly became aware that both required his professional help. He made it clear to them that hypnosis is not a magic bullet or necessarily a pathway to the objective truth. Rather, it is the truth *as the subject perceives it,* and may or may not be consistent with objective reality.

Betty recalled in a diary account:

When Barney and I presented ourselves to Dr. Simon in December 1963, we had many questions about hypnosis. What was hypnosis? Dr. Simon told us that no one really knew what it was. However, the kind he used was not the same as "stage hypnosis," which we had seen in public demonstrations, but a special technique he had used as the chief of neuropsychiatry for men returning from the war front in the 1940s. Later, Barney asked Dr. Simon what a hallucination was, so Dr. Simon gave him a demonstration. Barney "saw" the office door open; "saw" a little white dog come into the room; "felt" him jump up on his lap and begin licking his face; and finally, "saw" him go back out into the hall. Barney saw and felt the dog, but all the while he knew it was not real; it was imaginary.

More accurately, Dr. Simon had learned this technique as a consultant in neuropsychiatry to the General Dispensary in New York, in order to assist the dispensary dentist with the reduction of pain and anxiety in his patients. Dr. Simon explained his special technique, which he found particularly helpful in the treatment of amnesia and conversion hysteria (when a psychological trauma converts to a physical disability), in the October 1967 issue of *Psychiatric Opinion.* He had attained a high rate of success in treating patients when former therapists had failed to bring about an amelioration of psychiatric symptoms. It was through the use of his authoritative personality (some would say authoritarian) that he was able to penetrate traumatic pseudo-memories and less critical memories that precipitated amnesia or psychically generated physical symptoms. By arriving at the crux of the matter, Simon was able to relieve his patients' symptoms.

Dr. Simon began a three-week period of conditioning the Hills to enter a deep hypnotic trance—the stage of somnambulism. Had they not been good hypnotic subjects, Dr. Simon would have employed narcosynthesis to open up the area of conflict. Sodium amytal or sodium pentothal, commonly referred to as truth serum, would have been administered to open up the area of conflict, often in conjunction with hypnosis. However, this would have been less desirable because the area of conflict would have been opened up under less controlled conditions than is possible with hypnosis. Therefore, hypnosis was the preferred method of treatment. He established cues that would eliminate the time-consuming induction sequence and accelerate somnambulism, the level required to effectively impose posthypnotic amnesia. This tool would have to be employed to ensure that Betty and Barney could not share hypnotic recall until after all hypnosis sessions had been completed. It would also serve as an emotional shield to protect the Hills from their traumatic memories until they were ready to integrate them into full consciousness. This process would take several months.

Dr. Benjamin Simon.
Courtesy of Dr. Richard Simon.

Hypnotic suggestibility scales had been devised as a means of determining the extent to which a subject responds to hypnosis. Although they consist of various measures for each stage of induction, the first stage is usually determined by the subject's compliance with a simple task, such as imagining the force of a heavy weight held in one's hand. If the subject's arm lowers, he or she has reached level one. The suggestion that a subject will not experience pain when a needle is inserted into his or her arm signifies the attainment of a deep trance level.

In earlier times, hypnotic suggestibility was thought to be an indication of a subject's willingness to comply with a hypnotist's directives. More recently, new studies have refuted these earlier beliefs. A 2005 article by Michael R. Nash and Grant Benham in *Scientific American Mind* discussed "The Truth and Hype of Hypnosis." New hypnosis studies have shown that not everyone is susceptible to hypnotic suggestion, and motivation does not necessarily play a role in the success of induction. It seems to relate more to an individual's ability to concentrate and to become absorbed in activities such as reading or listening to music. It is unrelated to gullibility, hysteria, psychopathology, submissiveness, or imagination. Skeptics have charged that it is simply a matter of having an especially vivid imagination. However, empirical studies have shown that many "imaginative" subjects are poor candidates for hypnosis. Therefore, when we learn that a hypnotic subject is highly suggestible, it does not indicate that he is malleable or compliant. It means only that he is more hypnotizable.[3]

It is interesting to note that several research studies indicate that those who suffer from traumatic stress are more highly suggestible to somnambulism (the deepest level of trance) than the general public. Betty and Barney were both able to reach the level of somnambulism, although Barney's trance was slightly deeper than Betty's. Only 20 percent of the population can reach this deepest level of hypnosis at which the subject can effectively assimilate the traumatic experience and reintegrate it into conscious memory. The Hills were excellent subjects.

Nash and Benham discussed a 2004 study by James E. Horton of the University of Virginia's College at Wise, and Helen J. Crawford of Virginia Polytechnical Institute and State University. Using magnetic resonance imaging they attempted to determine whether or not brain structures play a part in an individual's responsiveness to hypnosis. They observed that the anterior part of the corpus callosum, the large, white-matter structure that connects the left and right brain, was 32 percent larger in highly hypnotizable subjects. This part of the brain inhibits unwanted stimuli and plays an important role in focusing attention. It would be interesting to image the corpus callosum of patients who have a post-traumatic stress disorder psychiatric diagnosis to test this finding. If this group is more suggestible, it would seem to follow that this area of their brain is more highly developed.

Traumatic amnesia, also called dissociative amnesia, is the total or partial inability to recall an event associated with trauma or extreme stress. These memory gaps, spanning from a few minutes to a few days, usually occur during the horrors of war, natural disasters, or accidents. This amnesia for the event is usually psychologically induced to protect the victim from memories that cannot be safely integrated. Most people who experience traumatic amnesia, such as the Hills, are aware that they have a period of missing time. The amnesia acts as a circuit breaker to prevent them from feeling overwhelmed. The resulting memory loss may be confusing and distressing for the individual who experiences it, just as it was for the Hills. Hypnosis and drug-facilitated interviews are employed by a psychiatrist to reduce the anxiety associated with the period of amnesia, and to guide the patient through the painful experience or conflict. The doctor must use extreme caution to prevent the creation of false memories through suggestion or to stimulate extreme anxiety that could lead to an increased level of trauma. This was of utmost importance to Dr. Simon in his treatment of patients with traumatic amnesia. Recent research has suggested that although the content of the recovered memories may or may not be accurate, it most frequently is. However, we cannot assume that it reflects real events unless another person independently confirms it.[4]

Dr. Simon treated Betty and Barney for dissociative amnesia related to their inability to recall a period of missing time following a close encounter with a UFO. As we mentioned, they first became aware of a period of missing time on the morning of September 20, 1961, when they arrived home from an all-night drive through the White Mountains of New Hampshire. When Barney glanced at his wristwatch upon his arrival home, he noticed that it had stopped. Upon entering his house, he noticed that the kitchen clock read a little after 5 a.m. They had arrived home later than expected, even allowing for periods of slow driving and their observational stops. Characteristic of traumatic amnesia, Barney experienced extreme stress and denial over his inability to account for the apparent missing time. Six days after the event, Betty wrote a letter to NICAP Director Donald Keyhoe to report their close encounter with an anomalous craft and Barney's emotional reaction to this period of amnesia. She wrote, "At this time we are searching for any clue that might be helpful to my husband, in recalling whatever it was he saw that caused him to panic. His mind has completely blacked out at this point. Every attempt to recall leaves him very frightened. We are considering the possibility of a competent psychiatrist who uses hypnosis." This letter proves that Betty and Barney were immediately aware of a period of amnesia associated with the sighting of a craft that was at least as large as a four-engine plane, silent, and flying in a very erratic pattern.

Both Betty and Barney Hill were excellent hypnotic subjects. They reached a deep trance level characterized by highly focused and selectively attentive response. University studies have demonstrated that mental functioning in this deep trance stage does not correlate to the characteristics of light-stage hypnosis. There is an alteration of language processing in deep trance that we do not see in light trance: Words are interpreted much more literally, and communication focuses on words themselves rather than ideas. There is also a decrease in critical judgment and an increase in incongruity.[5] As we come to understand the Hills' responses to Dr. Simon's questions, we will find many examples of literal interpretation, including a return to earlier biographical periods that invoked an acute emotional response. In deep hypnotic trance states, the Hills were cognitively aroused, yet dissociated from irrelevant cues. Because they were able to hyper-focus, Dr. Simon was able to facilitate their recall of the events of September 18–20, 1961, in great detail.

Empirical studies have demonstrated that although test subjects recalled accurate information, they may have unwittingly manufactured details that were not present previously. However, this is characteristic of recall in general. We remember those events that are most significant to us and forget those we identify as trivial. But if an event is so disturbing that it assaults human consciousness, our mind undergoes the adaptive process of repression or distortion. Simply stated, conscious recall and hypnotic regression both display similar characteristics: They are more of an adaptive process than a videotaped recording. As hypnosis.com puts it, "Each act of recall is a fresh creative process and not a memory retrieval of some fixed item from storage."[6] When extraordinary memories seem to defy what is commonly accepted as plausible, the individuals and the trained psychiatrist must rely upon their own experiences to determine the reality of the recall. They cannot simply be discarded as highly improbable. The memories must be viewed within the biographical context in which they occurred; further evidence to substantiate the claim must be examined. The focus of this book is to do just that.

There has been abundant skepticism over the ability of trance subjects to differentiate between real and imagined information recovered through hypnosis. These charges stem from the fact that good hypnotic subjects can experience trance-generated visual and auditory hallucinations, just as Barney did with the hallucinated dog. Empirical studies have revealed that hypnotic suggestion is capable of tricking the brain into registering a hallucinated sequence as real: The part of the brain that is responsible for reasoning and memory is equally active during a hallucinated auditory sequence and the real, audiotaped event. However, when test subjects were instructed to imagine the audiotaped sequence, the brain did not register it as real.[7] One important point is worth mentioning: The majority of individuals who have experienced trance-generated hallucinations do not register them as real events after the hypnosis session has been terminated. For example, Barney did not establish the false memory that he had encountered a real dog.

The use of hypnosis to recover repressed memory has engendered more controversy than any other issue related to hypnosis. Cognitive science has established that most people are able to discern between fantasy and reality; however, certain fantasy-prone individuals have come to believe that information confabulated during a hypnotic session is real. This mistake is particularly prevalent when adults are hypnotically regressed to early childhood. Although autobiographical memories usually remain intact, real events are often contaminated with fantasy material to fill in the gaps. This ability to confabulate under hypnosis has led to false memories that have resulted in personal trauma and legal intervention. In the Hill case, we are not examining decades-old memories. Only 28 months had passed since the UFO encounter, and Betty and Barney had retold their conscious, continuous memories of the event numerous times.

Elizabeth Loftus, Ph.D., from the University of Washington in Seattle, spearheaded the effort to determine how false memories are formed through external suggestion. She found that law officers and clinical psychologists sometimes ask their subjects to use their imaginations to construct hypothetical events that do not exist in reality. This exercise has led to false confessions and criminal accusations.

In a 1997 *Scientific American* article, Loftus described how these questionable techniques came under fire in the late 1980s, following a legal test case that involved a nurse's aide from Wisconsin. The woman experienced an extreme stress reaction following her daughter's traumatic event. A psychiatrist applied time-regression hypnosis and other suggestive techniques, including imagination exercises called guided imagery to inadvertently create false memories of childhood events. This psychiatrist's poor judgment and lack of skill induced false memories including satanic worship, cannibalism, bestiality, and rape. Under this medical doctor's care she was diagnosed with dissociative personality disorder following the recovery of more than 120 personalities. This psychiatrist's questionable therapy led his patient to believe that she had experienced severe childhood sexual and physical abuse. When reason returned, she realized that the psychiatrist had used suggestive questioning under hypnosis to plant false memories. In 1997, she settled out of court for $2.4 million in a malpractice lawsuit. It is this type of experience that has cast hypnosis in a poor light.

Her suspicion regarding the type of imagination exercises that resulted in false memory formation in the Wisconsin case led Loftus and her colleagues to design research studies to explore the formation of false memories. In one study they asked test subjects to rate the likelihood that they experienced certain events during their childhood. Two weeks later, they instructed the participants to imagine that they had participated in certain fictitious events using imagination exercises. In one study, 24 percent of the participants developed a false memory that the imagined event had occurred. It is interesting to note that 12 percent of those who did not participate in the imagination exercise also developed a false memory. External suggestions received from others were instrumental in constructing false memories. However, they did not occur in 76 percent of the experimental subjects and 88 percent of the control group. Further research has confirmed that time regression to childhood is not reliable in and of itself. The experienced evaluator can only differentiate true memories from false ones through corroboration.[8]

It is the malleability of memory and the fallibility of hypnosis that has cast hypnosis in a poor light and sent up red flags in the psychological research community. In a 1967 article in *Psychiatric Opinion*, Dr. Simon wrote, "In the investigation with the Hills, I had to be continually on the alert for distortions, honestly made by them, and had to test their revelations against the continuum of the entire picture. Even when they appeared to be 'lying' they were telling the truth, if one could work out the general semantics of the situation."[9] Throughout the hypnosis, Dr. Simon scrutinized the Hills' testimony for distortions, and questioned them extensively when he thought he had heard an inconsistency.

The reality of the Hills' abduction memories was less important to Dr. Simon than the amelioration of their symptoms. In the introduction to *The Interrupted Journey* he wrote, "The charisma of hypnosis has tended to foster the belief that hypnosis is the magical and loyal road to the TRUTH. In one sense this is so, but it must be understood that hypnosis is the pathway to the truth as it is felt and understood by the patient. The truth is what he believes to be the truth and this may or may not be consonant with the ultimate nonpersonal truth. Most frequently it is."[10]

In his 1967 article, he explained that he employed a special technique—not the consonant medical technique—and that his special technique was more "positive" and "certain."[11]

Having made this information clear to the Hills, commencing on February 22, 1964, Dr. Simon conducted individual hypnotic regressions with them. To ensure that information could not be shared, and to ensure confidentiality, he used a soundproof examining room. He proceeded very carefully, noticing that prosaic memories were recalled accurately prior to the exploration of the period of amnesia. When emotionally charged, traumatic memories were recovered, they often caused considerable agony. In these events Dr. Simon demonstrated sound professional judgment by bringing the sessions to a premature closure. It was not until all hypnosis sessions were completed in April 1964 that Dr. Simon removed the posthypnotic amnesia in small segments for the purpose of assimilation and integration into the Hills' conscious memories. This was accomplished in conjunction with traditional psychotherapy, which lasted until June 27. Thereafter, Dr. Simon and the Hills remained in close contact through telephone conversations, letters, and periodic visits.

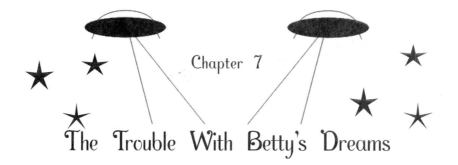

Chapter 7

The Trouble With Betty's Dreams

It is clear that, throughout the Hills' psychotherapy, Dr. Simon continually tested his hypothesis that Barney had absorbed Betty's dream material and produced fantasies to fill in the period of missing time. He used suggestion and persuasion in an attempt to convince the Hills that their abduction memories were not objectively real. However, throughout the hypnosis sessions, Betty and Barney remained unshakable. They insisted that they were reliving an actual experience that followed a continuous course from their conscious memories of the craft making contact with their vehicle, through a series of beeping or buzzing code-like sounds, until they saw a fiery orb on the ground, and later heard a second series of beeping sounds in Ashland, New Hampshire. The conscious memory of the huge UFO, Barney's face-to-face contact with humanoid beings through his binoculars, his fear that they were about to be captured, and his sharp turn off the highway formed a continuous memory to the abduction site.

Skeptics have used Dr. Simon's dream hypothesis to argue that the abduction has no foundation in reality. They contend that Betty's nightmares match her and Barney's hypnotic recall of abduction almost exactly. Given our current knowledge of the fallibility of hypnotic regression and the formation of false memories, it becomes essential that we seek independent confirmation to determine their veracity. This will be accomplished through a comparative analysis of the Hills' hypnotically recovered memories versus Betty's dream material. It seems prudent to examine the content of Betty's dream material before we proceed to the hypnosis transcripts. This material will be scrutinized in an attempt to explore the formative process of false memory creation. Then, the biographical context of the recovered memories will be scrutinized and evidence will be examined.

Days after the Hills encountered an anomalous object in New Hampshire's skies, Betty was awakened mornings by a series of frightening nightmares, which she jotted down on a note pad. Although the nightmares failed to follow a sequential story line, Betty rearranged them in logical order. Thus, she developed a frightening account of abduction by aliens from another solar system. Incorporated into her nightmares were events of which she and Barney were consciously aware. They had already reported a huge, fiery, bright orange ball that seemed to be sitting on the ground, silhouetted by evergreen trees. They consciously recalled turning to each other with the troubling words, "Oh no, not again," but consoled themselves with the explanation that it was only the setting moon. She asked Barney if he now believed in flying saucers and he replied, "Don't be ridiculous." They had also completed a formal Air Intelligence Report to Pease Air Force Base that described the unconventional craft and its two sets of mechanical code-like buzzing sounds reflecting off the trunk of their 1957 Chevy. However, the nightmares contained information for which Betty had no conscious memory.

A fiery orb on the ground. By artist David Baker. Courtesy of Mary Jane Baker

These nightmares so troubled Betty that she sought a professional opinion from her supervisor in the State Office. In a taped interview with Kathy, Betty said, "My supervisor in child welfare came out of the State Office, oh maybe three days in two weeks. When she was going to be in Portsmouth for two days in a row, she would stay overnight. Barney would be working nights so she and I would usually go out to eat and she would come back to the house and we'd sit around and talk. We did this for a while, and then, I brought [the nightmares] up because it was bothering me. I showed her the report that Walter Webb had written and she was very, very interested. She seemed to be open-minded about it. Then I told her about the dreams and we would talk about them for a while. One day she told me, 'Well Betty, for heaven's sake why don't you realize that this has actually happened to you?' She said, 'This must have happened, because if had not happened, then you wouldn't be reacting this way.'"

Betty's nightmares contained details of being stopped and surrounded by space people with primarily human characteristics. The men in her dreams were taller than the petite Betty: 5 feet to 5 feet 4 inches in stature, with large chests and prominent, Jimmy Durante noses. Their hair and eyes were dark. Only one spoke, and that was in English with a heavy foreign accent. Their complexions had a grey pallor with bluish-tinted lips. All of the men were dressed alike in light navy blue/gray trousers and short jackets that gave the appearance of having zippers, though none were seen. They all wore low boots and military caps.

In Betty's nightmares, they took the Hills to a clearing in the woods and onto a darkened, landed disk where they were subjected to unconventional physical examinations. Nail clippings, skin scrapings, ear wax, and hair samples were collected on clear glass or plastic slides, then covered and wrapped in cloth. Betty was given a classic neurological examination that included an EEG, but without a tracing machine. Next, her dress was removed and a 4- to 6-inch long needle was inserted into her navel, causing her to experience great pain, twisting and moaning. When the leader noticed that this pregnancy test was causing discomfort, he leaned over Betty and waved his hand in front of her eyes. Immediately the pain subsided, and Betty became appreciative and realized that she had found a new friend.

Next, she engaged in a conversation with the leader who smiled and apologized for frightening her. Suddenly, some of the men hurried into the examining room using words and tones that she could not identify. When the leader followed the crew out of the room, she became concerned that something had gone wrong with Barney's testing. But when the examiner returned and checked her teeth, she realized that they had removed Barney's dentures. She explained to them the reason for Barney's loss of teeth and the effects of the aging process. These human-like men shook their heads in an unbelieving manner.

Later, in the nightmare sequence, Betty searched for a souvenir to take back with her to prove that she hadn't lost her mind. She found a large book full of symbols written in long, narrow columns. After joking with her, the leader agreed to give Betty the proof that she needed to confirm that her abduction was real. When the remaining crew members discovered that she had the book, they took it from her, and she became very angry. Then the leader apologized, stating that he saw no harm in giving it to her. However, he had been overruled. The crew had decided not to permit Betty and Barney to remember their experience, and therefore, the book was taken away.

When Betty queried the leader about his planet of origin, he pulled an instructional map of the heavens down from the wall. It contained numerous points of light, connected by curved lines. Some were heavy, others light; some were broken, and some connected stars in a series of lines. The leader displayed the very human trait of sarcasm when she asked him to point out our sun on his map. He refused and snapped the 1960s-era instructional map back into place.

"The Capture" by artist David Baker. Courtesy of Mary Jane Baker.

In Betty's dream, after the completion of Barney's examination, all of the men accompanied both of the Hills back to their vehicle, where they watched the ship become a bright, glowing ball that turned over three or four times and sailed into the sky. Betty was exuberant. The primary question that has been a hot topic of debate for more than 40 years is, did Betty's frightening dreams reflect reality, or were they no more than wish-fulfillment generated by Betty's fantasies?

Betty didn't tell her supervisor about another dream that recurred off and on for a period of time after her sighting. She thought it was irrelevant. However, she discussed it with Dr. Simon at the end of her hypnosis sessions. It gives us a key to Betty's subconscious fears. The dream is as follows:

I would dream that Barney and I were somewhere, not home, but we were maybe on vacation or something. I would look out the window and there would be waves and waves of UFOs coming; not just one. The sky would be all lighted up with them. I would say, "Oh Barney, come on, let's go out. They're back. Let's go out and see them." Then they would start doing something. I don't know if they were dropping bombs, or what, but the whole world would be on fire. It would be all in flames, like a bombing, I suppose—I've never seen one. And then, I would become very frightened and say that they wanted to destroy us or capture us, or something like that.

Before we move ahead to the hypnosis transcripts, it is imperative that we explore what science has learned about the nature of nightmares. It wasn't until the 1960s, when Vietnam War veterans reported their traumatic nightmares about war events, that the distinction between ordinary nightmares and traumatic nightmares was made. The research shows that posttraumatic nightmares are repetitive and vivid. They reveal more memory of the traumatic event than ordinary nightmares. In fact, these nightmares can be an exact replay of the traumatic event. The event can also replay during a waking period as flashbacks. Traumatic dreams are a normal way of working through the memory of trauma.[1] They follow a predictable sequence: First come dreams that are characterized as exact recall of the event. Then they morph into different scenarios that incorporate the intense emotion felt during the traumatic event. Last, the dreams mimic other forms of life experiences but include aspects of the traumatic memory.[2] This may have been what happened in Betty's case.

Yet we cannot be certain that trauma caused Betty's dreams. Some researchers have conjectured that the Hills' captors hypnotized or somehow altered their memories through the employment of advanced technology we are only beginning to investigate. One important key to understanding the psychological dynamics behind Betty's dreams might lie in Betty's subconscious reaction to her hypnosis sessions. Although Dr. Simon employed the posthypnotic suggestion of amnesia after each of the Hills' sessions, Betty experienced troubling dreams during the ensuing week, as did Barney. The dreams contained some elements of the UFO encounter and abduction, but in many respects were entirely different.

For example, in the week following Betty's first hypnotic regression she had two nightmares. One was about water—perhaps a lake and a shoreline. But she couldn't recall anything else. The second was more memorable. It was about a light, similar to the light of a flashlight, that was bouncing all around. It would bounce toward Betty, and then it would retract. She felt as though she was in great danger from the light—that it would shine on her and something terrible would occur when it did. As the light approached Betty she screamed and woke up.

In late spring 1964, prior to Betty's last hypnosis session but while her amnesia was still in place, she experienced another frightening dream. Betty told Dr. Simon:

> We were riding along and I could see this object going through the sky with light in it and I was all excited. I told Barney, "There they are." You know, we're finally going to meet them. They land and we see them land, and we're quite excited about this. And then, I see them in the road. Before this, I have no fear whatsoever. I'm looking forward to meeting whoever these people are. But the moment I see them in the road, I'm hollering in my sleep, saying to myself, "Oh my God, they're not what I expected." They don't look like I expected them to look. They look like people but they're sort of grotesque. I became very frightened.

Although Betty's dream was vague, it contained elements of her hypnotically retrieved memories of abduction. She had already relived the trauma of the roadblock and subsequent capture, but they had not yet emerged as part of her conscious recall. However, on a subconscious level she seemed to be working through her distress. One can only speculate about the true source of her ordeal. Either she was working through the nightmare of a real capture by aliens, or her subconscious mind had created a disturbing fantasy, first as primary nightmares, then as confabulation in deep trance regression.

Now, we will move forward to a comparative analysis of the Hills' hypnotic recall vis-à-vis Betty's dream/nightmare material. A thorough analysis of all the available material is necessary for one to determine the true nature of the Hill UFO encounter and subsequent abduction. *The Interrupted Journey* by John Fuller presented a neat, chronological account of the Hills' journey. However, a substantial portion of the couple's testimony was omitted from the book, and this has led to speculation, confusion, and distortion. Dr. Simon asked the Hills to recall portions of their trip over and over again, and with each retelling, new facts came to light that filled in missing portions of their stories. Only a handful of researchers have ever heard the complete story.

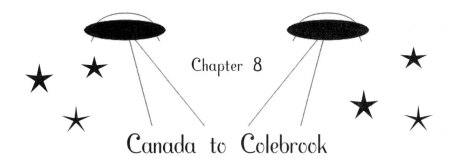

Chapter 8

Canada to Colebrook

An analysis of the Hills' separate recall regarding their abduction would be lacking without a detailed inspection of their individual claims under hypnosis. To facilitate this dissection of material, Kathy transcribed the 10 surviving hypnosis tapes recorded by Dr. Simon and given to her by Betty for this project. Through careful scrutiny of their individual recall, we can ascertain whether or not the Hills' memories of specific places and times meshed, as one would expect them to, had the event actually occurred. It is also important to draw comparisons between Betty's and Barney's compliance with Dr. Simon's directives and their individual descriptions of events, particularly those that were not part of their conscious, continuous memories. As a result of Dr. Simon's command that the Hills should recall all of their experiences, emotions, and thoughts, the transcripts contain an abundance of emotionally charged material during the abduction scenario. For the purpose of this analysis, much of the emotional content will be removed and our primary focus will be upon descriptive content and accuracy of recall.

It is our contention that a clear and precise analysis can only be performed when all of the details surrounding the event are examined. Therefore, for the first time, tapes of all 10 hypnoanalysis sessions will be exposed to scrutiny. For the reader's convenience, when applicable, we have referenced similar text in John Fuller's *The Interrupted Journey*. However, the hypnosis tapes were owned by the Hills and Dr. Simon, and temporarily loaned to Fuller for his book. None of his transcripts of the hypnosis sessions, or his comments, were used in this book. This work is entirely original and derived from Betty's copy of the audio tapes.

The primary focus of this investigation will be to compare Betty's hypnotically retrieved recall to that of Barney's. Then, the hypnosis transcripts will be scrutinized against Betty's written account of the nightmares that she experienced shortly after their consciously recalled UFO encounter in 1961. Due to the problematic nature of hypnotically retrieved material regarding verification of its authenticity, we will examine it for correlating data that the Hills could not have discussed prior to the hypnosis.

Betty Hill and John Fuller.
Courtesy of Kathleen Marden.

Our investigation will begin with the Hills' hypnotic recall of the events of September 18, 1961, one day prior to the UFO encounter. We will have the opportunity to inspect the Hills' individual recall of their journey through Canada and to compare it for correlating accuracy. Betty's and Barney's unique personality characteristics, language patterns, and organizational abilities will emerge to give the reader insight into the Hills' private lives. In the end, it will result in a comprehensive overview of the much misunderstood UFO encounter in New Hampshire's White Mountains and the events leading up to a purported alien abduction. Let us begin with Barney's first hypnosis session.

On February 22, 1964, Dr. Benjamin Simon began his study of Barney's experiences by inducing a deep hypnotic trance. Over the previous few Saturdays, he had conditioned Barney to enter a deep trance and had established cues to facilitate a quick path to the deepest level attainable. Simon's commanding voice ordered:

All right then, trance Barney. Go deeper and deeper asleep...far asleep...deeper and deeper, fully relaxed. All muscles are relaxed. Deeper and deeper asleep...deeper asleep, deep asleep. When I touch your hand your arm will become rigid like a bar of steel...rigid. It cannot bend or relax; very rigid. Now, when I touch the top of your hand you will lose all sensation. You will not feel this pin...no pain whatsoever. Now as I stroke your hand, the sensation becomes normal. The arm relaxes. You go deeper and deeper. Now you are in a very deep sleep. Your memory is now sharp, very sharp. You will remember everything...everything that has occurred; all of your experiences. You will not be anxious or distressed but you will remember everything and you will tell me everything. I want you to go back now to your vacation in 1961 when you were in Montreal.

When Dr. Simon asked him to describe the motel in Montreal where he and Betty stayed on the night of September 18, Barney responded that they did not stay in Montreal, adding, "It was approximately 112 miles from Montreal." When queried about his failure to remember the town or the name of the hotel, Barney explained that they arrived at night, and due to the darkness, he did not notice the motel's name.

In an attempt to elucidate, Barney added, "It was out in the country. In this small area we did not see any town marks and the car was making a lot of noise. It was Betty's car that we were driving. We stopped at a service station and they told me the car had not been properly greased. So they greased the car and this eliminated the noise. Then we decided that we could not continue to Montreal and that we should look for a place to spend the night. And, that's when I saw this motel and did not pay any attention to the name."

The car repair had interrupted their trip and thrown them off their schedule. As darkness fell, Barney (the driver) became tired, so he decided to spend the night at a motel and continue on to Montreal the next morning. Although he had never been denied access to lodging, he knew that racial prejudice was prevalent in the early 1960s, and he was uncertain about Canada's policy on civil rights. He was all too aware of the hostility of white people toward blacks, particularly when there was an interracial couple, so he was concerned about whether or not the motel would accept them. In 1961, it would not have been unusual for a racially prejudiced motel owner to deny lodging simply by stating, "sorry, no vacancy." The fact that they and their dachshund, Delsey, were immediately accepted came as a welcome relief, and they settled in for a much-needed rest.

On March 7, 1964, Dr. Simon placed Betty in a deep trance using precisely the same technique he had used on Barney. But unlike Barney, who gave a precise response, Betty failed to follow Dr. Simon's exact instructions to give details of her trip from Niagara Falls to Montreal. Instead, she jumped ahead in time to the afternoon of their arrival in Montreal. When Dr. Simon directly asked Betty if they had spent the previous night anywhere, she responded as if her train of thought had suddenly been interrupted. In a hurried manner, she stated only that they had stayed "at this motel down by the Thousand Islands and left there in the morning and went to Montreal" (approximately a two-hour drive). She didn't mention the car repair or any of the information that Barney so carefully and precisely offered, nor did she express her thoughts or feelings. Instead, she placed her emphasis on Montreal.

Under individual questioning by Dr. Simon, Betty and Barney both agreed that they lost their route to St. Catherine's Street in downtown Montreal. However, their individual recall of the event is inconsistent and out of sequence. Betty gives the impression that they stopped at two garages to ask for directions, whereas Barney mentions pulling to the side of the road to check his map before proceeding to St. Catherine's Street.

Barney testified, "I approach the city from a different direction than I thought I should on the map. I pull over to the side and I ask Betty, 'Where are we? Can we see ourselves positioned on the map?' And, I see my mistake by this fork and I had continued to the right when I should have made a very sharp left turn, which would have brought me into the city in a different way."

Both Betty and Barney told Dr. Simon about a gas station attendant who did not understand English and assumed they wanted to use the toilet facilities. However, Betty placed this stop early in the afternoon, prior to their drive along St. Catherine's Street, whereas Barney says it occurred in the confusion of the afternoon traffic. This is an excellent example of the fallibility of memory. Although there is no doubt that the Hills became lost as they attempted to maneuver through downtown Montreal, their recall of the sequence of events is not identical.

These apparent discrepancies occurred numerous times during the Hills' testimony, but questioning by Dr. Simon in subsequent sessions eventually led to an accurate account. However, these inconsistencies have never come to light, and this has led to distortion and misunderstanding of the Hill abduction story.

On first account, the Hills' descriptive recall of the sights on St. Catherine's Street meshes almost perfectly. Betty and Barney observed the stylish fashions in storefront windows, and Betty, who had a keen memory for facts and figures, recalled the price of a mink coat that she admired: $1,895. Barney added, "I am parked by the side and we are admiring the buildings and we both are talking about the way the women are dressed and how stylish Montreal is." Barney noticed representatives of his own race on the streets of Montreal and was pleased by this. The Hills exchanged thoughts about finding a hotel near St. Catherine's Street where they could take in the nightlife. But, on second thought, they reasoned that Delsey would more likely be accepted in a motel on the outskirts of the city. So they attempted to locate a route that would take them out of Montreal.

Betty and Barney both described the difficulty they experienced while attempting to maneuver through Montreal's heavy traffic and confusion. Barney spoke of being quite a distance from the downtown section when he lost his route and stopped for directions at a French-speaking garage. When this attempt failed, he located a police officer directing traffic, who spoke English very haltingly, with a strong accent. But he gave Barney the directions, and Barney was able to locate his desired route to the outskirts of Montreal.

Betty, in contrast to Barney, did not identify the police officer, but seemed to be referring to him when she stated, "And then we got lost again and Barney got lost again and a *man* told him how to go. But, I guess we took the wrong turn because we went over a bridge and found ourselves outside of Montreal. And we kept going. We talked about turning around and going back because we hadn't done any sightseeing in Montreal, but we kept driving, thinking we would get a motel first."

She still anticipated that they would find a motel for the night, oblivious to the fact that Barney was thinking, "The cars are driving all over and I think we want to get out of the city as quickly as possible. I decide the traffic is still too congested and it's about the hour that most people are getting off from work. I want to avoid this as much as possible and put distance between me and the city of Montreal." Barney has made the decision to leave Montreal, but Betty is unaware of his agenda. He does not have a detailed city map, and without one, Montreal can be a very confusing place...especially because all of the signs are in French. He has already become lost twice and does not want to venture back into the congested city traffic.

As they drive on, the roads become narrower, and they are finally in a country setting. It is early in the evening and they are hungry, so they stop at a roadside stand for hamburgers and hot dogs, potato chips, and coffee. Barney relates, "They do not speak any English and they think my wife is French." Betty concurs with Barney's assessment of the situation, as evidenced by her statement that the woman at small drive-in restaurant spoke to her in French, adding that she thought Betty was French. They both speak of removing Delsey from the car while they eat at a picnic table. Barney, a frequent watch-checker, noted that it was about 5:30 in the evening, and he wanted to be on his way.

The couple continued their drive through Quebec en route to New Hampshire, but decided stop for a snack and coffee at a restaurant in Coaticook, approximately a 75-minute drive from Colebrook. Betty explained to Dr. Simon, "It was dark and we got into this town and stopped to eat and, oh, the restaurant was all right. It wasn't too good. The waitress could only seem to speak a little English."

In his initial interview, Barney skipped over his stop in Coaticook, but later returned to this point in time as he quietly thought about it 72 miles south in New Hampshire. Barney testified, "I stop in Coaticook, Canada, and we decide to eat and we go into...I cannot get close to the restaurant, so I park on the street and we must walk to the restaurant." Barney goes on guard when he sees men sporting duck-tail haircuts, suspecting they might be hoodlums. He anticipates hostility, but is pleased to find "there is no hostility there." To the contrary, it is a "pleasant restaurant" with "friendly" people. A language barrier is the only difficulty he experiences.

It is not clear whether or not the Hills actually consumed a full meal at the French-speaking restaurant in Coaticook. We know only that they had to point to what they thought they wanted on the menu, but their lack of familiarity with the French language caused them to order potato chips when they anticipated French fries. They were served, but Betty mentioned her dissatisfaction with the food, stating, "It wasn't too good."

A careful analysis of the hypnosis tapes can only derive the fact that they stopped briefly before continuing on the last leg of their trip through

Canada and on into New Hampshire. This episode differs from John Fuller's account of the suspected hoodlum encounter. He morphed the Coaticook incident into the Colebrook incident, although they were actually two entirely different restaurants and experiences. He simply passed over some of the Coaticook restaurant testimony.

The Hills' dialogue is equivocal concerning their drive from Coaticook to the New Hampshire border. It suggests that they may have lost their route again after they left the restaurant, but it is not entirely clear. They had intended to follow Route 147 to the border, crossing in Norton, Vermont. Then they would travel east on Route 114 for approximately 23 miles to the New Hampshire state line. However, we suspect that they turned onto Route 141 and entered Vermont at Canaan/Hereford near the New Hampshire border. Barney interjects the somewhat confusing statement, "114. It's dark....It's not a good road but it's a short distance to New Hampshire and I see signs for Colebrook." Betty fills in the missing piece of the puzzle by explaining, "And I think that we got off from the main road somehow because we went to the Customs...and stopped at the Customs....And, he asked us how...well, he said that they didn't get many tourists at this Customs because it was out of the way. Most people went to a better-traveled highway and I don't know how we made the mistake and got onto this road." It is impossible to ascertain whether or not Barney took Route 141 when he exited Coaticook, rather than continuing on Route 147 to Route 114, but it is a possibility. Did Betty simply anticipate that they would travel along a larger highway than Route 114 proved to be, or did Barney transpose the route numbers 114 and 141 and take the smaller route? We know only that it turned into a well-maintained gravel road lined with prosperous dairy and vegetable farms.

Today, near the U.S. border, a resort area with a beautiful lake is lined with attractive cottages and an inviting chateau accommodation. The structures appear old enough to have been there in 1961. Barney spotted a resort of this description and contemplated stopping for the night, but decided that, because his energy level was high, he would drive into New Hampshire. Although he was apprehensive about traveling through a desolate mountainous area during the off-season, due to the possibility of an automotive breakdown, he decided to continue on and perhaps stop at one of New Hampshire's motels or cabins.

We will never know for certain that Barney followed Route 141 into Canaan, but the question is inconsequential. Route 141 is a more direct route to Colebrook, but was nevertheless a smaller road in 1961. John Fuller deleted this portion of the hypnosis from *The Interrupted Journey*, probably because it only would have added confusion. The time factor would have been comparable, regardless of which route they took.

It would seem fortuitous if Barney confused these two routes because he was concerned about going through U.S. Customs, and a less traveled entry point, perhaps, facilitated his journey into New Hampshire. He explains to Dr. Simon:

> I have a gun in the car. It's a .32 pistol and it is hidden in the well of the trunk of the car, with the trunk mat over it. I left Portsmouth in the morning...about five o'clock. It was dark and I secreted the gun in the trunk. The Canadian official of the Customs building did not look at my car...just the dog and we had papers proving that we had brought the dog into Canada. And he waved us on pleasantly. But the American Customs asked me to open the trunk and he looked at our equipment and he said, "What is this?" and I said that many times when we are on the highway we would stop and cook our food. This is our cooking equipment. He said, "A good idea, and I hope that your trip was pleasant." And he waved us on.

Later, Dr. Simon asked Betty if she had any concerns about anything at Customs. She replied, "No, except the trunk of the car was so untidy and somewhere we heard a weather report, and this is what made us decide to go back to Portsmouth, rather than stay overnight." She, as did Barney, mentioned that the border guard seemed curious about their reason for entering the United States at this small, less-traveled crossing. Betty seemed to be ignorant of the fact that Barney had hidden her handgun in the trunk of her '57 Chevy Bel Air. Although she became aware of the pistol's presence later that evening, she seemed unconcerned about it at this juncture.

On the morning of September 17, 1961, Barney thought about a trip he had taken to Detroit and Niagara Falls, Canada, with his first wife and children. When Barney became tired, they had been forced to spend the night in their vehicle, and at that time he wished that he had taken a gun for protection. It was this memory that prompted him to take along Betty's gun this time. (Betty owned a gun because she enjoyed participating in target practice on her parents' farm.)

As stated earlier, Betty found her food at the Coaticook restaurant to be unsatisfactory, so she and Barney were anxious to find a restaurant where they could consume a late-night snack and cup of coffee before they began the last leg of their trip. They seemed relieved to find themselves in the familiarity of New Hampshire, on a route they were accustomed to traveling, and in a comfortable environment with people who spoke English.

Their brief stop at a Colebrook restaurant was both relaxing and refreshing. Barney wondered why the dark-skinned waitress was not very friendly, whereas the others in the restaurant seemed "friendly" or "pleased." He told Dr. Simon, "I wonder if she is Negro and she is wondering if I know she is passing for white." Barney quickly finished a hamburger while Betty savored a piece of chocolate cake and coffee. He stated the he felt "welcome and alert," albeit "somewhat impatient with Betty to finish her coffee." He noted that the restaurant clock and his watch both indicated that it was 10:05 p.m., and estimated that they would arrive at home in Portsmouth by approximately 2 a.m. Betty independently confirmed his statement by reporting to Dr. Simon, "There was a clock above the door of the ladies' room and it was 10 o'clock and we finished eating and left."

In 1961, facilities in New Hampshire's North Country closed at 11 o'clock, so this would have been their last chance to recharge for their trip south. Today, most travelers take Interstate Routes 89 or 91 through Vermont, but these highways had not been constructed in 1961. Route 3 through Colebrook was the major north–south route. Today, Colebrook restaurants close by 10 o'clock, and earlier on week nights.

Kathy, while researching the Hills' journey, visited Colebrook to investigate the route the Hills followed and to measure their time sequence. An investigation of Colebrook's restaurants was undertaken to check the validity of their memory of a clock above the ladies' room door. The Wilderness Restaurant, located in Colebrook's downtown area, has nail holes above the entrance to the toilet facilities, suggesting that a clock once hung in that location. Fully 46 years have passed since the Hills snacked in Colebrook, so many restaurants may have come and gone. However, this restaurant exhibited evidence that would confirm the Hills' statement that they checked the time on the clock above the ladies' room.

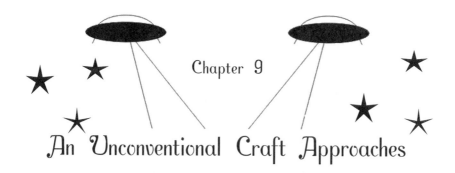

Chapter 9

An Unconventional Craft Approaches

As Barney drove south on Route 3, Betty rode silently, observing her surroundings. This Great North Woods area of northern New Hampshire was dotted with sprawling farm homes, acres of cornfields, and yards full of logs waiting to be milled. They passed through a valley edged with small, tree-covered mountains along a two-lane highway lined with railroad tracks and skirted by the Connecticut River. After they had traveled approximately 27 miles south of Colebrook they passed Groveton, elevation 884 feet above sea level. Eight miles south of Groveton, at an elevation of 867 feet, lay the village of Lancaster and its well-known fairground.

On March 7, 1964, Dr. Simon probed Betty's detailed memory of her trip through northern New Hampshire. She stated she was somewhat startled by a truck that passed, dragging part of its exhaust system and creating sparks on the surface of the road. Next, she stated, "The moon was bright and not quite full but very bright and alive." (The waxing gibbous moon would be full in six days, and high, thin cirrus clouds, generally not noticeable to an untrained observer, covered about 50 percent of the night sky. We do not know if the eastern sky, western sky, or half of the entire sky had cloud cover.) North of Lancaster, near Groveton, Betty observed a star below the moon on the lower left-hand side. As the couple passed through Lancaster, they entered a wide valley with rolling hills. Smaller, tree-covered mountains lay to the west, and the craggy granite peaks of the Mount Washington range could be observed to the East. Moments south of Lancaster, she noticed there was a bigger star up above this one that had not previously been there. She pointed it out to Barney, and continued to watch it as it seemed to grow bigger and brighter.[1]

In 1961, the Hills told NICAP's Walter Webb that it first appeared to be a falling star—only it fell upward. Betty's omission of this element is somewhat confusing, but if we examine her prior testimony to Dr. Simon, her failure to give a richly detailed account of her trip is apparent. This was a reflection of Betty's communication style throughout most of the hypnosis sessions.

In 1966, the Air Force's Blue Book consultant, J. Allen Hynek, interrogated Betty about this point at Dr. Benjamin Simon's home in Arlington, Massachusetts.

Hynek was the official astronomical consultant to the U.S. Air Force's Project Sign, and later Project Blue Book from 1948 to 1969. He earned his doctorate in astronomy at the University of Chicago and was the director of the Lindheimer Astronomical Research Center at Northwestern University, and chairman of Northwestern's astronomy department. He also served as associate director of the Smithsonian Astrophysical Observatory in Cambridge, Massachusetts, as well as heading its NASA-sponsored satellite tracking program. Later, realizing that the UFO hypothesis had not been disproved, Hynek founded the Center for UFO Studies. He spent the remainder of his life engaged in the scientific investigation of unidentified flying objects.[2]

Simon had induced a deep hypnotic trance to initiate Betty's recall. Hynek revealed that she observed the planet Jupiter on the lower left side of the moon and the bright moving object above it, directly left of the moon. Jupiter was the brightest planet in the sky and would have stood out among the other, less brilliant celestial bodies.

In 1976, skeptic Robert Sheaffer suggested that Betty and Barney, in all probability, observed the planets Jupiter and Saturn—not a UFO. He had used a sketch Betty had drawn of the UFO in relation to the moon when she first sighted it, to claim that she had actually only observed two planets. He argued that Betty's failure to mention three brilliant celestial objects and her poor observational skills proved that her UFO was, in reality, the planet Jupiter.[3] However, he failed to take into account the fact that Betty described two bright objects to the left of the moon, whereas Saturn was positioned below and to the right of the moon. Nor did he offer an explanation for the object's apparent movement and expanding size.

Following Sheaffer's argument to its logical absurdity, Betty argued that if one were to accept the skeptical version of her observation, Jupiter would have left its orbit around the sun, decreased in size as it descended towards the White Mountains, and traveled across the moon's face, while Saturn remained stationary in the sky.

At 10:30 p.m. on September 19, 1961, Saturn, a first-magnitude celestial body, could be seen almost directly below the moon. The planet Jupiter, two and one-half magnitudes more brilliant than Saturn, was positioned three degrees below the moon and above and to the left of Saturn. The U.S. Air Force initially came to Sheaffer's conclusion, but later, with additional information, changed its assessment to "insufficient data."

Returning to March 7, 1964: Betty told Dr. Simon that after she observed the expanding point of light for several minutes, she became puzzled and curious. She had passed by a mountain that obstructed her view, and when she saw the star again she thought it had moved, but she wasn't sure. When she noticed that Delsey was somewhat restless she asked Barney to stop beside the road.

Barney's February 22, 1964 account of this incident is as follows: "Delsey's not squirming; she's still under the seat. I don't see a spot to stop, but I've passed several places where I could have pulled off safely from the main highway. But I say, 'Well, I will stop at the next one.' And I have not stopped and Betty said, 'Look, there's a star moving' and I look and I see the star."

Barney located a roadside viewing area near Mt. Cleveland about 20 miles south of Lancaster, just south of Twin Mountain, and pulled to the side of the road. He retrieved Delsey's leash and removed her from the vehicle, while Betty jumped out of the passenger side with her binoculars. As Barney glanced toward the moving star, he walked Delsey to the car's trunk, as he told Betty to hurry up so he could use the binoculars.

On March 21, 1964, Dr. Simon pushed Barney for more information about the stop. Barney stated, "I went to the trunk of the car and opened it and took out a gun I had concealed there, and I put it in my pocket. And then, I said, 'Give me the binoculars.' And I looked and I could see that this thing that I thought was a plane had made a turn to the left toward Vermont and kept turning, and started coming right back."

Betty's account of the first observation point is nearly identical to Barney's, with only one minor exception: In her initial interview, she reported that it was she who walked Delsey before she retrieved binoculars from the car. This is inconsistent with Barney's statement that it was he who walked the dog. But under further questioning by Dr. Simon, she later recalled that it was indeed Barney. It is important to note that Dr. Simon did not point out this discrepancy to Betty. He merely directed her to retell this event.

Dr. Simon failed to probe the rationale behind Barney's decision to remove the gun from the car's trunk. But on March 7, 1964, Betty filled in the missing piece of the puzzle. She told Dr. Simon, "There were a couple of trash barrels, and Barney said we should look out for bears. This was his idea."

New Hampshire's wilderness area is a natural habitat for a variety of forest animals, including black bears, moose, deer, and cats of prey. Barney, who had to relieve himself, walked Delsey into the wooded area. Bears would have been naturally attracted to the easy meal picnickers had left behind in the trash barrels, so Barney carried the gun as a cautionary measure.

Next, Betty told Dr. Simon that in Barney's opinion they were observing a satellite, but she "knew" it wasn't. Through the binoculars she had seen the odd-shaped object travel across the face of the moon, flashing multicolored points of light. Although she had never before observed a satellite, she thought it was too close and too large to fit his explanation.

By the time Barney returned from the wooded section, the enigmatic craft had already passed over the moon's face. He took the binoculars again, while Betty and Delsey returned to the car, and he observed a row of windows in what he, at first glance, assumed was a small aircraft similar to a piper cub. Barney told Dr. Simon, "I had only seen this happen when I was in Philadelphia and I used to be a mail truck driver, and there was a box located near the international airport. And just where I would stop, I would see planes coming in to land with their lights on. And it was a very funny feeling seeing this large thing coming to land, and I thought of that when I was standing on the highway...that this thing is coming right toward us and I said, 'Come on Betty, let's go'"(March 21, 1964).

His skeptical attitude and pragmatic thinking style caused Barney to assume that his eyes were deceiving him. He reasoned that although the craft appeared to be unconventional, it had to be a piper cub in a landing pattern or possibly on a crash course. He even pondered the possibility that it might be a commercial airliner or a military jet. Wanting nothing more than to continue with his drive home to Portsmouth, he became angry and impatient with Betty. However, the craft's unconventional nature sparked his curiosity and caused him to continue to watch it as he drove along Route 3.

As Barney continued on his journey down Route 3 through the narrow mountain pass that forms Franconia Notch, he observed Cannon

Mountain, with its Aerial Tramway, only five miles south of the Mt. Cleveland lookout, near where they made their first observational stop. Betty observed the restaurant on top of Cannon Mountain. As the object passed above it, she noticed that the lights in the restaurant extinguished. Assuming that the restaurant was closing for the evening, in the darkened car she glanced at her watch. Her hypnotic testimony reveals, "It was, I think, 10 minutes past 11. I thought that if anybody were up there they would be able to get a good look at this object. It went right behind the restaurant, and there is a lookout tower in that area. When I was watching it to see what this object would do, I didn't see it." She thought that, perhaps, it had descended into the valley between the two mountains or turned its lights off. But as she rode past the Old Man of the Mountain, it was there. She described it as looking as though it were bouncing along the mountain's ridge. Momentarily, she would lose sight of it, but then it would appear again.

It is apparent from the Hills' testimony that both were cognizant of the unconventional behavior associated with the craft's movement. As they continued along Route 3, Betty focused upon the object's movement while Barney halted the car briefly several times to observe it from the driver's seat. He described how it moved in a stair-step pattern, rising vertically, and then moving horizontally for a short distance before it dipped down. And as it did this, he noticed a row of lights on it that seemed to tilt and level off. It didn't bank in a swooping motion as a plane would, but the cigar-shaped object seemed to shift from a horizontal position to a vertical one. As he drove on he had a peculiar feeling that it was spinning.[4]

From her vantage point in the passenger seat, Betty had an unrestricted opportunity to view the unconventional object. Her March 7, 1964 description corroborated Barney's testimony. She told Dr. Simon, "It was turning. It was rotating, and it would go along and fly in a straight line for a short distance, and then it would tip over on its side and go straight up."[5]

Next, he sighted the familiar landmark The Old Man of the Mountain, New Hampshire's state emblem. Still convinced that he could find a conventional explanation, Barney pulled off onto a scenic turnout to the right of the highway just south of the Old Man of the Mountain profile, probably into a hiking trail parking area. Reasoning that it moved too rapidly to be a piper cub, Barney attempted to convince himself it must be a military jet. He stepped out of the car, angry with Betty and intent upon proving the conventional nature of the craft. However, although he estimated the object was only a thousand feet away, he could not hear the hum of a motor.

Barney thought of a frightening incident with a military jet while he was bathing with his sons at a state park in French Creek, Pennsylvania. The hotshot pilot had dive-bombed the area and pulled up close to the park, producing an explosive sound, possibly a sonic boom. Barney was angry that the military pilot had behaved so irresponsibly, endangering the people below.

On March 21, 1964, as Barney recalled the military's reckless disregard for the citizens below, he reported, "I began to feel very alarmed and hoped for some traffic...some car...or to see the State Police come by and say, 'Look at [that]...it's following us.' But no one came by and I felt very uncomfortable."

Betty questioned whether vibration of their vehicle on the road was causing a distortion in her visual observation, making it appear that the craft was unconventional, when actually it was not. After their stop she concluded that the road vibration could not account for the erratic movement of the craft.

Back on Route 3, the Hills described the craft's unconventional movement. Barney thought of a paddle with a rubber band attached to a ball. He stated, "You hit the ball and the ball goes straight out and comes straight back without a circle." Betty added, "And as they got closer, there seemed to be more of this jumping back and forth in the sky."[6]

Both Betty and Barney reported that, during this time frame, the craft rapidly changed direction, ascended and descended vertically, and hovered motionless in the sky, spinning and tilting upon its side. As we analyze Betty's and Barney's descriptions of the craft's flight characteristics, we can see that, although each chooses his or her own unique language to describe it, their descriptions are almost identical.

Six miles south of Cannon Mountain, Barney momentarily halted his vehicle at a parking area near the Flume, but left when he discovered that the trees blocked his view of the craft. Finally, only 13 miles south of his first observation site, he saw two wigwams, signaling that he had arrived at Indian Head. Feeling comforted by this location, "less in the barren hostility of the wooded area,"[7] he searched his memory for a familiar open area that would afford him an unobstructed view. Moments earlier, he had been annoyed with Betty because she had become excited by the proximity of the unconventional craft. He knew that she was usually reticent to express strong emotions, so her unremitting interest signaled something significant. She was prodding him to look at the craft, but he couldn't because he had to watch the road.

When Dr. Simon told Barney to continue on with his account, he became extremely distressed, asking to be permitted to wake up. But when Dr. Simon denied his request, assuring him that it wouldn't trouble him, Barney's voice became shaky. He said, *"It's over my right. God, what is it? And I try to maintain control so Betty cannot tell I'm scared. God, I'm scared!"*[8]

When Dr. Simon attempted to reassure Barney that the memory wouldn't hurt him, he broke into frantic screaming that rapidly turned into hysterical sobbing. Prior to this outbreak of emotion, the trip had gone rather well. Although Barney expressed concern from time to time about the hostility of white people toward blacks, his interactions with Caucasians had been friendly and pleasant. Although he had grown increasingly concerned about the unconventional nature of the craft, he felt comforted by the presence of motels and tourist attractions. He simply did not want to proceed to the next step in his journey, one of his last conscious memories of eye-to-eye contact with the occupants of a large, hovering UFO.

But he was forced to continue forward to a slight curve in the road just one mile south of Indian Head. He had no choice but to stop his vehicle in the middle of the road because the anomalous craft that his mind had refused to acknowledge was right there, large and hovering slightly to the right of Route 3. Barney said it looked like a "big, big pancake with windows and lights—not lights, just like one big light." It was obviously not a commercial plane, because the curved sides of this hovering disk were tipped with red lights. Additionally, it was completely silent.

Although Betty was too busy watching the road to observe the craft hovering over the field, she described how the object suddenly shot ahead of them and swung around in front of the car. It was no longer spinning, and she could see a lighted double row of windows and red lights on each side of the disk-shaped craft. Her recall of this conscious memory was nearly identical to Barney's.

Skeptics have quoted a statement allegedly made by Dr. Simon on the Larry Glick show in the mid-1970s that Barney was "screaming and groveling on the ground" prior to UFO sighting, allegedly due to his growing fears. There is not one iota of evidence on the hypnosis tapes to support this claim. Barney's first emotional outburst occurred when he was forced to recall his sighting just one mile south of Indian Head.

Early photo at the field south of Indian Head where Barney observed the craft and its occupants.
Courtesy of Kathleen Marden.

Barney's first account of his close-up observation of the craft was punctuated with the highly charged release of repressed emotions. A full account can be found in chapter five of *The Interrupted Journey*. However, a previously unpublished excerpt reveals Barney's highly charged emotional state. On March 21, 1964, he testified under hypnosis to Dr. Simon:

> This is ridiculous! Oh, it's huge! Oh my goodness. Oh, my God. I can see it. It's there! And there are lights! Oh, jeez, I don't believe this! I don't believe this! I don't believe this! It's huge and there are people there and they're looking back at me. Oh my God, help me! If there is a God, help me! Coming closer, I'm coming closer. There's a man up there and he's not gonna let me go away!

Oh! Oh! It's big...80 feet. Look at it! Oh, look at it...two red lights. They're on the side of it. It's like a pancake...it looks...I'm not going to say it...I don't believe flying saucers are...[real]. I'm not gonna say it. I don't ever want to say that word again.

Barney immediately went on the defensive, screaming, "I've gotta get my gun!" (which he had placed in his jacket pocket during his first stop). Barney added more detail in an earlier regression when he informed Dr. Simon that he picked up his gun from the floor and shoved it into his pocket. "And I got out of the car with the binoculars and I stood with my left arm on the door and my right arm partly on the roof of the car." He looked and before he could get the binoculars up to his eyes, the object shifted in an arc. It continued to have a forward look, facing him as it swung, but did not rotate from its position as it glided to an adjacent field. Barney walked across the highway in disbelief, shaking his head and trying to blink his eyes. He lifted the binoculars to his eyes and looked on unbelieving.

In hypnotic regression, Barney was able to add more details to the description of the craft's occupants than he described to NICAP's Walter Webb in 1961, only a month after the sighting. Briefly, he described the round-faced man who reminded him of a redheaded Irishman, and the evil-faced leader. He was a "not too big" man dressed in a military-style cap and black shiny jacket, with a scarf dangling over his left shoulder. His haunting, slanted eyes—a type that Barney had never seen before—were seemingly communicating the telepathic message, "Stay there and keep looking. Just keep looking and stay there. And keep looking. Just keep looking."[9] Filled with terror, Barney pleaded with God to give him the strength to pull the binoculars down so he could flee toward his car.

Individuals who are not familiar with the characteristics of deep trance, mentioned earlier, misinterpret this description as indicating that Barney was actually observing human, perhaps military, personnel. However, we must remember that Dr. Simon had directed Barney to express all of this innermost thoughts and emotions. Exhibiting the characteristics of deep trance, Barney mentioned three events from his past that seemed emotionally comparable to his present situation. He felt threatened by the facial expression of the round-faced crewmember who reminded him of a redheaded Irishman. His past experience with the Irish had been one of racial prejudice, but Barney remarked that this facial expression seemed friendly.

However, the man in the black, shiny jacket reminded him of a Nazi. A veteran of World War II, Barney recalled the threatening stare that reminded him of a Nazi officer and the precision of movement as the crew moved to a panel.

Finally, Barney remembered pouncing upon a tiny bunny when he was a boy on his aunt's and uncle's Virginia farm. The bunny felt that it was safely hidden from its captor's view, but in reality Barney was able to apprehend it. At about midnight on September 19–20, 1961, as he stood alone in the field with a gigantic unconventional craft hovering not more than 300 feet away from him, and approximately 50 feet in the air, Barney felt as exposed as that rabbit. Barney indeed was undergoing a classic abreaction to the horrifying experience that had been haunting him for the past 17 months.

On March 21, 1964, Barney, in a less emotionally charged account, described how, as he rounded a slight curve in the road, he was confronted with the sight of a huge, hovering craft above and slightly to the right of the highway. Forced to stop his vehicle directly in the middle of the road, he recalled:

> It was right there, large and hovering and I could not understand this. I knew I had my gun in my pocket and I said, "I will get out and get a better look." And I opened the car door, and tried to brace my arms on the door and on the roof of the car. And the motor was running and my arms were jiggling, so I stepped away from my car. And when I did, the object, which was to the right of the car on Betty's side, made an arc-like turn—or not a turn, but a swinging motion over to the left of my side. And I thought, "My God, what is this thing? It's got to be a helicopter to just stay suspended like that." And it's just not making any sound, so I started walking across the highway to look at it. And as I walked further away from the car I noticed with my binoculars that there were 11 men now, I thought, looking down at me, and they suddenly made a turn to what I thought was a panel. I could see their arms going up and there was one that kept looking down, and I kept going closer. I could see two red lights coming out from the tip of this thing that did not look like a plane at all, or a helicopter. I could see a long something coming down from the center and I kept going closer and closer. I thought, "My God, what is this thing?!" I felt myself being told to come closer and I

was greatly confused by this and I blinked my eyes and I thought, "This can't be real." And I shook my head and turned away, and looked back and said, "Oh, God its there. What is this thing?" I tried to put my hand toward my gun and I could not put my hand there. I cannot understand why my hands keep going up with the binoculars. I was told to keep the binoculars up and keep looking up, and keep coming closer. No harm would come to me. [He then pleads with God in a great emotional outburst.] I opened my hands and the binoculars fell around my neck, and I ran screaming back to the car that they were going to capture us. And yet, I could not understand what they wanted to capture us for. I thought I should report this to the police if ever I could find a call box or anything, or a restaurant open.

While Barney was in the field, Betty waited impatiently, looking out the front and back windows of the car for approaching vehicles. None passed. Four or five minutes later, when Barney hadn't returned to the car, she stretched across the front seat and called, "Barney, come back here! Barney you damn fool; get back here! Ugh, come back here! [Crying profusely now] Barney, Barney, Barney, get back here you damn fool! What's wrong with you?"[10]

Concerned for Barney's safety, Betty had started to slide across the seat to push the door open. Her calls had gone unanswered and she was determined to go after him, but at that moment Barney came running. He threw the binoculars on the seat next to Betty, and in a hysterical laughing or crying state, told her they had to get out of there or they were going to be captured. As he fled from the field, the craft shifted location again, this time directly over the car. Because the motor was running, he shifted into first gear, stepped on the gas, and took off rapidly.

Accounting for driving speed (about 15 mph) and distance (14 miles), and allowing for observational stops, the Hills were now running at least 30 minutes behind schedule. They could expect to arrive home at approximately 2:30–3 a.m.

As Barney drove, Betty rolled down her window and slid her body through the opening. With her head and shoulders extending upward, she attempted to locate the craft, but she saw only blackness. She could no longer see the stars overhead or lights on the craft. In Dr. Simon's office on March 28, 1964, she realized it was directly overhead.

With the craft in pursuit, the Hills traveled rapidly south on Route 3 past the familiar sight of Clarks Trading Post, with its trained bears and gift shop. Then suddenly the craft emitted a series of code-like, electronic buzzing sounds that seemed to bounce off the trunk of their '57 Chevy.

Betty continued her late spring dialogue: "So, I closed the car window and then, there's this bee-bee-bee-beep on top of the car and the whole car vibrates. And I say maybe it's an electric shock of some kind and I'm touching the metal of the car, but I don't feel any shock. I just feel vibrations. And Barney says, 'What's that? What's happening?' And I say, 'I don't know…I don't know what it is." I wish I knew the Morse code."

Almost immediately, the Hills entered a period of rapidly fading consciousness, retaining only vague memories of passing through the village of North Woodstock. Barney's amnesia was nearly complete, though Betty recalled fleeting memories of familiar sites. As they traveled along Route 3 through North Woodstock and beyond, they would have observed a valley that expanded to the east, meeting smaller, tree-covered mountains. Trees lined the steep embankment to the west, and periodically a house perched on the side of the road. Immediately to the east of Route 3, railroad tracks ran parallel to the highway, and a series of three bridges stretched across the Pemigewasset River, allowing access to Route 175. Betty recalled only a vague memory of a railroad-type bridge. The valley was wide and Route 175 ran parallel to Route 3 through the town of Thornton. Betty noticed a familiar pumpkin head (which she later realized was for the Jack-O'-Lantern Golf Resort) as they traveled south with the craft pacing them from above. The craft was no longer within their visual range and they hoped that it had left them. As we examine the next chapter we will see that the Hills' hopes were quickly dashed.

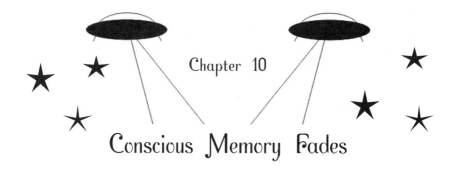

Chapter 10

Conscious Memory Fades

With the UFO overhead, emitting electronic buzzing sounds on the trunk of their car, Betty's and Barney's conscious memories began to fade—Barney's more rapidly than Betty's. They were left only with the hazy memories of a sudden, unplanned left-hand turn off Route 3 and over a railroad type of bridge, an inexplicable roadblock where they were signaled to stop, and a huge, red-orange, flaming moon sitting on the ground. Their next fully conscious memory occurred in Ashland, New Hampshire, when a second series of electronic buzzing sounds, the same as the first, apparently brought them to full mental acuity. Throughout the ensuing months, as they began to remember more and more, these memories would come to haunt them. Repeated attempts to find a rational explanation for them resulted in more questions than answers.

Our examination of the Hills' hypnotic recall of this period will begin with Betty, who did not have visual contact with the occupants of the craft, as Barney had in the field. It is believed that her conscious memory of the events following the stop at the field persisted until sometime after the craft emitted buzzing sounds upon the car. She recalled vague memories of a pumpkin head at the Jack-O'-Lantern Resort, 8 miles south of the field in Lincoln. The brakes squealed as Barney came to a near stop on the highway and maneuvered a sharp left-hand turn over a steel bridge. There was also a roadblock, but this memory was faint and distant from her. It seems that these buzzing sounds were a significant factor in the process of partially eradicating the couple's memory—full memory returned only after they heard a second series of electronic buzzing sounds some 17 miles south of the their turn onto Route 175 in Ashland.

Betty's hypnotic recall began just north of the bridge. On March 7, 1964, she remembered riding along in an unfamiliar area with no recollection of how she arrived there. She sensed that something was going to happen, but she wasn't frightened. Suddenly, without warning, the car slowed and made a sharp left-hand turn off the highway onto a narrow road. All conversation had stopped, but Betty assumed that if they became lost, they'd come out somewhere.

Barney's account of this time frame is consistent with Betty's. He stated that, as he was hurrying to get away, he drove perhaps a few miles before he noticed he was not on Route 3. In a March 21, 1964 hypnosis session he stated, "I made a turn and I never knew this. I don't know why I had to make that turn, and I was lost. I saw I was on a strange area of highway and I had never been there before. And I was being stopped. I was very uncomfortable, but somehow the eyes [that seemed to have penetrated his consciousness and prevented him from taking self-initiated action] were telling me that I should be calm and that I would not be harmed. And to relax...and I saw these men coming down towards me...."

Dr. Simon, with incredulity in his voice, asked Barney if he hadn't just felt or dreamed that he encountered men in the road. Barney responded with an emphatic, "No, I did *not* dream this!" Dr. Simon, in amazement, asked, "There were men down the road that actually stopped you?" Barney forcefully replied, "Yes!" Then, Dr. Simon pursued his line of reasoning by asking Barney if this hadn't been just an impression or a dream. But Barney remained steadfast in his insistence that the event had actually occurred. It was not a dream or a fantasy. To support his contention, Barney added, "They were there and I did not know this. I never knew this because I was hypnotized by Dr. Simon and he told me that I would remember, and I remembered."

Skeptics contend that when Betty and Barney saw a star-like light in the sky that seemed to be following them, they became frightened and turned off the main highway onto narrow mountain roads, attempting to evade the imagined UFO. But we have just presented documented evidence that Barney did not make a conscious decision to leave Route 3. The vehicle seemed to turn through the influence of an external force. Barney, who knew he was in a dangerous situation, had been actively seeking the assistance of a highway patrolman. He did not intentionally leave a straight section of the main highway to follow a less populated, more desolate route.

Betty then reported to Dr. Simon that they were traveling along when they came to a sharp curve in the road, and as they went around the curve, there were many tall trees on her side. Suddenly, she noticed men standing in the highway and thought that perhaps their car had broken down. Barney had to stop, and the men separated into two groups and started to approach the Hills' car. The motor died, the car stalled, and Barney tried unsuccessfully to start it. He said he thought it was the men in the craft again and Betty became terrified, weeping profusely. As the men approached the passenger door, Betty attempted to escape and run into the woods to hide. However, the moment she grasped the handle to open it, the men came up and they opened the car door. There were three small men—two in front and one behind them, with another standing behind the cluster of three.

Betty Hill at the capture site.
Courtesy of Kathleen Marden.

Allowing for observational stops, momentary halts, and periods of driving at less than 30 miles per hour, the roadblock occurred approximately one hour and 30 minutes after the Hills left the roadside rest stop at Mt. Cleveland. It was about 12 miles southeast of the field near Indian Head where Barney observed the craft's occupants through binoculars.

Barney's description, though told from his own perspective, was nearly identical to Betty's. He described a group of men standing in the brightly illuminated highway. Without warning, a cluster of six men divided into two groups and approached each side of the car. He became frightened, but this time he didn't reach for his gun. He had the impression, he said, "If I did think of my gun I would be harmed." As three men assisted him out of the car, he felt two eyes coming close to his, seemingly pushing into his eyes, and he was helpless to resist. Then his mind went blank, he closed his eyes, and he thought of nothing more. One of his feet touched the ground and two men grasped him, supporting his weight as his feet dragged along the ground.

We can draw certain conclusions from these statements: Barney claims that what he "thought" was a cluster of six men in the highway split into two groups of three. Three went to him and three did not. Betty's testimony agrees with Barney's when she states that the men in the highway came in two groups. Each counts three men at their car door—two in front and one behind them.

In her dream account, Betty states only that eight to 11 men surrounded the car. However, each independently told Dr. Simon that the men split into two groups of three and approached each side of the vehicle. Betty counted a fourth behind the group on her side, but Barney closed his eyes rapidly and saw only three. In her dream, Betty sat motionless as the strange men opened the car door. However, her hypnotic recall reveals that she attempted to open the car door and flee into the woods. We can see that her dream, at this point in the sequence, lacks the detailed information that both she and Barney produced under hypnotic regression. Further, Barney offered details that could not have been absorbed by overhearing Betty tell investigators about her dreams. The dream hypothesis is failing to hold up.

It becomes apparent as we analyze the complete investigation of Betty's and Barney's encounter that much of the evidence in support of an abduction hypothesis has never been compiled—prior to this, we have had an incomplete picture of the entire sequence of events, and it is reasonable to assume that skepticism would prevail when all of the facts are not present.

Now let us proceed to Betty's hypnotic recall of her trip from the vehicle to the landed craft. Betty begins, "I'm thinking I'm asleep and I've got to wake up. I've got to wake up. I don't want to sleep. I keep trying. I've got to wake myself up. I don't want to sleep. And I try and I go back again. I keep trying. I keep trying to wake up. [Sudden increase in verbalization rate] Then I do! I open my eyes and I'm walking through the woods! I just open them quick and then I shut them again. Even though I'm asleep, we were walking [Sobs]."[1]

This portion of Betty's recall is nearly identical to her dream description: "I am struggling to wake up; I am at the bottom of a deep well and I must get out. Everything is black. I am fighting to become conscious. Slowly and gradually I start to become conscious. I struggle to open my eyes for a moment and then they close again. I keep fighting. I am dazed and I have a faraway feeling. Then, I win the battle and my eyes are open. I am amazed!"

Betty then told Dr. Simon that she was escorted along a path in the woods by two of the small men. An additional two men were in front of her, and when she turned her head, she saw Barney being assisted by two men. Barney's eyes were closed and he appeared to be asleep. Betty became angry and attempted to awaken Barney, but he seemed oblivious to his situation. It was as if he hadn't heard Betty's voice. A bit further along the path, Betty turned around and called his name again, "Barney, wake up!" But he didn't respond. Then the man who was walking beside her inquired, "Oh—is his name Barney?" And she turned around and looked at the man, and figured it was none of his business, so she didn't speak to him. When Betty failed to reply, the man reassured her there was no reason to be afraid. They only wanted to do a few tests, and when the tests were completed she and Barney would be returned to the car unharmed, and they could go about their way.

Betty added more detail to this account in a later session when she stated:

> We go...the path winds in the woods and it winds around...to the craft on the ground. It was metal...like an oval...or something like that. You know...like it wasn't shiny. It was a very moonlit night...it wasn't quite as clear as daylight, but I could see. It was on the ground and there was like a rim around the edge. The rim was a little bit above the ground, and there was a ramp that came down. It was big. There was a clearing in the woods with trees around it, except I think not big....I thought that I would get the hell out of there if I could. I couldn't seem to. This man was beside me. All I could say was, "Barney, Barney, wake up."

Now let us compare Betty's nightmares to her hypnotically recovered memories. The following is an excerpt from her first nightmare:

> We reached a small clearing in the woods. In front of us was a disc almost as wide as my house is long. It was darkened, but

appeared to be metallic. No lights or windows were seen and I had the impression that we were approaching from the back of it. We stepped up a step or two to go onto the ramp, leading to a door. At this point, I became frightened again and refused to walk. The leader spoke firmly but gently, reassuring me that I had no reason to be afraid. But the more delay I caused the longer I would be away from the car. I shrugged my shoulders and agreed that we might as well get it over with; I seem to have no choice in this situation.[2]

At first glance, this segment seems to confirm that Betty's dream is nearly identical to her hypnotic recall. Upon closer inspection, however, we find subtle differences between Betty's dream and her hypnotically recovered memory. The men in her dream were relaxed and friendly in a professional way. The leader was firm but gentle and reassuring when she refused to enter the craft. However, under hypnosis, the man behind her became angry when she resisted entering the craft. Finally, in her dream the man reasoned with her that the longer she remains uncooperative, the longer she will be away from her car, so she complies. This stands in stark contrast to the regression, in which she resists their attempts to force her onto the craft. Then, the humanoids grip her arms, and she becomes helpless to resist.

The apparent disparity between Betty's nightmare material and her hypnotic recall suggests that perhaps her traumatic dreams were part of the dream-state process of resolving conflict. Her nightmares repeated certain aspects of the traumatic event, whereas other elements were changed or missing. One must ask the question, did Betty create a false memory in order to protect herself from the horrific reality of her situation? Or, did Betty add confabulated details to fill in a gap where no biographical memory existed?

Kathy attempted to answer this question in a 2004 interview with Betty. We must remain cognizant of the fact that Betty's posthypnotic memory of this event was somewhat different from both the hypnosis and the dream. Her later account explained the damage that was done to her dress at the entrance to the craft. She recounted:

At first Barney tried to fight them off, but only for a short time. They had him under some kind of control. He couldn't get away. I'm still talking to Barney saying, "You damn fool. Why don't you wake up?" As we were being led into the craft, we were being held or controlled by the men. He had about six of them. There were ruts in the road. They are practically carrying him. When he was being taken through the woods the tips of his shoes were dragging on the ground. So, the tips of his shoes were scarred. With me it was different. I was more or less walking under my own power. Only at this point I'm thinking, "Who do these characters think they are? What do they think they're doing? I don't know where we're going, but I'm not doing it." I don't know if I was yelling or just thinking it, but I was objecting. I was resisting. And I got almost up to the craft when I started fighting. When they were holding me it certainly was not a weak grip. I know that they had a good, strong grasp on my arms. They bruised me a little bit. I had torn my dress in the struggle. It had a built-in lining and I was struggling so badly that the stitching on the inside of the dress had been torn out, so in places it was hanging down. When we got up to the craft, I was still struggling, but at this point, I sort of threw up my hands and said, "The heck with it. I don't have any control here. They've already got Barney close to being onboard, so I might as well stop my fighting and go ahead and behave myself." So, I went up to the craft...I only had a short distance to go, so I went up to this oval-edged door like you see on a ship, and Barney had already stepped inside. It was like a platform and it set on the ground, and then, there was a little spot that was up about six inches at the most. You stepped on that, over the six inches, and through this oval-shaped door. Inside the craft, we could see that there was a platform that circled the interior, and the rooms, as such, were higher than the floor of the interior.

Now, let us compare the content of this portion of Barney's hypnotic regression to that of Betty's, remembering that Barney was somnambulistic at this stage. On February 29, 1964, Barney recalled, "They were by my side and I had a funny feeling because I knew they were holding me but I couldn't feel them. I felt floating...suspended. I only became aware that I could not feel them when we were going up an incline, and then, I felt that I could not feel them. Yet, my arms were in a position of being supported. My elbows were out and I was moving, but I was not walking."[3]

In a later unpublished regression Barney added more detail:

I'm out of the car and I'm going down the road into the woods. There's an orange glow. There's something there....Oh! Oh! If only I had my gun. What do they want? The crazy eyes are with me. They're with me. We go up a ramp. My feet just bumped, and I'm in a corridor. I don't want to go and I don't know where Betty is. The eyes are telling me to be calm. I'll be calm. I'll be calm. If I'm not harmed I won't strike out, but I will strike out if I am harmed in any way. I'm numb. I'm numb. I have no feeling in my fingers. My legs are numb.

It is apparent that Barney's description is consistent with what one might expect from a person whose eyes are closed. He is numb and in an altered state, but his account supports Betty's. When his feet bump the opening to the craft he realizes that, although his legs are numb, he is being supported. This information suggests that the tops of Barney's shoes were scuffed along the path through the woods and when his feet slid over the raised opening in the doorway. This is further supported by his statement, "I am only thinking of mental pictures because my eyes are closed, and I think I am going up a slight incline, and my feet are not bumping on the rocks."

In a 1966 meeting in Dr. Simon's home with J. Allen Hynek and the Hills, Dr. Simon induced a deep hypnotic trance in both Betty and Barney simultaneously. Then he instructed the Hills to answer Hynek's questions. Hynek attempted to elicit specific details about the Hills' experience that had previously gone unanswered. Dr. Simon demonstrated his ability to "switch off" the auditory input to one person, while the other underwent interrogation. He used this technique from time to time during the 1964 hypnosis sessions whenever there was an interruption.

When Hynek inquired about the temperature inside the interior of the craft, Barney stated that it was different from the night air. It was cooler. Later, when Barney was "switched off" and Betty was asked the same question, her reply was consistent with Barney's. This detailed information cannot be found in Betty's dream sequence, and their stories correlate point by point in minute detail.

Now we will examine the content of the couple's individual memories of their experience onboard the craft.

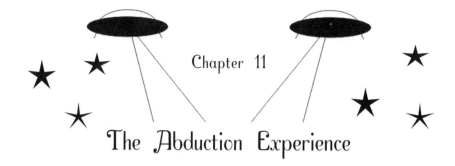

Chapter 11

The Abduction Experience

It has often been alleged that the richness of content in Betty's experience compared to the paucity of detail in Barney's suggests that he absorbed her dream/nightmare material. It is our contention that John Fuller's book, *The Interrupted Journey*, focused primarily upon Betty's complex abduction scenario, but omitted the more significant details of Barney's. In order to avoid repetition, Fuller often omitted entire segments of the hypnosis sessions, although Dr. Simon explored this material repeatedly. Additionally, sensitive areas of Barney's exam were modified or excluded completely to protect his privacy.

In this chapter, we shall examine a comprehensive account of the craft's interior and the physical examinations, including Barney's examination. We will begin with Betty's entrance into the examination room.

In her last hypnosis session she stated, "I went up the ramp and I went inside and there was a corridor. And there was a door and there was a light inside...and there was a room, and there was a light inside this room. It was a bluish light. And I wanted them to take Barney and me into the same room. When I got up to the door, Barney was behind me, and I started to go into the room...and I just started to...and they take Barney past the door. There were two men...the first two, and then, there were two men in front of me and two on each side of the door. The man who was beside me showed me the door, and I went through, and he came in behind me, and the other men stayed with Barney."

Barney's description of the examining room is consistent with Betty's hypnotic recall. He reported that it resembled, "a hospital operating room. It was a pale blue, sky blue." It is interesting to note that although both individuals recall a bright bluish light that seems to permeate the surface of the walls, Betty's dream sequence mentions a conventional "bright overhead light with a bluish shade." The Hills' hypnotically recovered description is inconsistent with Betty's dream material—Barney could not have absorbed this information from overhearing Betty's dream account. However, each independently recalled identical environmental characteristics.

Next, he told Dr. Simon that this room did not resemble the operating room where he had an appendectomy as a child. "I was carried into a room and I got on a table and I was afraid, but somehow, not afraid enough to run. I thought it would soon be over if they don't harm me."[1] Later, Barney added, "It looked like an operating table...or an examining table. I don't know. I just know that I could be supported fully on it and it was very clean...nothing elaborate...just that I could be on it, and my feet extended out from the bottom of it...overlapped it from the position I was laying in" (March 14, 1964).

On the same date Betty described it as follows: "It wasn't like the examining table that some doctors...I don't know if all doctors have the same kind of examining table. This was more like a long table but not awfully long [approximately 4 feet]. I guess it was like a regular examining table. It was light. I mean it was white or metal. It was metal. I know...it was hard. It wasn't soft or that type of thing." In this case, Betty's description is more detailed than Barney's, but their individual accounts remain consistent—and different from Betty's dream material. In "Dreams or Reality?" she mentions only that it is an examining table.

Barney's ensuing physical examination is rich with descriptive detail that has never before been made public. He narrates the exam as follows:

I felt my shoes being removed and my pants being opened. And, I could hear a humming-like sound that they seemed to be making. They pulled my pants all the way down to where my legs were. I could feel them turning me over and putting something in my rectum. It was like a tube. It was not painful. I thought it was just a little larger than a pencil. I felt it go in very easily and then it was withdrawn. They looked at my back and I could feel them touching my skin right down my back as if they were counting my spinal column. I felt something touch right at the base of my spine, like a finger pushing...a single finger. I could only hear this mum...mum...mum,mum,mum,mum, mum,mum,mum...mum [rapid humming] like sound and then I was turned over again. And, my mouth was opened and I could feel two fingers pulling it back. And then I heard as if some more men came in and I could hear them rustling around on the left side of the table I was laying on, and, something scratched very lightly like a stick on my arm.

And these men left and I was left with what I thought were three men....The two that had brought me in and the other one that seemed to follow these two men. I could tell that there was more than one person in the room. But only one man seemed to be moving around my body all the time.

Later, Barney recalled that the examiner had also checked his ears, adding that the examiner seemed particularly curious about his bone structure.

In another account Barney describes his abductors' vocalizations, noting, "Their mouths moved and I could see them." When their mouths moved sounds came out from them that Barney described as sounding like (quivering) "oh-oh-oh-oh-oh-oh. They opened their mouths but they were not talking to me." He said that they did not talk to him, but just made sounds when they communicated with each other. He had never heard this sound made by either human or animal.

Betty's account of her captor's communication is consistent with Barney's, as evidenced by the following: "Oh, he makes a sound...I don't understand it in English. The crew made different sounds...like ah-ah-ah-ah-ah [humming] that went up and down but it wasn't humming like we hum." The leader and the examiner "didn't make mumbling sounds like the crew. They were like words...like sounds of words." Betty stated that she heard these sounds in an unfamiliar language and understood it as if it were English. She could understand almost everything that the leader said, but only some things that the examiner said. Again, the Hills independently contribute detailed information that cannot be found in Betty's dreams.

"The Examiner" by artist Patrick Richard, based upon Betty's description. Courtesy of Patrick Richard.

As Barney continued to elaborate on the procedures used during his physical exam, he, in a conscious interview with Dr. Simon, explained, "I have the most peculiar feeling that something was placed against my genital parts. It was more as if it was in a solution of something that was there, that had substance to it...that had body to it." Barney said he felt "a tug or a pressure or something," but he told Dr. Simon that there was not an erection or an ejaculation, and no pleasure was associated with it. It is not entirely clear that the exam even included a reproductive component, although in a later session Barney mentioned that he suspected they were taking a sperm sample. His descriptions suggest that specimens were extracted from every orifice in his body.

One mystifying element that occurred during the hypnosis involves a concentric circle of wart-like growths that appeared on Barney's groin shortly after his UFO encounter. It was in the exact location where the cup-like appliance was pressed against him, and he had never before had these growths. In the spring of 1964, as Barney relived his physical examination at the hands of his abductors, his growths became inflamed and required surgical removal. Although his physician had initially diagnosed them as venereal warts, the specialist who removed the 21, three-quarter-inch growths, said that they were not. They didn't have the cauliflower appearance of venereal warts. In fact, they were not warts at all. They were removed more for cosmetic purposes than as a medical necessity.

Barney examined his groin on the morning of September 20, 1961. He felt that he had somehow been contaminated and was looking for evidence, but he did not observe an injury to this part of his body until January or February of 1962. Dr. Simon did not seem to draw a correlation between Barney's warts and his memory of a cup-like instrument being placed in their exact location. The hypnosis tapes indicate that Dr. Simon examined the lesions. However, he seems to have concluded that this was a mere coincidence. Barney recoiled in opposition to Dr. Simon's incredulity, insisting that he had "been touched."

Betty's exam was similar to Barney's. Her dress and shoes were removed, she was forced to lie upon a table, her skin was scraped, and her mouth as examined. Later, a neurological and a so-called pregnancy test were accomplished. Although Betty's account is somewhat more detailed than Barney's, she did not mention a rectal or vaginal specimen.

It is interesting to note that Betty's physical exam onboard the craft closely correlates with her dream material. It causes one to wonder, did Barney fail to mention portions of the entire examination to Dr. Simon, or did Betty confabulate, adding more procedures than actually occurred? Or did the examiner, as the Hills later stated, focus primarily upon Betty's skin and Barney's skeletal system? As we explore Betty's exam, we will note that although her dream material parallels her hypnotic recall, it is less detailed and somewhat different.

Betty's March 7, 1964 regression begins, "I go into this room and some of the men come in the room with this man who speaks English and they stay for a minute. I don't know who they are. I guess they're the crew, but they only stay for a minute. The man who speaks English is there, and another man comes in, and I haven't seen him before. I think he's a doctor. There's a stool...a white...is it white? I don't know if it's white or chrome. There's a stool and they put me on the stool. There's a little bracket. My head is resting against the bracket."[2] It is interesting to note that although Betty describes a scenario similar to her dream, the dream material does not contain a detailed description of the stool.

Next, the examiner began his medical procedure. Betty recalled:

I have a light blue dress on and they push up the sleeve of my dress and they look at my arm here, and they look at my arm. They turn my arm over and they look at it. They have a machine. I don't know what it is. They bring the machine over and they put it...I don't know what kind of machine. It's something like a microscope, only a microscope with a big lens. And they put a...I don't know. I had an idea they were taking a picture of my skin. And they both look through this machine here and here, and then they talk. I don't know...I couldn't understand what they were saying. And then they took something like a letter-opener, only it wasn't. They scraped my arm here...They scraped and they looked like little skin....You know how your skin gets dry and flaky sometimes, like little particles of skin? They put...there was something like a little piece of cellophane plastic...something like that. And they put what came off on the plastic. The examiner opens my eyes and looks in them with a light. And he opens my mouth and he looks at my throat and my teeth and he looks in my ears. And then he takes like a swab or Q-tip and he puts it in my left ear. And he puts this on another piece of material. The leader takes it and rolls it up and puts it in the top drawer. Oh, then he feels my hair, then the back of my neck. And they take a couple of strands of my hair and they pull it out and he gives this to the leader and he wraps that up and puts that in the top drawer. Then he takes something that may be like scissors. I don't know what it is, and then, they cut a piece of my hair here. They cut off a piece of it and he gives it to him. And then he feels my neck and through my shoulders around my collarbone. And then they take off my shoes and they look at my feet and my hands. They look at my hands all over and he takes...uh....The light is very bright and so some...I don't always...my eyes aren't open. I am still a little scared, too. I'm not particularly interested in looking at them. And so, I try to keep my eyes shut, and then, I do open...you know, not all the time. I sort of give myself a little relief by not looking at them. I shut my eyes and he takes something and he goes underneath my fingernail. And then he takes something...I don't know, probably manicure scissors or something, and he cuts off a piece of my fingernail. They look at my feet all over. I don't think they do anything to them. They just feel my feet and toes and all.[3]

This description of Betty's medical examination closely parallels her dream material. It is interesting to note that she revealed to Dr. Simon that her eyes were closed during much of this exam. She captured only fleeting glimpses of the procedures that were taking place. This information leads one to speculate whether or not Betty was actually filling in the visual gaps with dream material. Betty's exam may actually have been more similar to Barney's. Additionally, during this part of the hypnosis, her speech was rapid and facile, further suggesting that she was substituting familiar dream material, instead of re-experiencing the traumatic exam.

Weeks before Betty's death, Kathy attempted to extract the true nature of the event from her. Using a cognitive interview technique, she facilitated Betty's moment-by-moment recollection of the exam. Betty slowly and thoughtfully recalled the exam, adding that her head dropped down several times and they lifted it up into position. Then they opened her eyes and stared into them, giving her the impression that they were amazed. (Could this be a similar description to Barney's statement that the eyes pushed into his?) This suggests that she also was somewhat immobilized, though not as completely as Barney. We know from their treatment of Barney that the occupants had a propensity for the immobilization of resisters. It is therefore reasonable to conjecture that Betty was subjected to a mind-altering force that rendered her helpless moments before her physical examination commenced. Thus, her descriptive process was a visualization of what she thought was occurring, although her eyes were closed during much of this part of the exam.

Returning to 1964, Betty told Dr. Simon that at this point, the initial examination had ended, and the examiner informed her that he wanted to conduct a few simple tests. The first test would provide information about the differences between his and her nervous systems. In order to perform this test, Betty was required to remove her dress. Before she had a chance to stand up, the examiner grasped the tab on her zipper and pulled it down to her waist. (This does not explain how Betty's zipper became ripped.) Having slipped her dress off, now wearing only a slip, bra, and panties, she followed the examiner's directive to lie down on the examining table, which she mentioned was about the height of a desk. She assumed a position on her back and the examiner approached her with what appeared to be a cluster of needles. She said each needle had a wire running from it. There was, in Betty's words, "some kind of a gadget on the end of these needles" that reminded her of a large TV screen. The screen, Betty said, had "all kinds of lines or something like that." When Dr. Simon inquired about whether or not the needles hurt Betty, she reported that they didn't cause pain. The examiner simply touched the needles to her spinal column, behind her ears, and on several areas on her head, arms, and legs. Then they rolled her over onto her abdomen, pushed her slip up to her armpits, and touched her along her vertebrae.

This account was less detailed and somewhat different than Betty's 1961 "Dreams or Reality?" rendition. She dreamed about a machine that resembled an EEG, but her dream lacked the tracing monitor she described to Dr. Simon. The examiner gently touched needle tips to her temples, face, behind her ears, along her neck and spine, under her arms, and around her hips, causing a slight twitch in some areas. She assumed that a recorder of some kind was being used, but she didn't see one.

Using a cognitive interviewing technique, Kathy facilitated Betty's recall of this abduction-related test. Betty told her, "He decides to remove my dress. Now he is confused because he doesn't know how to remove my dress. So I sit up, and that's when he sees the zipper, but he doesn't know how to handle it. And so he starts tugging at it and I can almost hear the stitching rip. So I reach behind and start to pull the zipper down and then he seems to get the idea and he starts pulling the zipper down too. So, it did get torn in a few places, but not much."

When Betty removed her dress from her closet in April or May of 1964, she discovered that the fabric on the left side of the zipper, next to

"The Supervisor" by artist Patrick Richard.
Courtesy of Patrick Richard.

the metal teeth, was ripped in a 1-inch vertical tear. On the right, in the area where the dress fabric attaches to the zipper cloth, 2 inches of stitching was torn out.

Betty continued, "So he unzips my dress and pulls it off my sleeves and just drops it in a pile on the floor. So it stays there while he...[long pause] so then he starts feeling all up and down my spine." In this account Betty failed to mention the nerve conduction-like test that she experienced in her dream account and during regressive hypnosis. Her cognitive interview account closely resembled Barney's description of the examiner touching his spinal column as if to count his vertebrae.

The now famous pregnancy test marks the final stage of Betty's exam. UFO researchers have compared the insertion of a needle into Betty's navel to amniocentesis, a medical procedure now administered on a routine basis to determine the genetic makeup of a fetus. It can identify the presence of a chromosomal birth defect such as Down syndrome or identify the biological father when paternity is in question. The procedure involves the removal of amniotic fluid from a pregnant woman's uterus. In 1961, amniocentesis was still in experimental stages. It was not possible to grow human cells in the laboratory until the mid-1960s, and genetic testing on a fetus was not accomplished until 1968.[4] Betty could not have acquired this information prior to her frightening dream in 1961.

Skeptics contend that this part of Betty's exam came directly from the 1953 movie *Invaders from Mars*. Betty once mentioned that someone had invented this false information about her to promote a debunking argument. She was distressed by these false accusations, and told Kathy, "I might have seen part of some science fiction movie once when I was visiting your mother when you were a kid, but I don't know what it was, or even if I saw it."

In April of 1964, Dr. Simon asked Betty, "Do they look like any of the pictures of people you've seen from outer space, like Martians?" Betty replied, "I don't think I've ever seen any pictures."

The late UFO researcher/writer Karl Pflock conducted an extensive investigation of the Hill UFO encounter and concluded that the evidence pointed toward an alien abduction. He corresponded with Betty and Kathy for several years, and visited Betty in her home.

At the end of a meticulous investigation of Betty Hill, he concluded that there was no evidence to support the claim that she was a science fiction fan. Those who knew her well will unequivocally support Pflock's conclusion.

Karl Pflock graduated from San Jose State University in 1964. He served in reserve components of the Marine Corps and Air Force from 1960 to 1966, and was employed by the CIA from 1966 to 1972. From 1981 to 1983, he was a senior staff member for Congressman Jack Kemp. From 1983 to 1985, he was special assistant for defense, space, science, and technology to Congressman Ken Kramer. From 1985 to 1989, he served as the deputy assistant secretary of defense (deputy director) for Operational Test and Evaluation. He was awarded the Defense Outstanding Public Servant Award and the Defense Superior Achievement Award. In 1992, Pflock returned to full-time writing and independent research. Pflock died on June 5, 2006, from Lou Gehrig's disease.

Now back to the insertion of a needle into Betty's navel. One thing is clear: Betty exhibited such marked agitation during the needle insertion part of the medical examination that Dr. Simon decided to end the session. He noted, "She squirmed in her chair and wept profusely."

A week later, on March 14, 1964, Betty added details to her description of the needle by stating, "It was a long needle. I would say the needle was 4 inches long...6 inches maybe. There was a tube attached to it and they didn't leave it in very [long]...just a second." It didn't cause the kind of pain that one would associate with the insertion of a needle; it was far more painful. Betty compared it to the sensation of being stabbed by a knife.

Betty's dream material also included the insertion of a needle into her navel, but it was more detailed and in a slightly different sequential order. In her dream, the examiner told Betty that the test would be very helpful to them, but she did not mention this during her hypnotic regression. Also, he explained in advance that he planned to do a pregnancy test on Betty that would not cause her to experience pain. When he inserted the needle with a sudden thrust, Betty twisted and moaned in pain, causing both men to look startled. In response, the leader bent over and waved his hand in front of her eyes and the pain was completely gone. This is in stark contrast to the hypnotic memory of continuing to experience pain at the point of entry after the needle had been removed. In her dream, she became relaxed and appreciative to the leader; however, under hypnosis she remained markedly traumatized. Tears were streaming down her face and she showed signs of being in considerable agony. Dr. Simon was forced to end the session early due to the degree of agitation that had ensued.

Her comment that the needle felt similar to a knife suggests that the examiner might have performed a laparoscopic procedure on Betty, which requires that an incision be made slightly below the navel. A thin, flexible tube with a tiny video camera on the end is inserted into the abdominal cavity to examine the internal organs. The physician observes images that appear on a computer screen. Laparoscopy has achieved great success as a means of accomplishing minimally invasive surgery since the first experimental use of laparoscopy was performed with a cytoscope in 1901 by German surgeon Georg Kelling. He insufflated air into the abdomen of a dog as an experimental means of stopping intra-abdominal bleeding. However, his studies did not draw support from the medical community and were not widely known. In 1934, American surgeon John C. Ruddock used a primitive form of today's laparoscope for diagnostic purposes. Then, in 1953, Professor Hopkins revolutionized this procedure by developing a rigid rod lens system that consisted of a rod-like instrument with an attached telescopic lens, earning him the credit for the invention of videoscopic surgery. By 1970, gynecologists had introduced laparoscopic surgery into their practice, but it was not until the early 1990s that general surgery was widely performed in the United States using this technology.[5]

One can only conjecture about the procedure that Betty relived in excruciating detail in Dr. Simon's office during the winter of 1964. Although it seems somewhat similar to amniocentesis and laparoscopy, it is significantly different in two ways. First, the instrument that she described as the largest needle she had ever witnessed was introduced into her abdominal cavity through her navel. Earthly doctors perform this medical procedure somewhat differently: In modern amniocentesis, an ultrasound is employed to locate the position of the placenta and fetus before a long, thin, hollow needle passes through the lower abdomen into the uterus. Second, the uterus and ovaries are not located behind the navel, leading one to question the validity of performing an examination of the reproductive organs through this entry point. We can be certain of one significant factor: The average American had no knowledge of either procedure in 1961 or 1964.

This concludes the study of the Hills' hypnotic regression pertaining to their medical examinations. We have been able to draw similarities between the experiences of both individuals that would have been impossible for each to glean from the other, which suggests the occurrence of a real experience that each lived separately from his or her own perspective, yet simultaneously.

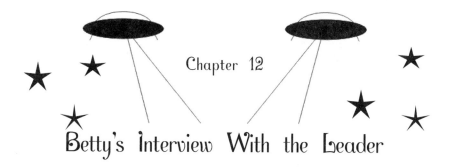

Chapter 12

Betty's Interview With the Leader

Betty's conversation with the leader is unique in character. It was part of her hypnotic regression and dream material, but was not experienced by Barney. The leader explained to Betty that only one medical examination could be performed at a time, apparently because there was only one physician on the craft. Reportedly Barney was enduring a medical examination during this time frame. An analysis of Betty's interview with the leader vis-à-vis her dream material should facilitate our understanding of this strangest and most contested aspect of the abduction experience.

On March 14, 1964, Betty informed Dr. Simon that when her physical examination had been completed, the examiner left the room, leaving her alone with the leader. She was grateful to him because he had stopped her pain, and now feeling comfortable in his presence, she initiated a conversation with him. She explained that her experience had been so outrageous that no one would ever believe that it had actually happened. In fact, she stated that most people didn't even know that he existed, adding that what she needed was some proof to take home with her. He told her to look around and maybe she could find something she would like to take. On the cabinet was a fairly large book. She put her hand on the book and asked if she could have it. He told her to look in the book, and she did. It had pages and writing, but it was different from any book she had ever seen before. In a deep hypnotic trance that day, Betty described it to Dr. Simon as follows: "It went up and down. It was different...it had short lines, and some were very thin and some were medium and some were heavy. They had some dots and they had straight lines and curved lines."

When the leader asked Betty if she thought she could read the book, she replied that she wasn't taking the book to read; it would serve as her proof that she and Barney had actually met people from another planet. She added, "So, he said that I could have the book if I wanted it, and I picked it up, and I was delighted. I mean, this was more than I had ever hoped for. And I'm standing there and I'm saying that I had never seen anything like the book, and that I was very pleased that he had given it to me, and that maybe someway I could figure out in time how to read it."[1]

When we compare this hypnotically retrieved information to Betty's dream sequence, we find that they are nearly identical. However, the dream recall is not nearly as rich with detail as the hypnotic recall, which suggests that she might have confabulated to add more detail to her account, but that is mere speculation. In "Dreams or Reality?" she wrote, "I suggested that what was needed was absolute proof that this had happened; maybe he could give me something to take back with me. He agreed and asked what I would like. I looked around the room and found a large book. I asked if I could take this with me and he agreed. I was so happy, and thanked him. I opened the book and found symbols written in long, narrow columns. He asked jokingly if I thought I could read it, and I said that this was impossible; I had never seen anything like it. I was not taking this for reading purposes, but this was my absolute proof of the experience, and that I would always remember him as long as I lived."

Next, Betty interrogated the leader about the location of his home base. She begins, "And so, then I said that...I asked him where he was from. I knew he wasn't from the Earth and I wanted to know, where *did* he come from? He asked me if I knew anything about the universe and I told him no, that I know practically nothing, but that when I was in grade school we were taught that the sun was the center of the universe and that there were nine planets. And then, later of course, we *did* make advances and I told him about seeing...I think I met him one time...about Harlow Shapley [an American astronomer]. And he wrote a book too. And I had seen photographs that he had taken of millions and millions of stars in the universe. But that was about all I knew."[2]

Then the leader crossed the room and pulled a map out of an opening in the wall and asked Betty if she had ever seen a map like it before. She walked across the room and leaned against the table, looking up at the oblong map with dots scattered all over it. Some were little, just pinpoints, and others were as big as a nickel. On some of the dots, there were curved lines going from one dot to another. Then, there was one large circle with several heavy, solid lines that connected it to another, slightly smaller, circle. When Betty asked the leader why some lines were solid and heavy, and others were dotted, he informed her that the broken lines were expeditions.

Next, Betty became curious about where the leader's home port was located on the map. When she asked him where he was from, he asked, "Where are you on this map?" Betty laughed and informed him that she didn't know, and he replied, "If you don't know where you are, there wouldn't be any point in my telling you where I am." Then he rolled the map up and put it back in the space in the wall and closed it.

Again, Betty's dream sequence is nearly identical to her hypnotic recall. In "Dreams or Reality?" she wrote, "Then I asked where he was from and he asked if I knew anything about the universe. I said, 'No, but I would like to learn.' He went over to the wall and pulled down a map." It is apparent that Betty's dream mimics 1961 technology: The leader pulls down a map reminiscent of classroom geographical maps, which he later snapped back in place. Under hypnosis, Betty said he removed the map from a hole in the wall. However, when she later consciously recalled this portion of the abduction in an interview with Kathy, the map became "almost like looking out a window about three feet wide and two feet high. The pattern was in the forefront. Other stars were there but not so noticeable. The stars in which I had an interest were those that were connected by lines, although three others were noticeable to me, maybe from the angle from which I was looking."

The Hills' hypnotic recall breaks down when Betty describes an incident involving the removal of Barney's dentures. Betty recalled, "All of a sudden there is a noise out in the hall and some of the other men come in, and with them is the examiner and they are quite excited. So, I ask the leader, 'What's the matter? Has something happened to Barney? What is it? It's something to do with Barney.' And the examiner has me open my mouth and he starts checking my teeth and they are tugging at them. And I ask them, 'What are they trying to do?' And the examiner said [copious laughter]...he said that they couldn't figure it out—Barney's teeth came out and mine didn't."

In a mid-April, 1964 interview, Betty told Dr. Simon, "While I was waiting, I was talking to the leader, and when I was talking with him, one of the men came in with Barney's dentures in his hand. This is very funny because Barney is very sensitive about this. Most people don't know he wears dentures and he doesn't like to have people know this. I thought, well he's going to be angry about this."

When the leader inquired about Barney's dentures, Betty explained that as people grew older they had to go to the dentist and have their teeth extracted and replaced with dentures. Referring to Barney's tooth loss, she added that he had to have dentures because he had a mouth injury that had necessitated the extraction of his teeth.

Curiously, the leader seemed ignorant of the human aging process. He asked Betty, "What's old age?" And she said, "'Well, it varies, but as a person gets older, there are changes in him, particularly physically. He sort of begins to break down with old age.' And so he said, 'Well, what is age?' What did I mean by age? I said that it is the life span, the lifetime that people lived. And he said, 'How long was this?' And I said, 'I think a life span is supposed to be about 100 years, but people can die before that, and most of them do because of disease or accidents'—this type of thing. That...and I think the average length of time was near, I don't know, 65 or 70."[3]

"The Leader" by artist David Baker.
Courtesy of Mary Jane Baker.

The leader indicated to Betty that he had no understanding of time or aging, so Betty told him that she didn't know exactly how it was figured out but it had something to do with the Earth's rotation, the position of the planets, and the seasons. But somehow she couldn't make him understand.

This portion of Betty's hypnotic recall is nearly identical, word for word, to her dream. However, with the exception of the removal of Barney's dentures (he remembered only that his mouth was opened), it is not part of Barney's experience. Our inability to correlate this hypnotically recovered information casts doubt upon its authenticity. It fills in the gap in the time sequence between Betty's physical exam and the completion of Barney's, but there is no independent verification.

The following scenario was also part of Betty's dream, although it appeared in a different sequential order. It too is suggestive of a fantasy sequence. She explained to the leader, "I said that we eat meat, potatoes, vegetables, and milk and all. So he asked me, 'What are vegetables?' And I said that this was a broad term and could cover a great variety of certain kinds of foods we eat. And I couldn't explain just what vegetables were. There were too many. So he said, was there one kind that I liked that I ate, and I said that I ate a great many, but my favorite was squash. So, he said, 'Well, tell me about squash.' So, I said, 'Well it was yellow, usually in color.' So, he said, 'Well what is yellow?' So I said, 'Well, I'll show you,' and I started walking around the room looking and I couldn't find anything yellow at all."[4]

There is an apparent contradiction in this sequence: Betty alleges that the leader can communicate with her in English, but he seems to lack even a rudimentary understanding of it. Additionally, he seems to lack familiarity with the concept of yellow. However, Betty describes the craft flashing multicolored lights as it passes in front of the moon. (This was part of her conscious, continuous memory.) One of these colors is amber, a shade of yellow. This portion of Betty's interview does not stand up under scrutiny. It is clearly characteristic of the rich fantasy material found in dreams...perhaps her subconscious mind's attempt to add acceptable elements to an otherwise traumatic event.

The star map is the only portion of Betty's interview with the leader that has been tested scientifically. Marjorie Fish and Stanton have engaged in an extensive investigation of this aspect of the abduction, detailed in Chapter 22.

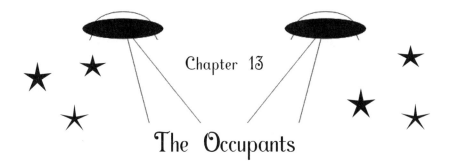

Chapter 13

The Occupants

There has been a great deal of confusion regarding the Hills' description of the physical characteristics of the spacecraft's occupants. This seems to stem from the paucity of information available from the descriptive literature. It is a common misconception that Barney observed the humanoid occupants only during a brief interval from his position in the field. In fact, Barney had a conscious, continuous recollection of observing humanoid forms wearing glossy black uniforms and black caps. Barney stated in his initial report to NICAP Investigator Walter Webb that the experience so jolted his reason and sensibilities that his mind evidently could not make the adjustment. A mental block occurred when he attempted to remember the facial characteristics of the humanoids standing in the window peering out at him. However, he noted the expressionless face of the "leader" and the smiling face of the occupant who looked over his shoulder from a control panel.

On February 22, 1964, Dr. Simon probed Barney's recollection of this event while under deep regressive hypnosis. Barney stated, "He's friendly looking and he's looking at me over his right shoulder. He's smiling. His face is round. I think of a redheaded Irishman." This reminded Barney of someone who projected warmth instead of the prejudiced hostility that Barney was accustomed to receiving from the Irish. He did not *literally* see a redheaded Irishman. This threatening figure merely reminded him of a past experience with the Irish. Moments prior to this hypnosis sequence, Barney was experiencing extreme emotional duress, punctuated by intermittent shrieks, whining, and heavy breathing. He did not want to penetrate the mental block that he had erected nearly two and a half years earlier. His subjective description was conceived in Barney's precathartic emotional state, and should not be understood as a literal portrayal of a redheaded Irishman.

The second humanoid creature that Barney observed from the field reminded him of an evil-faced German Nazi. Again, this was his subjective emotional response based on an earlier World War II era experience. However, augmented by hypnosis, his conscious recall became more detailed than it was during his 1961 interview with NICAP's Walter Webb. He was able to fill in the voids caused by his mental block. He had never noticed that the humanoid standing at the window, the one he called "the leader," was wearing a black scarf. As he focused in on the leader, he described his appearance as follows: "His eyes were slanted. I see it so...his eyes were *slant-e-d*...[hauntingly], but not like a Chinese."[1] Barney suddenly became terrified when he realized that he was observing unearthly eyes.

Stanton Friedman with alien bust. Courtesy of Stanton Friedman.

In addition to his observation from the field, Barney saw the physical characteristics of the aliens on at least two other occasions: once when they approached his vehicle on foot at the point of abduction, and again when he opened his eyes during his examination. These periods of observation gave him the opportunity to absorb details about the humanoid creatures' facial features, body structure, comparative size, language, and gait—descriptive elements that were partially recalled during hypnotic regression. However, Dr. Simon never asked Barney for a detailed narrative of these characteristics: They were a mixture of memories that Barney recalled consciously prior to hypnosis and details that flowed forth as he remembered additional information after the hypnosis.

Often, in skeptical literature, we will read that Betty described the aliens as being 5-foot-3 to 5-foot-4, with large chests and larger, longer Jimmy Durante noses. Their complexions were of a gray tone with bluish-colored lips and very dark, possibly black hair and eyes. These human-appearing men were dressed alike in grayish-blue uniforms with short slip-on boots. This description is actually based on Betty's nightmares, and does not conform to her hypnotically induced memories of the humanoid creatures. Under hypnosis, she was so emotionally distressed by their appearance that she panicked and later experienced nightmares. However, the passage of time tempered Betty's fear, and she later recalled detailed information about the aliens. As we shall see, Betty's post-hypnotic descriptions were remarkably similar to Barney's.

The late David Baker, a prominent New Hampshire watercolor artist, was the first to bring a precise forensic drawing of the aliens' physical characteristics before the public. A casual friend and fellow NICAP member, Dave shared Barney's interest in jazz music. In the months following the publication of *The Interrupted Journey,* the men and their wives occasionally met to attend jazz concerts in the White Mountains or to listen to jazz records. It was in September of 1967, during dinner at the Baker's home, that Dave asked Barney if a forensic artist had ever attempted to make a detailed sketch of the humanoid creatures who had abducted him. When Barney replied in the negative, Baker suggested that he would be willing to complete charcoal sketches of the humanoids based upon Barney's descriptions. During the next few hours, Baker completed 10 rough forensic drawings of the leader, examiner, and crew members, while Betty conversed in a separate room with Mrs. Baker.

Baker reported that Barney reacted with visible emotion as he eyed the sketches that the artist was completing. Then, later that night, when Betty viewed them for the first time, Baker commented, "She went walking down to the other end of the room, and just walked in tight circles and stayed by the window, very much upset."[2]

Then, on October 2, 1967, from his Jackson, N.H. home, Baker typed a letter of inquiry to Betty and Barney as a precursor to the completion of his watercolor paintings. He endeavored to put the Hills' detailed facial descriptions into a possible anatomical arrangement following known laws of bone structure. The Hills supplied the following information:

* The captors' enlarged eyes were slanted, and extended around the sides of their faces, indicating peripheral vision reminding one of cat's eyes, rather than Oriental eyes.

* They appeared to have a wide-cheeked, weak-chinned appearance suggestive of a Mongoloid face.

* They had an enlarged cranial structure. Hypothetically, this would be anatomically necessary to compensate for the loss of space that a normal-sized brain would require to accommodate such enlarged eyeballs.

* They gave the impression of immobility of oral muscle control. Barney realized that although from a distance he consciously recalled a smile by the humanoid who reminded him of a "redheaded Irishman," his captors, upon closer inspection, did not seem to register the human emotions of sadness or joy.

* A membrane was observed near the captor's mouth-opening when it was parted slightly. This membrane appeared to flutter when the humanoid creatures communicated with each other in a humming type of language not understood by the Hills.

* Although the iris seemed to fill up most of the creature's eyes, the small white area observed had a yellowish cast. The blinking of eyes was not apparent, suggesting the possibility that a membrane served to keep air and impurities out of the eyes, making lubrication of the orbs unnecessary.

* No ear cartilage was noted; only ear holes, possibly covered by a membrane.

* No hair was observed.

* Skin color was aluminum gray.

* Legs were spindly and chests were enlarged.

Baker conjectured that a tight, colorless membrane covering an alien's entire body could have served as protective gear for clinical or climatic reasons. He demonstrated the effect by pulling a tight silk stocking over his face in the Hills' presence. Later, he mentioned his great concern over the Hills' emotional reaction to the simulated effect.

Using his assumptions, a few weeks later, Baker produced a series of watercolor portraits, simulating to a degree the entities Betty and Barney encountered. He met Betty and Barney at the home of Dr. Simon, where he was able to question Barney under hypnosis to clarify the minute details about previously undisclosed characteristics of the alien's appearance.

Using an original process that he developed called the vitreous flux watercolor technique, Baker was able to complete four paintings on Masonite board, by applying several coats of paint to create texture before an image emerged. He completed fairly accurate, detailed paintings of "The Capture," "The Leader," "The Examiner," and the "Fiery Orb."

Betty later purchased three of the paintings—two of which are among the "Hill UFO Collection" at the University of New Hampshire. The third, the painting of "The Examiner," was mysteriously purloined from Betty's house prior to her death by an unknown thief. Recently, artist Patrick Richard produced a forensic painting of "The Examiner," using photographs of Baker's original as a guide."

In the mid-1970s, James Harder, Ph.D., director of research for the now-defunct Aerial Phenomena Research Organization (APRO) based in Tucson, Arizona (a nonprofit scientific and educational group dedicated to the eventual solution of the mystery of unidentified flying objects), began to work with Betty to gain additional information regarding the appearance and social characteristics of her abductors. Harder was a professor of hydraulic engineering with responsibilities in bioengineering at the University of California at Berkeley. A specialist in close-encounter cases, Harder was a trained hypnotist. He gained Betty's trust and was instrumental in documenting a more detailed description of the humanoid abductors after questioning Betty under hypnosis on January 19, 1976. Prior to this, Betty's intense fear of her captors' appearance prevented her from providing a detailed description. Over time, through posthypnotic suggestion, Dr. Harder conditioned Betty to become less frightened and to remember more.

Betty revealed that she saw eleven 11; 10, she thought, closely resembled each other with normal individual differences, but at least one was physically different from the rest. He was diminutive in size, approximately 3 1/2 feet tall. His head resembled a basketball, with an enlarged cranial structure, but a flat, large-eyed face. The vertical measurement of his ocular orbit was longer than wide, and the eye extended slightly beyond the human eye to the sides of the face. Either the iris was very dark or the pupil was extremely large, as it filled up most of the visible portion of the eye leaving very little white or yellowish-white showing. The nose was broad, flat, and small, with a thin, wide slit for a mouth. He had a very sturdy build with a thick neck, broad shoulders, and barrel chest. His hands had at least four short, stubby fingers and a thumb, but no visible fingernails. She said, "His fingers were sort of spread out. It is like two fingers are together, as if they grew together with a ridge between them. There is a little tiny short finger and a thumb. They are not like the leader's fingers. It looks like someone cut the tips of his fingers off. I don't know if he has three or four fingers."[3]

Betty sensed hostility from this humanoid creature as he waited in the darkened hallway outside her examining room. She stated, "He keeps staring at me, glaring. I want to kick him because of the way he is looking at me. He makes me afraid. If I kick him he'll know I'm not afraid of him." At one time, he approached the door and she could perceive sounds unlike any she had ever heard before. When she was leaving the craft he exhibited an angry appearance. His voice was raised as if in an argument, and the book that was to be her proof of the abduction was taken from her. His authoritative behavior caused Betty to rethink her prior interpretation of the social structure of the group. She suspected that perhaps he was the real leader or the military representative, and the occupant she and Barney referred to as the leader was actually an interpreter. One thing seems clear: His behavior indicated that he filled a supervisory role.

In 1980, through a referral from Dr. James Harder, Betty communicated detailed descriptive information to a mainstream scientist who wishes to remain anonymous. On April 8, 1980, she wrote the following to the scientist:

> As for the examiner, the one who did the testing of us was about 4 1/2 feet tall; his head shape was more like ours, and did not seem to be as large in size as the "little guy," but was more in proportion to his body size. Facial features were similar to the "little guy," but had a "bumpy" appearance. It is difficult to describe, but the skin was not smooth.
>
> The leader was the "good-looking" one—having a closer resemblance to us. His face was of a triangular shape, tapering down to a very small chin and jawbone. I observed a very small mouth and nose. His height was approximately the same as mine—5 feet.
>
> I think the eight crew members were similar to the leader and examiner, although I did not observe them closely, for they were in the dark most of the time. While I was being examined they remained in an unlighted corridor. As for height and appearance, they gave the impression of similarity.
>
> As far as I could determine, all lacked hair, eyebrows, and eyelashes. I did not observe the protruding part of the ear. Their skin seemed to have a gray tone. Their hands had four fingers and one thumb and were long and slender. I do not recall seeing fingernails, but during my examination, I was terribly frightened, and most of the time my eyes were closed. I did open them

occasionally, particularly when I thought they were getting some kind of equipment to be used in my examination. At that point, my curiosity overcame my fears. Frankly, I did not want to see their appearance.

Barney and I did attempt to withhold some aspects of their physical characteristics from the public. Since you are interested in their evolution, I will confidentially reveal some of these. When Barney was lying on the table, looking up, he saw inside the mouth of the examiner. There were no teeth, but possibly a small tongue. He also observed a membrane, which fluttered when the examiner spoke in his own language to his group. This was apparently used for communication. They also had the appearance of being top-heavy—their chest area seemed to be larger in proportion to their body build than ours, whereas their legs and hip region seemed smaller. When they walked outdoors, they did so with a rolling gait, as though they had sea legs, and were somewhat unsure of their balance. However, two of them carried Barney along without difficulty. For their size, they must have been very strong. I had the opportunity to observe very little walking onboard the craft, but from what I can recall, I didn't notice anything unusual about their gait, although the door was open. Additionally, outside, one of the crew members gave the appearance of gulping air— opening his mouth almost like a fish. This gave me the impression he was having difficulty breathing our air.

As for the craft itself, the air seemed cooler than on the outside. The night air was warm for that time of year, possibly as a result of the hurricane coming up the coast. I was wearing a short-sleeved dress, without a sweater, and was comfortable. But I *did* notice a temperature difference.

As for the lighting in the examining room, it was extremely bright, indirect lighting that seemed to shine through the walls and ceiling. The brilliant, blue-white light hurt my eyes at first, causing me to keep them closed for a while.

One aspect of the examination seemed to amaze them. Although I could not understand their communication with each other, I sensed their excitement when they examined my skin through what I thought was some kind of microscope. They seemed astonished. The examiner looked first; then the leader. Then they took turns. I assume they were examining my cell structure or genetic code. So many times since then I have wished I asked the leader if we were genetically related. Could they be our descendents? I suspect they are.

It is impossible to write all I have learned in the past several years in one letter. However, I have been developing an assumption pertaining to their origin. Based upon the work of Marjorie Fish and others, I assume they are from Zeta Reticuli, a planet which could be 6 to 11 billion years old. I have made the assumption that their home base has less sunlight, less gravity, and less water than Earth. Their planet could have adjusted to life without food as we know it. I think they are researching nearby star systems, of which we are one, but these systems vary in age from early development to far beyond us. They may be transporting forms of life from one planet to another to study their adaptability to new environments.

I hope I have not overwhelmed you with some of my speculative ideas. I have been pondering these areas for nearly 20 years, and my thinking has not always been easy. However, it is based upon knowledge gained, which is too lengthy for one letter. So, if you would like to speculate, it would be interesting to me.

Sincerely,

Betty Hill

On April 18, 1980, the scientist replied as follows:

In my correspondence with Jim [Dr. James Harder, APRO's director of investigations] I was tentatively of the opinion that perhaps type-A aliens (his classification), of the kind you met, may have been derived from us by other aliens and bred more or less as we breed domestic animals to produce desirable mental and physical characteristics. From your descriptions, this now seems unlikely to me.

To begin with the normal aliens (i.e. not the "little guy"):

1. The proportions of the head and the body of the examiner are indicative of a somewhat higher level of encephalization than in our species. I want to replot the curve derived for maximum terrestrial encephalization levels, based on better data, before evaluating the *relative* encephalization of the examiner.

2. "Skin not smooth—gray tone"—recent publications imply that in some desert animals, dark color is not related to heat-dumping, but to assimilating heat during periods of cold stress without the necessity of elevating metabolic rates. Of course, there is also a relationship between melanization and exposure to ultraviolet light.

3. The weak jaw of the leader could certainly be interpreted as evidence of ingestion of nonresistant food—or a preprocessed food. Cf. also small size of mouth.

4. Body size on Earth seems to be correlated with the abundance and ubiquitous availability of food. It is probably also inversely correlated with gravity.

5. The large chest would seem to suggest a proportionally greater need to ventilate. Due to low oxygen content of parental atmosphere? Or high metabolic rates? Or rarefied parental atmosphere? Or inefficient oxygen assimilation mechanisms (cf. Octopus)? The difficulty one crew member has in "gulping" air might suggest that the greater (?) density of our atmosphere increased air turbulence in his breathing apparatus which may have been too finely tubed.

6. "Sea legs"—If they were actually carrying your husband without some levitation device (which seems to be suggested in the book—cf. p. 155 of soft-back edition) they would have been strong. The limbs then have been powerful in spite of their small size. Was the peculiar gait then the result of imperfect adjustment to a somewhat weaker gravity?

7. The large eyes and brilliant interior lighting present a bit of a paradox. I'll try to check this aspect indirectly with some colleagues. However, you note that the corridors were unlighted. Could their eyes accommodate a larger range of illumination? I assume they wore no optical devices during the examination? Enclosed are Xerox copies of Gecko eyes to show the great range of pupil dilation. Is there any resemblance here to the eyes of the aliens?

8. The coolness of the interior environment and naked-ness of the skin suggests the desirability of heat flow from them into the environment. This would be con-sistent with high metabolic rates.

9. Your comment on their reaction to the cellular (?) con-struction of your skin is very interesting. Would scien-tists in a similar situation be more excited by fundamental differences or fundamental resemblances? Perhaps the latter, for fundamental resemblances would be more rapidly understood than fundamental differences. I suspect, personally, that much of the organization of the multicellular organisms derives from the nature of the cell. The appearance of the aliens is much closer to ours than is that of many other terrestrial organisms. Might not our fundamental building blocks be also simi-lar? I must admit, it would be too much if the DNA structure and gene loci arrangements were closely similar—I'd wonder if someone were stacking the deck on me!

There are some astonishing parallelisms, e.g.:

1. Their five-fingeredness, as basically in terrestrial verte-brates. Were their fingers unequally jointed as in lizards or about equally jointed (divided into equal segments) as in our case?

2. The fact that they had nostrils *and* a mouth, through which air is passed when speaking—cf. fluttering of membrane which is functionally a secondary palate? I wonder if the membrane is used in modulating sounds in the same manner as our tongue. The intercommuni-cation between the digestion and the respiratory sys-tems in the oral cavity at first blush is not the kind of coincidence that one would predict.

In speculating on the reason for the adaptive specializations of these creatures, we should probably keep in mind the possibility that they may have been dwelling in space stations for evolutionarily significant spans of time. Their morphology may derive from a mixture of temporally discrete suites of selective pressures. Thus, could the "sea-legs" behaviour be a result of adaptation or previous acclimatization to a rotating artificial gravity of a space station? Could the large chest be partly the effects of natural selection and reduced air pressure in space stations?

I find your ideas about Zeta Reticulians evolving in an older, relatively impoverished biological system appealing. As Terry Dickinson points out in his article, Zeta Reticuli is lean in metals relative to the solar system. I suspect, but am as yet unable to propose a quantitative relation, that the availability of nutrients is directly related to the rapidity of evolutionary rates. Thus the aliens you saw, assuming them to be indeed derived from this star system, are only about as encephalized as we are in spite of the relatively great age of their natal star system.

On April 30, 1980, Betty made the following comments in her return correspondence:

In reference to your comment #5, "The large chest would seem to suggest a proportionally greater need to ventilate," I know of two cases of face-to-face contact with aliens. After being in our atmosphere for approximately 20 minutes, both groups experienced great difficulty breathing. On both occasions, an alien said, "Help me, for my energies are running out." They had great difficulty in walking, needing to hang onto things to move, and slowly dragged their feet, walking and moving with great effort. They appeared as though they were about to collapse.

Comment #6—regarding their strength in carrying Barney, although they were smaller than us in size, I found them to be quite powerful. Barney was carried along by two aliens, one on each side of him, who placed their hands under his armpits. They were reaching up to do this. Barney weighed about 160 pounds. Another example happened when I refused to go onboard the craft and fought to get away. One alien took each arm and pulled me firmly onboard the craft. I was struggling to the point that my dress was badly torn.

Comment #7—their eyes: Barney and I said repeatedly that we had never seen eyes like theirs before. In some manner, both of us blocked out a full description of these. Whenever Dr. Simon said "eyes" to me, I burst out crying. Something about the eyes was terribly upsetting to me. Now, I have a hint as to the cause of my upset. When I looked at the eyes of the Wall Gecko, I became physically ill, a feeling of horror. I cannot say with certainty that the eyes are the same, but from my reaction to this, I suspect that they are. Often I would say that they had a similarity, in some strange way, to the eyes of a cat, but now I suspect it is a similarity to the eyes of a Wall Gecko. Now, while I am writing this, the same reactions are returning—feelings of being upset, ill, etc.— extreme fright. As for the gecko, I have no fear of reptiles, snakes, etc., so I am certain it is not that. I grew up in an area with many snakes and have often handled them.

As for their fingers, I remember them as being similar to our fingers, but I had a feeling of coolness when I was touched. Whether this was from a cooler body temperature, or from my own fears, I do not know.

I did not note any differences in the rapidity of their breathing. I was puffing from fighting to get away, but they seemed to be breathing normally. Also, I did not see any evidence of fatigue at the end of our encounter. I could not say whether their legs were bony, lumpy, etc. They were covered, but seemed smaller than our legs in that the pant legs were not as well filled out as with the average male, so I assume they were smooth.

I think they had an orifice in the place of ears, but I could not swear to this. Both the leader and examiner were wearing caps, with no protrusion of the external ear.

In total, Betty and the scientist communicated in letter form over a period of six months. This intellectual curiosity and depth of scientific knowledge has contributed significantly to the general public's understanding of possible alien environments. It is unfortunate that this type of speculation cannot be carried out in a public forum, but mainstream science is extremely conservative. One who strays too far from the narrow path of accepted dogma risks intellectual controversy and ostracism from the mainstream.

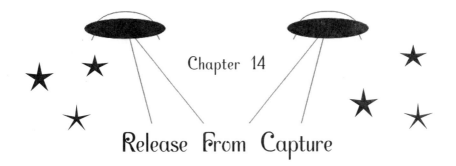

Chapter 14

Release From Capture

Upon the completion of Barney's medical examination, he was escorted back to his vehicle, while Betty exchanged words with the leader. She was furious because a member of the crew had overruled his decision to give Betty the strange 5 × 9 inch plastic-like book that would serve as proof of her abduction. Further, he informed her that the decision had been made to eradicate both individuals' memories of the abduction. At this point Betty defiantly rebuked, "You can take the book, but you can never, never, never make me forget about it, because I'll remember it if it's the last thing I ever do." According to Betty, the leader laughed and replied, "Maybe you will remember. I don't know. I hope you don't but maybe you will. But it won't do you any good if you do, because Barney won't. Barney won't remember a single thing. And not only that, if he should remember anything at all, he's going to remember it differently from you, and all you're going to do is get each other so confused, you won't know what's going on. It would be better if you forget it anyway."[1]

It is critical that we analyze Barney's hypnotic regression of this segment to compare his individual recall with Betty's, vis-à-vis her dream sequence. "Dreams or Reality?" indicates that she and Barney were escorted back to the car together and that the entire crew accompanied them. However, her hypnotic recall differs from this portion of her dream. Betty reported in this regression that her conversation with the leader continued until she arrived at her car. While several crewmembers escorted Barney to his vehicle, only the leader walked with Betty. If Barney had absorbed Betty's dream material, he would have reported that their return was simultaneous. However, this is not the case. He reported, "And I am walking and I am walking and I am being guided and my eyes are closed. And I open my eyes and there is the car and the lights are off and it is not running and Delsey is under the seat and I reach under and touch her, and she is in a tight ball. And I sit back and I see Betty is coming down the road and she gets into the car."[2] Later, Barney remembered sitting on his gun when he entered the car.

Barney has informed us that he had already taken his position in the driver's seat when he observed Betty approaching the car. Again, the correlation is consistent with Betty's hypnotic account of the event with one exception: Delsey's position in the vehicle. Barney mentions only that she was under the seat when he arrived back at the car. Betty, however, sees Delsey sitting on the passenger seat trembling all over.

In Betty's dream sequence, she and Barney walk to the car together and lean against the right-hand side of it—Barney against the front fender and Betty against the passenger door. Betty opened the door and removed Delsey, holding her as the UFO became a bright, glowing object, which turned over three to four times and sailed into the sky. Here we see more correlating data: Their hypnotic recall is consistent, but differs from Betty's dream account of the event.

Photo of a fiery red UFO taken by Betty Hill.
Courtesy of Kathleen Marden.

In the same interview, Barney told Dr. Simon, "It was a bright huge ball...orange. It was a beautiful bright ball. And, it was going and it was gone and we were in darkness." This huge, glowing orange ball was part of Betty's and Barney's conscious recall of the events of September 19, 1961, but they were uncertain of its origin. Betty's hypnotic description of the departing craft is more detailed than Barney's, but again, their accounts contain correlating data. Betty stated, "It's a big orange ball and it's glowing and glowing and it's rolling just like a ball. It must be...I don't know—water? Do they go under water? It goes down and then there's a dip, and then, *zoom*.[3]

Barney fills in the details of the next segment by describing his exit from the capture site. He maneuvers around a bend in the road, and later realizes he is back on Route 3 when the pavement changes to a cement road. He feels that he has been through a harrowing experience, but is greatly relieved to have been released unharmed. As he courses down Route 3 toward Ashland and the newly completed Interstate 93, he and Betty again hear a rapid series of beeping sounds and the car buzzes with vibration. Thinking that perhaps something had shifted in the car, Barney slowed the vehicle, but the buzzing continued. When it ceased, Barney attempted to create the sound and vibration. He told Dr. Simon, "I drove the car fast, and then would decelerate rapidly, and I would swerve over to the left of the highway and back to the right, and I came to a complete stop and accelerated rapidly, but I could not seem to get that sound. And we drove down the highway and we saw the route for the expressway...17 miles to Concord. And I drove to Concord and down Route 4."[4]

The second series of buzzing sounds were part of the Hills' conscious, continuous memory of the events on September 19–20, 1961. Betty mentioned them briefly in her dream sequence and described them in her hypnotic regression. It also marks the period when Betty and Barney have returned to full conscious memory. This event occurred in Ashland, approximately 17 miles south of their unexpected turn onto the steel bridge that took them to the abduction site. It is now apparent that Barney continued to pursue a prosaic explanation for these events. He drove the car from side to side, accelerated and decelerated, and came to a complete stop in an attempt to reproduce this perplexing sound. The radio was off, the car was well greased, the trunk was closed....There is no mundane explanation that can hold up under scrutiny for the sounds emanating from the rear of the vehicle.

In 2001, the late Karl Pflock proposed a new possible explanation for the buzzing/beeping sounds. Pflock advanced the hypothesis that when Barney, in haste, removed the gun from the trunk of his vehicle south of Indian Head, he failed to close it completely. Then, as he sped down what was probably a very bumpy section of road, the trunk rattled, causing the beeping sounds and the vibration. Pflock did not have access to all of the Hills' audiotaped hypnosis sessions, and therefore did not know that Barney had already taken the gun from the trunk south of Twin Mountain, approximately 14 miles north of the field. Before he reached the field south of Indian Head, Barney had driven over several road surfaces: the concrete on Route 3, his stops at the side of the road, and his turn-out onto a dirt road.

To further support his argument, Pflock claimed that in November of 1963, Betty told the Two State UFO Study Group in Quincy, Mass., that when she and Barney arrived home they discovered the car's trunk lid was closed, but not latched. After an extensive search we failed to find evidence of Betty's statement. It is not in any of the investigators records, on the audio tapes of the hypnosis, or in any of the Hills' extensive correspondence. However, Howard Roy's account of the Hills' discussion states that Barney noticed, upon arriving home, that the trunk was unlocked. There is no reference to the lid being ajar, and further inquiry with Betty revealed that the trunk was securely closed. Either Barney misspoke, or as is often the case, the written account of his talk was inaccurate. The misunderstanding probably stemmed from a comment Betty made regarding the condition of the trunk's contents when they arrived home. She thought that the trunk had been opened and their luggage had been ransacked. Perhaps this happened at Customs when they entered the United States.

Our investigation has turned up some interesting facts regarding the characteristics of a 1957 Chevy trunk and latch. Unlike the car's hood that had two latches, the trunk had only one. The second latch on the hood prevented it from flying open when the vehicle was moving. However, the trunk had only one latch, which opened with the insertion of a key into a round lock. Therefore, it was impossible for the trunk lid to be closed, but not latched: The 1957 trunk was counterbalanced with springs, making it slightly easier to open than to close. If the trunk was not securely closed, it in all probability would have opened when the vehicle hit a bump. It is unlikely that the Hills could have driven from near Twin Mountain to Portsmouth without noticing that their trunk was open, especially since Betty continued to watch for the UFO.

Furthermore, in 1961, Route 3 was a cement road. Concrete roads are constructed with evenly spaced expansion and contraction joints. Had the Hills' trunk been open, they would have heard an even, rhythmic, clicking sound. However, Betty and Barney described code-like buzzing or beeping sounds: beep-beep-beep-beep (rapid succession, then pause) beep-beep-beep-beep.

Now, let us proceed with the Hills' trip south. The couple turned off Route 3 and entered the new interstate highway in Ashland. They followed it south to New Hampshire's state capitol, Concord, before turning east for the 46-mile drive along Route 4, to their home in Portsmouth. Betty searched the sky from time to time but did not see the craft again.

When they arrived home, they checked their windup watches for the time and discovered that both had stopped running. Barney was in Colebrook when he last noted that it read the same time as the clock on the restaurant wall. Betty's was fully operational at Cannon Mountain. Barney checked the clock in his kitchen and noted that they arrived home a little later than expected. It was 5:20. He entered the bathroom to check his body for marks while Betty walked Delsey along the path to their home and listened to the chirping of birds in their yard.

Barney had a nagging feeling that something had been done to his groin, but nothing unusual was evident when he examined himself. Next, he peered through his bedroom window and searched the morning sky, suspecting that something was around, somewhere.

Barney informed Dr. Simon that he was tired when he arrived home, and therefore did not remove his luggage from the car. But Betty added, "Barney brought some of the things out of the car; not everything." He brought in the ice box and Betty immediately discarded the remaining food. She didn't want to touch anything, fearing that it might be contaminated. She worried about radioactivity, cosmic rays, and viruses, and because of this concern, she instructed Barney to put everything in the back hall.

Before Betty and Barney retired for some restorative sleep, they bathed and shampooed their hair. Finally, he and Betty retired, discussing how something very strange had happened to them. Betty kept thinking she wished she knew someone with a Geiger counter. Yet Barney's memory of the abduction was rapidly fading.

When they awoke later that day they agreed not to tell anyone—only talk about it to each other. They each drew a picture of the craft from memory, and when they discovered they were nearly identical, Betty called her sister, Janet, and told her.

Betty added the following detail:

Dot and Henry, who rent the upstairs apartment, came in, and they had suggested that we take....We didn't have a movie camera and they did and they suggested when we left that we take their camera. And well, we decided not to bother with it. So, Barney said something about well, maybe it would have been a good idea if we had taken their movie camera. And, I'm not sure just what he said to Henry...something about we had seen a strange object in the sky, and if he had the movie camera, maybe he could have taken some pictures. And then Dot had a...oh, I said to Dot I said, "Yeah, you know he saw a flying saucer and he doesn't want to admit it. And if he had pictures, he'd have proof of it"...something on this idea, I think. And ah, Dot...she herself has a belief in these strange flying objects and she was somewhat interested. And we told her that we had seen one, something in the sky...bouncing around, and that it had followed us for a while, and I think that's all we said. That's all she knows to my knowledge. And then, Barney and I kept saying that we weren't going to talk about it; that we were going to forget about it. But I couldn't. I couldn't stop thinking about it for a second. It was on my mind constantly. So I thought that I've got to talk about this a little bit, so I decided to call my sister, Janet. The chief of police was at her house and he said that we should report it to Pease Air Force Base. And I said that no, I didn't want to do that. And, then she said that maybe we should check some things out first. And she said, hang up and let me call the man next door. He's a physicist.

Kathleen Marden, Janet Miller, and Betty Hill at Christmas. Courtesy of Kathleen Marden.

I called Janet and just told her about how it followed us and...swung around in front of us. I did tell her about the lights and the fins and oh, about the beeping. Well, with Dot, I just told her that it followed us. I didn't tell her about the beeping at that time. I think maybe it would depend somewhat on the person I was talking with, too. And so Janet called back and said that the physicist who lives next door had said that I should take a compass and go out around the spot where the beeping was heard to see what would happen.[5]

Barney became increasingly irritated with Betty's excitement, refusing to cooperate with her effort to locate their compass. Finally, she retrieved it from her kitchen drawer and dashed out to her car, which was parked in front of their house. Barney went to the bedroom window and looked out at her as she circled the car, moving the compass toward the metal. Next, she stormed into the house demanding that Barney observe the effect the car apparently had on the compass. Barney retorted that any metal will cause a compass to react. But Betty pointed out 12 to 18 half-dollar-sized shiny spots on the trunk of the car that caused the compass to spin and spin. They hadn't been there the previous day and Betty suspected they were somehow connected to the strange buzzing sounds of the previous evening. Intrigued, Barney began to experiment with the compass. He moved it close to the spots and the compass would spin and spin, but as he moved it few inches away from the shiny spots, it would drop down.

It is common knowledge that any inexpensive compass will fluctuate when it is placed in proximity to the metal of a classic automobile. What we cannot explain is why the compass would spin when placed over the perplexing spots, but drop down when moved a few inches away from them.

Betty reported that the spots could not have been caused by the weather. They had the appearance of clear lacquer paint that had been applied with a template over the color. Later, when she waxed the car, the spots remained shinier than the car's surface, but during the winter they gradually faded away.

Dr. Simon queried both Betty and Barney regarding Webb's impression of the mystifying spots. They both stated that Webb was so busy with the initial interview, he had forgotten to look at the spots, and they had forgotten to show him the evidence. In a 1966 televised interview Barney stated, "Walter Webb did not see the spots." In a 2006 e-mail exchange Webb told Kathy, "You might be interested in this paragraph from my letter to NICAP's Dick Hall, dated Sept. 17, 1965: "I simply failed to attach much importance to the 'beeps' in '61, and it seems to me that I casually looked at the car but recall seeing nothing out of the ordinary. I believe there were spots on the trunk, but they didn't impress me at the time as being of suspicious origin." Later, he added, "My memory is simply too vague about that particular episode."

In April of 1964, the Hills' amnesia had been lifted and Dr. Simon altered the focus of the hypnotherapy sessions. He employed the use of hypnotic suggestion to attempt to convince the Hills that the content of Betty's dreams could explain the amnesiac period. Suggesting that Barney's empathy for his wife had caused him to absorb her dreams, he argued that they had experienced a mutual fantasy to fill in the gap. He asked Betty, "Now in all of these things that you feel happened, did it not happen in your dreams? Couldn't this all have been in your dreams?" To this Betty replied, "No." He inquired about why she felt so sure of it. She replied, "There were discrepancies. It was different." She felt that the star map held particular significance. He pointed out the obvious discrepancy that the leader, who seemed to speak our language, did not have a basic understanding about aging, dentures, routines, and so on. When challenged, Betty became confused and distressed, breathing heavily and becoming congested.[6] She insisted that the abduction was different from her dreams, that there was much more than she had told Dr. Simon. She pointed out that her captors were different than the men in her dreams. They were shorter, had large, bald heads and penetrating eyes, and were dressed differently. Their bodies seemed strangely out of proportion and their appearance was frightening. As her traumatic amnesia lifted, Betty remembered the physical description of her captors in greater detail.

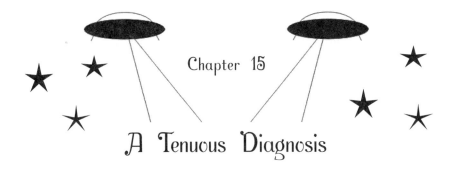

Chapter 15

♉ Tenuous Diagnosis

Throughout the hypnoanalysis, Dr. Simon faced the daunting task of attempting to separate fantasy from reality. He repeatedly interrogated the Hills for clarity whenever inconsistencies surfaced in their hypnotic recall, attempting to puncture the veracity of their recall. Direct questioning revealed that whenever they appeared to be fabricating information, there was a logical explanation that filled in the apparent discrepancy. However, as a scientist, Dr. Simon was faced with the task of accepting the reality of an unprecedented UFO abduction, or finding a more tenable psychoanalytical explanation. If he accepted the Hills' testimony as real and this information became public, his professional reputation would be at stake.

Dr. Simon must have weighed heavily his responsibility to resolve his patients' trauma against the acceptance of the factual content of the recovered memories. If the abduction hypothesis were true, how could he possibly relieve Barney's fears? The occupants had threatened to take retribution against Barney if he ever revealed information about them. If this abduction had a foundation in reality, how could Barney's anxiety diminish? On the other hand, if Barney had merely absorbed the content of Betty's nightmares, due to his empathy for his wife, his anxiety could be relieved, assuming the hypothesis was correct. Yet each time Dr. Simon attempted to puncture the Hills' recovered memories, he encountered an obstruction. They consistently refuted his conjectures.

He seemed willing to accept the idea that the Hills' UFO sighting was real, as evidenced by his letter dated March 8, 1965. Betty had informed him that a United Nations representative had contacted her about his own sighting. Dr. Simon replied, "I am not surprised to hear about the UN representative's interest in these things. They are a fairly universal phenomenon and have been seen in all parts of the world." In another letter dated December 8, 1966, he contends, "I have steadily held that you probably did have an experience with this sighting." His stated opinion seems to suggest that, at that time, he accepted the consciously, continuously recalled portions of the UFO encounter as reality.

However, abduction by space aliens was more difficult to accept.

Dr. Simon's inability to accept the ET hypothesis overshadowed his interpretation of the Hills' hypnotic material. Therefore, throughout the psychoanalysis, he remained dubious about the value of their preamnesiac conscious memories, and instead focused on Betty's nightmares. He attempted to convince Barney that he had merely absorbed Betty's dreams, as evidenced in the following conscious, post-hypnosis interview. The Hills had discussed their memories of being onboard the craft the previous morning at the breakfast table. Barney stated, "Geez, I get the chills. I get the chills even now. I was telling her I can see it so clearly. This much I have always realized that somewhere...this was prior to coming here for hypnosis...that I had always realized that somehow there was someone stopping us and I never could put any sense to it. In the truthful answer, trying now not to conceal my feelings of being ridiculed, I would say that it is something that happened. But, I put a protective coating on me because I don't want to be ridiculed."

Betty and Barney with Betty's parents, Florence and Raymond Barrett.
Courtesy of Kathleen Marden.

When Dr. Simon discussed the possibility that Betty had influenced Barney, he countered this conjecture by stating, "When I was standing out there [in the field] I knew that Betty wasn't influencing me. What I was thinking is how I would rather not talk about it. Okay, we saw something; now let's get in our car and drive about our business. This irritated me when she kept saying, 'Look, its right over there.' I would slow down and take a peek and see this object still was out there. This greatly irritated me, so I said, 'What are you trying to do, make me see something that isn't there?' Knowing that it *was* there and not wanting it to be there. This is why I've been confused."

Next, Dr. Simon explored Barney's perception of the content of two nightmares that Betty had experienced during the previous week. In these terrifying dreams, Betty saw what appeared to be a moon-like object over a body of water, and then a yellow-lighted object that appeared to rapidly depart. Barney responded:

If this was a dream that she had, it is only an extension of something that I *do* know and *did* see. Eliminating the water, from what I'm seeing, this large object was sitting there and then it started moving off and going very rapidly away. This too, I always knew about before hypnosis. But, much of this I wanted to forget very badly. I always had a fear after this sighting that a great disaster…now how can I explain this disaster…that there was harm that could come to Betty and me by pursuing this…even trying to investigate. So, I've always been the reluctant person. I had been told to forget by these men. I know it wasn't a dream. This is something that could really serve no purpose, and I have to forget it. *"You will forget it. It can only cause great harm that could be meted out to you if you do not forget."* It was the same type of force that I felt in the field that was causing me to come closer, even though I wanted to run away. This was inside of me. I wasn't creating this power. When I arrived home in Portsmouth on the same day, I had this feeling of foreboding that something would happen. That Betty…let's forget this. Let's forget the portion of even having seen the sighting from Groveton all the way down to Indian Head, because no good can come of it. When I was talking to Walter Webb [in October, 1961] I found that something was very strange about the whole thing. I can go right up to this point and I remember running back to the car. But, just what I had done….

I didn't pursue this any further with Walter Webb because I felt a tremendous pressure...A tremendous pressure to....Let's drop this thing Betty. You have your report Mr. Webb. Let us forget it and this was the extent of that.

I used to privately think about this. Betty was in the car with me. We were together when she asked me, "What did you see? What did you see?" I only said, "It's going to capture us"; I knew that. If you can have an explanation about something that you know is about to happen....I knew if I stayed out there on the highway I would be captured. She just said, "Well, what did you see?" and I didn't answer her. The next thing I could always remember is seeing this big object sitting in the road. And my first remark was, "Oh God, not again." Betty was saying, "It's the moon." And I said, "Yes, it's the moon." We both thought how peculiar it was that the moon was going away and then I didn't say anything else and she didn't say anything else. And then what was so surprising is that we weren't moving. I just wasn't moving. I'm talking now prior to hypnosis. This is the only way I have ever seen this situation. So, I thought afterwards that the reason I wasn't moving was because I had apparently brought my car to a halt to negotiate some kind of turn or something. This is why I wasn't moving, and this I accepted. As we drove on further, Betty remarked to me, "Well, now do you believe in flying saucers?" I said, "Don't be ridiculous, Betty."

Was I hallucinating, or in the event of a dream, thinking that it is part of reality? And yet, even if you could answer this question, I basically know that what had happened *happened*. And this is why I think the whole thing is so ridiculous. What happened happened, and that is why I even hesitate to ask the question, except for reassurance.

Dr. Simon replied, "Well, as I said before, I don't want to go into any great detail at this time. All these things can happen...anything can happen when you come right down to it. I can reassure you that you have nothing to fear, but I want to reserve a more concrete answer for sometime in the future as we develop this thing more and more into consciousness. I'll begin to work with both of you as you continue to remember the things that came out only under hypnosis. We'll open up more and more as time goes on. We want to get it into consciousness to the extent that you can tolerate it without anxiety, and this will come."

As more and more of the hypnotic material penetrated the Hills' consciousness, Dr. Simon attempted to facilitate the reduction of their stress. However, he remained persistent in his effort to challenge the Hills, suggesting that they had perhaps shared a fantasy; that Betty's nightmares had been transferred to Barney. The only difference between the hypnotic recall and the dream sequence, he stated, was the ramp at the entrance to the craft. Betty had informed him that, in her dream, she ascended a step or two before she set foot on a ramp. In her hypnotically recovered memory, there was only a ramp, no stairs. But Betty insisted there was so much more than she had spoken to Dr. Simon during the hypnosis sessions. She possessed detailed information not in her dreams that she insisted filled in the missing time and memory gap. Additionally, she pointed out that the men who abducted her were different than she expected. Based upon her dream recall, she expected them to be "cute," but in her recovered memory they were "sort of grotesque."

Deciding to set aside what the Hills deemed to be apparent inconsistencies between their own interpretations of their hypnosis experience and that of Dr. Simon, they attempted to accept his suggestion. But the acceptance of a fantasy hypothesis was short-lived. Betty recorded in her diary that initially, for a week or two, they felt as if a weight had been lifted from them. But this feeling was short-lived. Almost simultaneously, Betty and Barney realized that they could no longer deceive themselves. More than anything else, they realized that they "had been touched," and this feeling unleashed intense emotion in both of them.

It became abundantly clear to the Hills that Dr. Simon's opinion had failed to account for the objective evidence. During the hypnosis, Betty remembered that she had removed her torn dress and placed it in her closet on the morning of September 20, 1961. Subsequently, she had forgotten it, but during the hypnosis she recalled the struggle that tore the hem and lining and the ineptitude of the leader as he attempted open her zipper. After the hypnosis, she removed the dress from her closet and found that it was blanketed by a mysterious pink powdery substance. This dress later underwent forensic analysis several times. The Hills were perplexed by Betty's missing earrings that suddenly reappeared in a bizarre manner. And what had caused the deep scrapes on the tops of Barney's shoes and the lesions on Barney's groin? If they were not captured by aliens, then what *did* happen to them during the missing two hours for which they developed amnesia? The hypnotic regression had supplied the answers to all of these questions, so how could Dr. Simon account for this if the abduction were not real? The Hills were no longer able to find relief in the idea that it was merely a fantasy.

It has been reported by several investigators that Dr. Simon postulated that sexual symbolism could explain some of the content of the Hills' hypnotic recall. According to the reports of some researchers, he spoke of material indicative of latent fears and desires and interpreted the Hills' experience in Freudian terms. For example, the needle that was inserted into Betty's navel was symbolic of anxiety over her barren womb. The penetrating eyes symbolized Barney's anxiety over the disapproving eyes of others regarding his interracial marriage. Barney's physical examination, in Freudian terms, could signify latent homosexual feelings and fear of attack upon the genitals. The threat that danger would come to Barney if he spoke of the abduction could point to his perceived threat that harm would befall him because he married a white woman.

Although UFO researchers and skeptics have reported Simon's Freudian interpretation of Betty and Barney's testimony, a letter written to Betty by Simon on December 8, 1966, calls this claim into question. Betty had written a letter to him expressing concern over remarks allegedly made by Dr. Simon that had later been quoted in an article that appeared in *FATE Magazine.* Along with her letter she mailed a photocopy of a letter that contained a reference to Dr. Simon's Freudian interpretation of the Hills' UFO encounter. He replied as follows:

> The author seems to make a fanciful, what I suppose would be called "Freudian" analysis of your experience, whereas Mr. B. [name deleted by author] uses the term Freudian in a most pejorative sense to sneer at me on the basis of something which he has read in a magazine of which I would never think of reading nor would my friends. Let me say at the outset that I was not interviewed by anyone connected with *FATE* nor do I know anyone connected with it, nor did I make any such remarks as Mr. B. attributes to me. I do not consciously use the word Freudian either as a noun or as an adjective and I do not speak of Freud in any other sense than that of one who has worked in the field of psychiatry and human behavior and who has contributed greatly to our understanding of human psychology. Mr. B. does not seem to understand the difference between interpretation and description of phenomena. At no time have I interpreted your dreams or

experiences, nor do I propose to. I called to your attention and to Barney's the probability that people would do so, as did the above-mentioned author, and I am sure many others. This is something we have to tolerate.

Dr. Simon continued by explaining that the writer seemed to have derived "many inferences from scant evidence." This methodology of dialectic discussions between "believers" and "nonbelievers," in his opinion, would not answer any of the questions surrounding the UFO mystery or the Hill case in particular. He further expressed his disapproval of the methodology of some skeptics with his comment, "the excavation of little items does no more to solve this complex problem than does Dr. Donald Menzel's 'production of phenomena' that could explain UFOs or Phillip Klass's electronic plasma hypothesis." He added that, although they might explain some phenomena, they could not explain the Hills' experience. Attacks by the process of "minimal extraction" could not answer the many questions that exist. He added, "I have steadfastly held that you probably did have an experience with the sighting. I think the study of this should be in the hands of objective scientists (among whom I include myself), and not the object of dialectic discourse in which invective and pejorative are the means of evaluating data."

The question of Freudian sexual symbolism is perplexing. NICAP investigator Walter Webb's "Final Report" contains a reference to it, and it has been a topic of discussion through time. Clearly Dr. Simon has denied making the remarks attributed to him and expressed disapproval concerning either the misinterpretation of his statements or the fabrication of statements later attributed to him. Further, he seems to have little tolerance for those who narrowly interpret the complex subject matter involved in the mystery of the Hills' abduction memories, and who, based upon scant evidence, debunk it. On the other hand, Walter Webb was a careful scientist who meticulously conducted a long-term investigation of the Hill experience. He met with Dr. Simon and listened to the hypnosis tapes with Betty and Barney's approval. There is no reason to believe that his documentation is inaccurate. It seems that this aspect of the case will remain a mystery.

In this time frame, Dr. Simon and skeptical investigators searched for alternative hypotheses to explain away the UFO abduction conjecture. Skeptics reported that Dr. Simon had concluded Barney's passive, highly suggestible personality gave way to the more dominant Betty's feeling that her dreams reflected a real event. Others stated that Dr. Simon felt that Barney, being sympathetic toward his wife, over time came to believe that her nightmares were subconscious memories of a real abduction. Dr. Leo Sprinkle, the director of counseling and testing and professor of counseling services at the University of Wyoming, mailed a personality inventory to the Hills, which they completed in 1967. The results, on file in Betty's records, give us an accurate interpretation of each of the Hills' personality profiles, and puts to rest the notion that Barney was submissive or highly suggestible. On the "Adjective Check List" (Gough & Heilbrum, © 1962), Barney did not score outside the normal range on measures of suggestibility, self-confidence, self-doubt, excitability, inhibitions, disposition, conformity, and anxiety. His only highly statistically significant score was in the area of "intraception." On this, he scored in the high range as a capable and conscientious person who derives pleasure from exercising intellectual talents. He was above average in the areas of perseverance, responsibility, achievement, self-control, commitment to truth and justice, sincerity and dependability, self-discipline, and hard work. He also had a better than average interest in the opposite sex in a healthy and outgoing manner.

Dr. Simon's reported assessment of Betty's personality was more on the mark. Her scores were highly statistically significant in the areas of perseverance, aggression, and autonomy. She scored a few points higher than Barney on the dominance scale, although he scored above average. This suggests that although she attempted to dominate Barney, his strong-willed personality countered her efforts. He openly disagreed with Betty, often judging her opinions as ridiculous. This led to constant good-natured bantering between them. It is a good indicator that she did not convince him that he was observing a UFO or that her dreams were his reality. She predictably scored high as an individual who acts independently of others' social values and expectations. This is reflected by her entrance into an interracial marriage in 1960. She also scored within the highly statistically significant range on individualism, optimism, spontaneity, and independence. She, as did Barney, scored above average on measures of achievement, self control, responsibility, and commitment to truth and justice. It seems that the Hills were remarkably normal.

When their therapeutic sessions ended, Dr. Simon gave the Hills a copy of their hypnosis tapes. He suggested that they should listen to them, as repeated exposure might reduce their level of trauma. Betty and Barney did not want to listen to the tapes alone, so they phoned Air Force officer

Ben Swett and arranged to join him and his wife at their home. Colonel Swett's sworn testimony documents the night they listened to Barney's first hypnosis session together. He wrote:

> I was skeptical at first, but hearing what was on those tapes, plus the fact they didn't want any publicity, convinced me that they were telling the truth. For example, under hypnosis, Barney described seeing the UFO hovering close to the ground near the road. He got out of the car, walked toward it, and looked at it through binoculars. Something like a man was looking at him out of a window—right into his eyes—and started putting thoughts into his mind: He says, "Come a little closer—Don't be scared"— uh—I used to talk to rabbits like that—when I was hunting them. Just before the point on the tape where Barney started screaming, "I've gotta get outta here!" and ran back to the car, the physical Barney jumped up and ran out to our kitchen and vomited in the sink. I thought that would be pretty hard to fake.[1]

Betty and Barney asked Captain Swett to listen to their tapes and to determine if he thought that they could somehow reflect a dream or a fantasy created in their minds. His sworn testimony states:

> I listened to all the tapes. That took five nights. I made a lot of notes and went back to several tapes to make sure I had them right. Then I cross-checked comparable elements, distilled the whole thing in my mind, and decided what I believe. What they recalled under hypnosis consistently (and persistently) supported the hypothesis that their experience was real. But Dr. Simon didn't believe in UFOs and wasn't about to. He kept leading them toward any other explanation, and thus strongly suggested their experience wasn't real. That is why they were so ambivalent and why their trauma had not been resolved. On the positive side, the fact he did not believe them (did not suggest it to them and tried to lead them away from it), greatly increased their credibility and thus supported the hypothesis that what they remembered was real.

Swett returned the tapes to the Hills, told them he believed their experience was real, and explained why he thought so. Then he went to their house several more times for what amounted to informal counseling sessions in which he tried to help them look at the entire incident more objectively.

Swett's support reduced their anxiety about the reality of their abduction, but Barney continued to ruminate about the fear of reprisal. Betty wrote, "He wondered if they would come back and punish us. In my attempt to relieve some of his feelings, I would scoff at his suggestions. How would they find us? What would they do? How would they find out about our hypnosis? UFOs were not everyday occurrences, and they were probably on their way back to wherever they were from, and would never return. We had nothing to fear; I was sure we would never see them again."

The Hills also permitted NICAP investigator Walter Webb to listen to their hypnosis tapes and to discuss them with Dr. Simon under an agreement of confidentiality. On July 13, 1964, Webb wrote a letter stating:

> Last night I listened to the last tape at Dr. Simon's home. We both agree that the first encounter with the UFO really happened (he and I differ on just what sort of craft was seen). Regarding the second encounter, I believe Dr. Simon does have a highly plausible theory that could account for the alleged abduction. But, the dream theory has not eliminated all doubt in my mind as I had hoped it would. Unlike most UFO 'contactee' claims, this one is particularly hard to explain because the first encounter appears to be true, and if the first encounter actually took place, with all of its extraordinary features and implications, then I feel we cannot positively rule out the possibility, however remote, that the second encounter did, in fact, occur. Dr. Simon admits he cannot prove that his dream theory is correct but, on the other hand, spaceship abduction cannot be proved either.

In the next paragraph he added, "The doctor knows very little about the UFO subject. So far he considers the notion of extraterrestrial visitation a bit fantastic. In refusing to even examine the available evidence supporting the space hypothesis, Dr. Simon has demonstrated a narrow, rigid outlook on the subject. He also has certain preconceptions about the appearance, behavior, and motives of alien visitors."

Senior Atmospheric Physicist James E. MacDonald expressed a similar view in a letter he wrote to the Hills on October 6, 1967. He explained that he would have enjoyed hearing an extensive version of the Hills' case firsthand, but he was engaged in a meeting with Dr. Simon and two Harvard astronomers. He continued:

We spent a long evening going over various aspects of the UFO problem, and did get a brief opportunity to hear some selected portions of the tapes Dr. Simon played. I tried to emphasize to Simon that he probably should be paying much more attention to the preamnesiac parts of the total account. After hearing a bit of the tapes where you go back through the initial sighting out in the field, I am most impressed. So is Simon, as far as I can tell. As I stated on the WNEW-TV program, the later portions are entirely too complex for me to have any opinion on them. But the first part, where the hypnoanalysis matches your conscious recall in reasonable fashion, seems to me to be quite significant. I asked Simon if, in his experience with battlefield trauma cases, he had ever encountered a degree of terror comparable to that which seems to come through in your part of the tapes. He indicated that he had not heard anything quite the same in battlefield cases. When I then asked him if he did not feel this implied that it was a real sighting, he said he felt that it probably was. I then pressed him on this, pointing out that the implications would be profound, and he retreated a bit from that position. I would not presume to be able to state his precise viewpoint on this, but I hope that he and you go over this again sometime.

Although his work with Dr. Simon left many unanswered questions, it seemed to relieve some of Barney's psychosomatic symptoms. He was able to become much more proactive and he plunged into his civil rights work. He also continued to pursue the question, "Is there evidence to prove that we were really abducted?"

When Betty and Barney discussed their belief that a real abduction had occurred with Dr. Simon, he told them that anything was possible. However, if a real abduction had occurred there would be a physical capture spot. They became more determined than ever to find it. Almost immediately Betty and Barney resumed their search of the White Mountains. They began to take weekend camping excursions with Betty's parents, who owned a travel trailer. They would spend long afternoons driving and searching, but to no avail. Then, on Labor Day weekend in September of 1965, they crossed the Kancamagus Highway to Lincoln and turned south onto Route 3. Almost instinctively Barney made a left turn onto Route 175, and both Betty and Barney immediately recognized the area. They became very alert, anticipating the approaching turn onto the gravel road.

They proceeded slowly until they found the area where the roadblock had occurred. Directly beside them was the path in the woods that Barney had drawn in Dr. Simon's office. They followed the path through the woods until they came to a clearing covered with soft beach sand. Betty immediately recognized this as being identical to the sand she walked on the night of her capture. They stood in awe as they realized that Barney's drawing matched this area precisely, with the exception that his car was facing in the opposite direction. They began to examine the ground and the surrounding landscape for evidence. Tire tracks made by a car and several charred and broken limbs lay inside the perimeter. A small, dead, blackened spruce tree stood in the middle of the clearing. Betty wrote, "That night after the second encounter, I was very well aware that the car was pulled off the road—I am positive of that. Now I believe that the car had been turned around and headed back towards Route 175."[2]

This supporting evidence, albeit circumstantial, that their abduction memories reflected objective reality, was reassuring to the Hills. They were thereafter less troubled and more secure in their belief that the abduction was real.

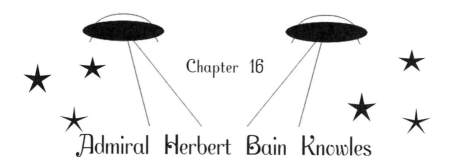

Chapter 16

Admiral Herbert Bain Knowles

It was through Betty's friend Lauri D'Allessandro that the Hills met Rear Admiral Herbert B. Knowles and his wife, Helen. They were invited guests at a buffet luncheon at their home in Eliot, Maine. The invitation stated that Admiral Knowles was a member of NICAP's board of directors. Initially they were apprehensive about attending the gathering, but Mrs. Knowles assured them that all of the guests who would be present were knowledgeable about UFOs. She added that many of those in attendance had also experienced UFO encounters. The Hills were reluctant because they were attempting to normalize their lives and return to their prior interests. Their civil rights activities were increasing and they were firmly committed to the promotion of social justice issues. However, the possibility of acquir-

Rear Admiral Herbert B. Knowles and his wife Helen. Courtesy of Kathleen Marden.

ing additional information about UFOs was intriguing, and they decided to attend.

Rear Admiral Knowles had retired from an outstanding career in the military. Born in Maine in 1894, he graduated from the U.S. Naval Academy in 1917, as an ensign. He served in the submarine service during World War I, aboard the early R-boats in the Orient. After the war, he taught at the Naval Academy in the engineering department.

During World War II, he commanded several submarines before taking command of The USS Neches and the USS Heywood, troop transport ships. Onboard the USS Heywood, he landed troops for an amphibious assault in the Tulagi, Guadalcanal area, in August of 1942. The Heywood repelled frequent air attacks and shot down an enemy plane while shuttling troops and supplies. She also evacuated wounded American troops and Japanese captives. After The Heywood underwent repairs in January, 1943, Knowles carried fighting men in an amphibious assault on Attu, Aleutian Islands. Then, he returned the Heywood, with nearly 500 wounded veterans, to San Francisco before transporting occupation troops to Kiska.[1]

Next, he was given command of transport in the South Pacific and his flagship was the USS Monrovia. It was an attack transport that carried 55 officers and 1,352 enlisted men.

Rear Admiral Knowles retired from military service in 1947 after decommissioning the Naval Station at Portland, Maine. In his retirement he joined the National Investigations Committee on Aerial Phenomena and served on its board of directors. As a result of his interest in UFOs, he became interested in Mrs. Frances Swan, a contactee who lived near his Eliot, Maine home. She claimed that she was communicating telepathically with two extraterrestrial civilizations that were orbiting Earth. He became a curious reader of the "contactee" accounts that were published in the 1950s, including books by George Adamski, Orfeo Angelucci, Dino Kraspedon, and Brian and Helen Reeve. (Betty inherited all of these books upon Admiral Knowles's death.)

In a letter dated January 14, 1980, Helen Knowles recalled the 1954 period when Mrs. Swan came to her door to inquire about how to address a letter to the Department of Defense. She wrote, "Herbie not only helped her out, but personally endorsed her letter after he read it. Then, because its contents were of vital national importance, he addressed a personal letter to Washington, which brought a group of departmental 'top brass' to our home."

An office memorandum from the director of the FBI dated August 2, 1954, informs us that letters were mailed to Maine Senator Margaret Chase Smith, who forwarded the information to the Secretary of Defense. Copies were sent to the Army, Navy, and Air Force. A letter also went to President Dwight Eisenhower.

The letter spoke of telepathic communication that Mrs. Swan was channeling via automatic writing from the commanders of two alien space ships. According to Mrs. Swan, the ships, which were 150 miles wide, 200 miles long, and 100 miles deep, carried 5,000 150- to 200- foot-long mother ships. Ship M-4 was allegedly commanded by "Affa," who hailed from the planet Uranus. The commander of the second ship, L-11, came from the planet Hatann and was named "Ponnar." Mrs. Swan stated that these telepathic communications with Affa and Ponnar were for the purpose of protecting the planet Earth from destruction caused by the atomic bomb and the hydrogen bomb, which disrupt the magnetic field of force that surrounds the earth. They stated that if these magnetic fault lines are breached, it would affect the entire universe. Their stated purpose was to repair the fault lines in the Pacific Ocean that were in immediate danger of breaking.[2]

According to the office memorandum, Mrs. Swan stated that whenever she was having contact with the people in outer space, she would get a buzzing sound in her left ear to indicate that they were "on the line." She complained that since the initiation of contact on May 27, 1954, she had no control over the transmission of messages the people from outer space were communicating to her. The painful and annoying buzzing sound in her ear would come at all times of night and cause her to lose sleep. This occurred until an arrangement was made to schedule communications at 8 in the morning, noon, and 6 in the evening seven days a week.

According to the FBI memorandum, when Washington's top brass visited Mrs. Swan at her modest, middle-class home on July 24–26, 1954, they found a woman who allegedly was receiving messages through thought control from "outer space." They noted that she could engage in automatic writing for four or five hours at a time, without becoming fatigued. The content of these messages was allegedly far in advance of Mrs. Swan's education or training. Seemingly, Affa and Ponnar could use Mrs. Swan's eyes and ears to see and hear through the use of a mechanical device. All conversations were said to be relayed to the people in outer space. One of the top brass stated that when he asked a question, even before Mrs. Swan had a chance to relay it, she began writing the answer down on paper. The "top brass" also heard buzzing sounds in their ears, but were not able to receive transmissions or messages. The aliens stated that the transmissions were related to flying saucers, life on other planets, life in the hereafter, prophesies in the Bible, the location of their own planets, and their reasons for being here.

The FBI memorandum stated that the agents were "looking for proof" and wanted to attempt contact with the men from outer space. Mrs. Swan indicated that they could communicate on any frequency, provided that they notified her first. Then, she would advise the people in outer space and they would accommodate the level of frequency. The official government representative stated that he could make no commitment as he did not know how far the Navy would go. However, he indicated that he wanted to schedule an experimental contact, through high frequency, on August 1, 1954. On that date, the spaceship was reportedly going to come within 100 miles of the Earth to facilitate communication. The G-man also inquired about the possibility of making physical contact with the people in outer space. This was agreed to as long as the protection of the space people could be guaranteed. The space commanders indicated that 5,000 "bells" or "flying saucers" would "appear in force, in close proximity, over many nations around the world in late August of 1954." The Naval intelligence contact experiment failed to produce the desired result. They were not able to establish psychic contact with the space commanders under Mrs. Swan's guidance. In the end, the Office of Naval Intelligence and the Bureau of Aeronautics took no official action in the matter due to the paranormal nature of Mrs. Swan's communication with the space people. Her letters were added to the "crank file."

Astronomer and computer scientist Jacques Vallee, Ph.D., referenced in his book, *Forbidden Science*, some "extraordinary notes taken from a classified report" that J. Allen Hynek, Ph.D., Air Force consultant to Project Blue Book shared with him in confidence. The report was written by an extremely competent Air Force officer, Colonel Robert Friend, who held the rank of major when he was responsible for Project Blue Book. It told of a meeting at a CIA office in Washington of July 9, 1959, under the direction of Arthur Lundahl, seven CIA officers, and a representative from the Office of Naval Intelligence. Three days prior to the July 9 meeting, Naval Intelligence officer Commander Larsen had discussed the Frances Swan/Naval Intelligence contact experiment of August 1954 with Lundahl and CIA officer Neosham, at the CIA. They encouraged Commander Larsen to repeat the experiment, and this time he was successful. He received a message from Affa, who instructed the three to look out the CIA window. All three men observed a circular object with a darker center and lighter outer rim. Neosham phoned the Washington airport radar and was informed that "electromagnetic signals were unaccountably 'blocked' in the direction in question."[3]

In 1980 Mrs. Knowles wrote, "I have been encouraged to pick up the pieces and put them together in a book, stressing the log that we kept at the time, together with extremely pertinent scientific data handed us by the lady who received messages from outer space and not understanding them at all." Kathy contacted Herbert Knowles's sister to inquire about the location of the log and book. She reported that Helen had never written it. Further, the log seems to have been lost after Mrs. Knowles's death.

In the true spirit of scientific investigation, a courageous Canadian government official, Wilbert Brockhouse Smith (1910–1962), had taken an interest in Frances Swan. He may have learned about Mrs. Swan through Admiral Herbert Knowles, with whom he had a close personal relationship.

Born in Lethbridge, Alberta, Smith was a Canadian radio engineer. He graduated from the University of British Columbia with a B.Sc. in electrical engineering in 1933 and an M.A. in 1934. He was an electronics expert who invented a high-speed radio direction finder used in World War II, a new type of voltmeter, and a regenerative noise filter. At the outset of his career he worked to improve the technical side of broadcasting facilities in Canada, and was involved in the formation of the Canadian Association of Broadcast Consultants, which often advised the Federal Department of Transportation. He was also a liaison between the DOT and the Canadian Radio Technical Planning Board. In 1939, he joined the Federal Department of Transportation. He engineered Canada's monitoring service during World War II, and in 1947, took charge of establishing a network of ionospheric measurement stations.

On September 15, 1950, Smith made discreet inquiries through the Canadian Embassy staff, when he attended a North American Broadcasting conference in Washington, D.C. Lt. Colonel Bremmer, a military attaché, arranged an interview with Dr. Robert Sarbacher, an electrical engineer and guided missile scientist, who was a consultant to the U.S. Research and Development Board. Sarbacher claimed that prior to his conversation with Smith, he was briefed at Wright-Patterson Air Force Base about the recovery of material from a flying disk that crashed in the western United States. In the 1980s, Stanton was the first UFO researcher to locate, talk to, and meet with Sarbacher. Sarbacher confirmed that he had spoken to Smith in 1950, and that Smith's notes and memo were accurate, and not hoaxed. Smith's archives contain handwritten notes referring to the content of his discussions with Sarbacher.

For a two-week period between committee meetings and at night, he met with Major Donald Keyhoe, USMC retired, an aviation journalist and author of UFO books, who in 1957 took the helm of NICAP. He told Keyhoe that he and a group of Canadian government engineers and scientists were unofficially experimenting to use the electricity of the ionosphere for propulsion. Later, after he obtained clearance to discuss the project with Keyhoe, he told him that Canadian scientists had been working for some time on the Earth's magnetic field. He added that if their initial conclusions were correct, they offered an explanation for the interesting properties that have been reported in connection with the flight characteristics of UFOs.[4]

On November 20, 1950, Smith wrote a "TOP SECRET" memo titled "Geomagnetics" to the controller of telecommunications, informing him that for the past several years he and others had been engaged in the study of various aspects of radio wave propagation. He stated that they were on the track of a means whereby the potential energy of the Earth's magnetic field may be abstracted and used. This provided the potential of introducing a new technology; a linkage between our technology and that by which saucers are designed and operated. He added the following:

> I made discreet enquiries through the Canadian Embassy staff in Washington who were able to obtain the following information:
>
> a. The matter is the most highly classified subject in the United States Government, rating higher even than the H-bomb.
>
> b. Flying saucers exist.
>
> c. Their modus operandi is unknown, but concentrated effort is being made by a small group headed by Doctor Vannevar Bush.

d. The entire matter is considered by the United States authorities to be of tremendous significance.

e. I was further informed that the United States authorities are investigating along quite a number of lines which might possibly be related to the saucers, such as mental phenomena, and I gather that they are not doing too well since they indicated that if Canada is doing anything at all in geomagnetics they would welcome a discussion with suitably accredited Canadians.[5]

In the same memo, Smith submitted a proposal to set up a special project, later named Project Magnet, to develop a new technology that grew out of his conversation with Robert Sarbacher. In the early 1980s, Arthur Bray, the conservator of Wilbert Smith's personal collection, made Smith's handwritten notes regarding this meeting public. Smith had informed Sarbacher that he was doing work on the collapse of the Earth's magnetic field as a source of energy, adding that he thought his work might have some bearing on flying saucers. Sarbacher informed Smith that U.S. scientists had not been able to duplicate the UFO's performance. When Smith asked if they traveled here from some other planet, Sarbacher replied, "All we know is that we didn't make them, and it's pretty certain that they didn't originate on Earth." When Smith asked if there was a way in which he could get information, particularly as it might fit into his own work, Sarbacher replied, "I suppose you could be cleared through your own defense department and I am pretty sure arrangements could be made to exchange information. If you have anything to contribute we would be glad to talk it over but I can't give you any more at the present time."[6] In his 1983 discussion with Stanton, Dr. Sarbacher confirmed that Smith's rendition of the meeting was accurate.

Another memo found in Smith's file was a Top Secret request for C.G. Edwards to obtain a security clearance for Smith to talk to U.S. authorities about the subject. There is evidence that the clearance was granted, although it is not in government files. Dr. Omond Solandt, who was then the head of the Defense Research Board of Canada, admitted in writing that Smith's theory was discussed with Dr. Vannevar Bush (1890–1974). Bush had been named chairman of the U.S. Research and Development Board on September 24, 1947, the date of the infamous Truman-Forrestal memo establishing Operation Majestic-12 (MJ-12), a Top Secret research and development/intelligence operation responsible directly and only to the president of the United States, and created in direct response to the crash and recovery of an alien craft near Roswell, New Mexico, in July of 1947. Operations of the project were carried out under the control of the MJ-12 Group, established by a special classified executive order of President Harry Truman, upon the recommendation of Dr. Bush and Secretary of Defense James Forrestal. Bush was also named to head the group evaluating a possible atomic bomb test by the USSR in September, 1949.[7]

Dr. Bush had been a professor, then dean, and then vice president at MIT before he entered an interesting career in the U.S. government. He is said to have been the most influential researcher in America. He built the most powerful computers in the 1930s and was Roosevelt's chief advisor on military research, and a member of the War Council. From 1939 to 1941, he served as chairman of the National Advisory Committee on Aeronautics, which became NASA in 1958. He headed the Office of Scientific Research and Development from 1942 to 1948, which was responsible for the development of the proximity fuse, radar, sonar, and many dozens of other devices that helped win the war. In the summer of 1940, he took control of America's secret development of the atomic bomb, while he held down a job as chairman at Carnegie, a leading scientific institution whose chief traditionally advised the government on technical matters. He was a member of a Top Secret elite group of six who set policy, including the president, vice president, the secretary of war, and Army Chief of Staff General Leslie Groves—the man who monitored and oversaw technical progress toward the bomb. When he ran into a snag because of funding issues, Roosevelt and his budget director solved it by creating the first "black budget" in the nation's history. He brought physics, engineering, and the military together for the technical innovation that he believed was the most important factor in national security, and it was his leadership that ultimately helped to win the war.[8]

Vannevar Bush's Canadian counterpart, Dr. Omond Solandt, chairman of the Defense Research Board, met with Smith on November 20, 1950. He agreed that work on a classified project on geomagnetic energy should proceed rapidly, and offered to provide laboratory facilities, the acquisition of equipment, and specialized personnel for incidental work in the project.[9] After his retirement, Solandt admitted that he and Bush frequently had conversations about UFOs, but did not reveal the particulars. He usually denigrated Smith, suggesting that he was not a good scientist, and that his experiments were not successful due to incorrect measurements and uncalibrated equipment. Yet, in contrast to Solandt's appraisal, Wilbert Smith was posthumously awarded the Lieutenant Colonel Keith S. Rogers Memorial Engineering Award in recognition of a lifetime of dedicated and distinguished service to the advancement of technical standards in the Canadian Broadcasting Industry, presented by the Canadian General Electric Company. Solandt's history of fabricated statements seem to stem from his desire not to divulge classified information, but Smith's archival materials make Solandt's role clear.

In 1952 Smith was appointed to Project Second Storey, a Canadian government committee set up to consider the UFO problem and to recommend government action. This was through the efforts of DRB Chairman Solandt, who asked staff member Harold Oatway to form a committee to investigate the flying saucer reports that were being reported in the Canadian press. Several of these reports were made by service personnel involving disk-shaped craft over Royal Canadian Air Force bases.[10]

On June 25, 1952, Smith submitted an interim report on Project Magnet stating that it appeared evident that flying saucers are emissaries from other civilizations. He added that they operate on magnetic principles that we have failed to grasp due to our failure to pay enough attention to the structure of fields in our study of physics.[11] Then on August 10, 1954, the controller of telecommunications issued a form letter authorized as a press release admitting that the DOT had engaged in the study of UFOs. He stated that even though considerable data had been collected and analyzed, it was impossible to reach any definite conclusion. Thus, Project Magnet was terminated, and Smith continued his research without official government sanction.

Smith engaged in a secret experimental project designed to communicate with occupants from UFOs through a contact (Frances Swan) who provided him with information. Swan's alien sources told him that all matter is held together by "binding forces." She said that there are areas of reduced binding that present a danger to planes, causing them to literally fall apart. By building a "binding meter" according to the principles given to him by Swan, he was able to locate regions of reduced binding. He recommended to the government that further investigation be conducted, but because he had obtained his information from alleged extraterrestrial beings that channeled it through Francis Swan, he was unable to obtain official recognition for his work.[12]

Two of the more notable guests present at the luncheon were Adele Darrah and her husband Tom, a retired U.S. Navy commander and close personal friend of Admiral Knowles and Frances Swan. Also present was Mrs. Murl Smith, the widow of Wilbert Smith who died in 1962, and Edie and Buck Buchanan from Ottawa, Canada. Buck was retired from the Canadian Military Service and Edie worked for the Canadian Parliament. Betty and Barney were surprised to see their friend Lauri D'Allessandro, and even more amazed to learn her purpose for being there.

The apparent objective of the luncheon meeting was to attempt to identify a small piece of metal that had been cut from a large anomalous object. Wilbert Smith had been contacted to investigate the flaming object that fell from the sky and landed on the banks of the St. Lawrence River. It was huge, weighing several tons, and initially all efforts to cut it were unsuccessful. Now Webb's widow would ask Lauri D'Allessandro to attempt to identify the object through psychometry or remote viewing. She was blindfolded, and the object was placed in her hands. She informed the group that it had fallen in flames from the sky, landing on the shores of a body of water; that it had been studied, and that no one had been able to identify it. She thought that it might have come from a UFO. Then, her blindfold was removed, and Murl Smith revealed the history of the object. Betty was astonished. She had no idea that Lauri was psychic and had never seen psychometry practiced before.

Later, Murl Smith and the Hills attended a conference on antigravity research in Warner, New Hampshire, where science fiction and scientific exploration merged. Betty wrote that she was awestruck that thousands of dollars were awarded to scientists engaged in this research.

Admiral Knowles attempted to introduce Frances Swan to the Hills, but she refused to meet them. Betty wrote about Mrs. Swan as follows:

A few miles from Portsmouth is a woman who claims she is in contact with the occupants of UFOs, through automatic writing. Almost daily she sits and receives messages. Although she and I share some of the same friends, we have never met. She refuses to meet me, for she believes that Barney and I met the wrong ones—the evil ones, the ones of wrong vibrations. Hers are different types, who are kind, loving, concerned for all; who give her messages of brotherhood and the Kingdom of God. Barney and I both agreed that we had never seen those of a different vibration! But, in those days, we had never heard of George Adamski.

With the introduction of the Hills, the contactee movement of the 1950s had come face to face with abduction. This was also Betty's first introduction to the contactee movement, but over time she met numerous individuals who described beautiful people dressed in long, flowing robes with blond hair and blue eyes who delivered Biblical messages of being chosen and blessed. She wrote:

> In going into their personal backgrounds, I found that all of them have been involved in psychic phenomena! They are involved in ESP experiments, dream interpretations, astral projection, meditation, mind control, and the spirit world. They attend classes, keep up to date with the latest books, and compare experiences with their friends. Their experiences seem to share a similarity. They are sincere, honest people who seem to believe that some kind of strange phenomenon is happening, which they label, UFOs. There seems to be a very definite correlation between the phenomenon of the contactee and the availability of centers for psychic development.

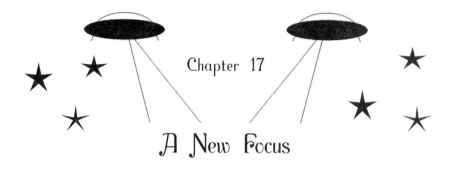

Chapter 17

A New Focus

After six months of long weekly treks to Dr. Simon's office in Boston, the Hills' lives once again normalized. They enjoyed active social and community involvement, promoting liberal social and political issues. The Unitarian church held an important position in their lives, and they attended regularly. They remained active in its couples club, whose membership, according to Betty, largely comprised officers from Pease Air Force Base. Together the group promoted civil rights activities and their collective political agenda. Through the church, Betty and Barney became envoys to the United Nations. They also continued an active role in the NAACP, where Barney fought against discrimination as legal redress for that organization. He presented several speeches throughout the seacoast region, and was a frequent guest speaker at the Portsmouth Naval Shipyard. Betty attempted to erase the abduction memory and to throw herself into her work and community affairs. She worked tirelessly to achieve Democratic Party success in the ongoing political campaign. Their work on voter registration and the organization of University of New Hampshire students to further the democratic presidential campaign effort achieved success in November of that year.

Betty, Barney, and their niece, Kathy, were invited guests at Lyndon Johnson's inaugural ceremonies in Washington, D.C. in January 1965 (see photo appendix). It was an enriching experience that they could never forget. They toured the U.S. House of Representatives and received a pass to attend a session of the Senate. Then they were treated to a guided tour of the Capitol Building. Their visit to the East Wing at the White House was especially impressive. The luncheons, parties, and inaugural ball were superb. Inaugural activities included a reception honoring the vice president and Mrs. Hubert H. Humphrey at the Shoreham Hotel, the Young Democrats' reception and dance at the Mayflower

Hotel, the inaugural concert at Constitution Hall, the official inaugural ceremony in the standing-room-only senate section, the parade opposite the Presidential Reviewing Stand, the Citizens for Johnson-Humphrey cocktail buffet at the International Inn (by special invitation), and the Inaugural Ball (by special invitation). Sandra Dee and Bobby Darrin were guests at the same ball. They visited President Kennedy's grave at the Arlington National Cemetery and the Tomb of the Unknown Soldier. On the trip home they visited Barney's sister and brother-in-law in Philadelphia and took their niece to the Liberty Bell and other historic sites.

New Hampshire Delegation at the LBJ Presidential Inauguration. Betty and Barney Hill are in the front row on the right; Kathleen Marden is the third from the left in the back.
Courtesy of Kathleen Marden.

Barney's dedication to political and community involvement afforded him a certain level of comfort. He was able to focus on social justice issues and to exercise his strong intellectual talents for the betterment of society. Yet whenever the UFO quagmire surfaced he became upset. If it was necessary for him to listen to the audiotapes of himself under hypnosis, he became visibly distressed and angry. The experience remained very painful to him, and he could not reconcile his complete loss of control. He particularly disliked baring this private and extremely embarrassing part of his soul to UFO researchers, even in the interest of promoting scientific knowledge.

The Hills continued to correspond with Dr. Simon, with whom they wished to express their dissatisfaction with the results of their treatment. Betty was disappointed that the hypnosis did not give her the assurance that her memory of the men in the road was only a dream. The actual memory of what occurred between the first and second sets of beeps was anticipated, but never answered. Adhering to Dr. Simon's suggestion, she told herself, time and time again, that they were not captured; that it was only a dream. But then something new would pop up and she would lose her focus.

According to Betty, Barney was particularly angry with Dr. Simon, who assured him, on several occasions, that it was impossible to lie or deceive under hypnosis, but then discounted his testimony on the tapes. Added to this was his disappointment that for seven months he drove to Boston every Saturday morning at great personal expense for what now seemed fruitless. In a letter to NICAP's Walter Webb dated August 23, 1965, Betty wrote, "Barney feels that Dr. Simon deceived him by assuring us on several occasions that the truth, the whole truth, and nothing but the truth would be on those tapes. And then at the end, he decided that it was a dream I had, although he had a copy of my dreams, and was able to compare the differences. Then, he explained Barney's part of the sessions by saying that he was suggestible to my dreams! The whole experience has been an upsetting, time-consuming, and expensive project."

Betty had become convinced that the hypnosis proved she had been abducted, and therefore, did not experience the kind of conflict that plagued Barney. Physically, she manifested a nasty case of hives upon hearing the tapes, but felt that healing would come when she and Barney became conditioned to the emotional outbursts that reflected their abject terror at the hands of their abductors. In her opinion, the tapes were a true documentation of a horrifying experience that played out in traumatic nightmares. She wrote to Webb:

> I am convinced that those tapes are true. I am also convinced that I did dream about my experience, which was a form of hypnotic recall and a fairly common experience in like situations,

according to my abnormal psychology courses at college. In fact, in my thinking, the dreams actually helped to convince me about the authenticity of the tapes. Therefore, I do not have any conflict, as my problem is resolved—it really happened. I do get somewhat upset hearing the tapes because I do have an emotional reaction to the actual experience, as I feel some of the same feelings that I did that night. In other words, I relive the experience.

Barney has a different reaction. In fact, he has several. First of all the experience is very painful to him still. We have talked about this with a friend, a psychiatric social worker, on several occasions, and she feels that Barney gets upset because of his reactions on the tapes, which are contrary to the way he thinks about himself. On the tapes he is fearful, crying, helpless, frightened, etc. In other words, he is not very "masculine" to his way of thinking. When Barney becomes upset, he seeks approval by asking if the person [listening] believes the tapes. Actually, he is asking that the person understand his position; his reaction to the actual experience. He is asking if the other person might react in the same way in the same experience. If the person shows doubt about the tapes, he feels that the person believes that this would be a normal reaction to an everyday situation for him.

Those who knew Barney well did not doubt his courageous, charismatic leadership style. He was not the wimp he feared others would perceive him to be, due to his intense expression of emotion under hypnoanalysis. He had expressed the powerful emotions that any man would feel under life-threatening circumstances. The idea that he was passive and suggestible to Betty's ideas or that he absorbed her nightmares and built a fantasy around them was, to those who knew him well, nonsense. His conflict arose when he laid bare his soul for no useful purpose. However, he set aside his subjective emotions to promote a better understanding of the abduction phenomenon among investigative scientists. Simultaneously, he persevered toward the resolution of social and political injustices in the real world. He projected a positive, proactive stance in all of life's endeavors.

In addition to working full time at the U.S. Post Office as a city carrier, Barney devoted indefatigable energy to the advancement of civil rights. His outstanding leadership was recognized on both state and federal levels. On May 21, 1965, Barney received a letter from the United States

Civil Rights Commission in Washington, D.C. The letter advised him that he had been appointed to the New Hampshire State Advisory Committee to the U.S. Commission on Civil Rights for a term ending December 31, 1966. Then, on July 9, 1965, the Democratic city chairman for the City of Portsmouth addressed a letter to the executive councilor of the Second District nominating Barney to the Human Rights Commission for the State of New Hampshire. It read as follows:

> I have been asked to forward the name of a prominent Negro leader of Portsmouth for consideration by Governor King as a nominee to the Human Rights Commission recently formed under a bill passed by the Legislature and signed by Governor King. It would be a great help if you could submit his name for the Governor's consideration and the approval of the Governor's Council.
>
> Mr. Barney Hill, 954 State Street, Portsmouth, New Hampshire, a postal worker, is eminently qualified to serve on the Human Rights Commission as a representative of the Negro race.
>
> Mr. Hill is an active member of the Portsmouth Chapter of NAACP, now serving as the Legal Redress Officer. He is presently on the Executive Board of the New England Regional Chapter of NAACP.
>
> Mr. Hill's sincere interest in human rights has been recognized on the national level by being appointed to the New Hampshire Advisory Board of the U.S. Civil Rights Commission.
>
> On the local level Mr. Hill has been very active and effective in convincing his people of the necessity of registering as voters and making their voice heard by voting in all elections. He is convinced that the Negroes will take their rightful place in society through the educational process and steady and persistent pressure.
>
> It is the consensus of the Democratic City Committee that Mr. Hill's name and qualifications should be submitted to the Governor. We respectfully request your assistance and Executive Councilor of our District. We trust that you will concur with our recommendation.

Barney's next courageous contribution to society was to develop an adult education program and to resolve racial issues in cooperation with the Diocese of Manchester, N.H. He addressed committees throughout the state and promoted the conditions for racial equality. In short, Barney worked tirelessly for the advancement of a just and humane society.

The knowledge that they had located the abduction site gave the Hills some consolation that Dr. Simon's opinion was incorrect. The degraded condition of Betty's dress signified that something extraordinary had occurred, that could not have happened during a continuous drive home on the night of September 19–20, 1961. They began to reexamine the evidence to look for scientific verification that their recovered memories were real. They approached this with the full support of their families and friends.

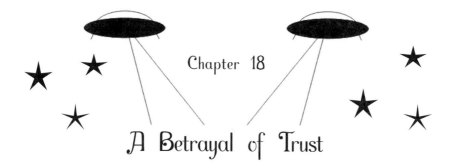

Chapter 18

A Betrayal of Trust

Ironically, just as Barney and Betty were seeing a light at the end of a tunnel that they never intended to enter, a dark shroud was thrown over them. In August, their friend Adele Darrah informed them that John Luttrell, a reporter for a Boston newspaper, had interviewed her. She remarked that he seemed to think that Pease Air Force Base had paid for their sessions with Dr. Simon, and had then sworn the Hills to secrecy. Nothing could be further from the truth. Betty wrote to NICAP's Walter Webb, "I guess he [Luttrell] has discussed us with everyone we have ever met in Massachusetts. But we have decided that we are *NOT* going to be involved in his story. He told Adele that he was assigned by his editor two months ago to do a story on us. We are letting people know that we do not want the story published."

In a phone call to Barney, Luttrell revealed that he knew most of the personal facts about their lives and requested an appointment to discuss the article with them. Betty wrote in her memoirs, "We told him that we would not be home on that date, and asked if he thought our experience might be published. If so, we objected to this. I told him that I might lose my job as a child welfare worker with the State of New Hampshire, if he published this. We were fearful of how it might affect our lives. We made our position known that we did not want our experience to be published. Later, we learned that the reporter came to our house and sat on our front steps." However, he was disappointed to find that after a sweltering ride and a 90-minute wait at their doorstep, the Hills failed to appear. Despite the Hills' adamant objection to his article, he remained persistent. In a letter dated August 19, 1965, Luttrell wrote, "I am endowed with enough determination to try it again and wondered whether we could get together at your convenience sometime on Sunday, August 22? Meanwhile, I've been talking with "Lorry" Dallassandro in Weymouth, and if the Hills prove to be anywhere as nice as she describes, meeting both of you will indeed be a pleasure. She thinks exceptionally highly of both of you and she, too, agrees that your experience is perhaps one of the most significant ever to occur anywhere."

The Hills were not as "nice" as Lauri assumed they would be, when it involved the invasion of their privacy and the dissemination of confidential information pertaining to their lives. But Luttrell attempted to reassure them by writing, "Rest assured that my motives lie only in the realm of information, and I have no intention of commercializing upon what's happened to the Hills." The Hills did not bite. Instead, Barney contacted two lawyers in an attempt to force the reporter, the publisher, and the editor to cease and desist. To his great displeasure, the lawyers informed Barney that as long as medical confidentiality was not violated and the story was treated as a news item, they could not legally bar its publication.

Betty wrote to Walter Webb, "I do not know what effect publicity would have on Barney's position in so many of the things he is doing. There is a possibility that he *might* be appointed to the State's Human Rights Commission which is being set up here; and he has just been appointed to the U.S. Civil Rights Commission, and he is director of the board of directors of the Poverty Program, and several other things." Clearly, any association with the lunatic fringe would destroy his credibility in the public eye. As a testament to NICAP Investigator Walter Webb's professionalism and personal integrity, he refused all of Luttrell's requests for an in-depth interview about the Hills.

When the article did not appear in September's *Boston Traveler*, Betty and Barney breathed a sigh of relief. They thought that they had successfully warded off this living nightmare. What they didn't know was that Luttrell had an audiotaped copy of their confidential talk to members of the Two State UFO Study Group. Nor did they know that friends and NICAP members were violating confidentiality by discussing their hypnosis sessions with a newspaper reporter. Further, they did not know that Luttrell had discussed their case with Air Force officers at Pease, and had obtained a copy of their Blue Book file. Then, Luttrell had surreptitiously, and without Walter Webb's knowledge, acquired a copy of his confidential "Final Report" on the Hill case dated August 30, 1965. Unknowingly, they had been betrayed on many levels. Perhaps those who betrayed them had been deceived by Luttrell, just as he had attempted to deceive the Hills.

Their greatest fear was realized on Monday, October 25, 1965, when in the middle of the night, Barney received phone calls from Europe about his UFO experience. He phoned Captain Ben Swett at Pease Air Force Base at 4 a.m. with panic in his voice, stating that an unscrupulous reporter had publicized his confidential information. Later, he found himself surrounded by the media outside the Portsmouth Post Office. Someone thrust the front page of the *Boston Traveler* toward his face, revealing the Headline, "UFO Chiller—Did They Seize Couple?" John Luttrell had succeeded in committing the ultimate betrayal by ignoring the Hills' repeated requests for confidentiality. His series of articles constituted a gross intrusion into the Hills' private, personal lives. He could not have succeeded without the collusion of Betty's close friends in whom she confided the details of her hypnotic material. This was an unforgivable violation of confidentiality by members of a UFO research organization. It forever plunged Betty and Barney into the public eye, a fate that they sought to avoid. It opened them up to public criticism, stereotyping, armchair psychoanalysis, and forever condemned them to a position within the lunatic fringe. Their prior accomplishments, their outstanding achievements in the community, and their personal stability and integrity suddenly dissolved in the eyes of those who sought to discredit them. They suddenly were thrust into the realm of the incredible.

Luttrell and his newspaper had commercialized their plight and sent them into a tailspin. The media surrounded their home, filled their front hall, and hounded them with telephone calls. When Betty arrived home, she wondered if one of the neighbors was having a dinner party, for cars were parked all around the house. She opened the front door and walked in to find herself surrounded by the media. She reminisced, "I asked Barney, 'What is happening?' He told me he was talking with someone from London. Someone handed the newspaper to me, and I saw the headlines. I took the newspaper and locked myself in the bathroom. I was stunned, unbelieving. I noted it was going to be a series to run for five days. When we were asked for our comments, we said that we needed to wait until we had read all of the series."

"In the midst of all of the calls, we received one from a friend stationed at Pease, who offered us dinner and sanctuary from the press. So at about 8 p.m. we excused ourselves and went to Pease Air Force Base, to Captain Ben Swett's house for dinner. Friends at the base joined us, and I will always remember that we found sanctuary that night at an Air Force Base with Air Force personnel."

When Betty arrived at the New Hampshire Division of Welfare Office the next morning, the press greeted her at the door. They wanted to photograph her at work, but fortunately for her, the State Office denied permission on the grounds that her private affairs were separate from her professional employment. However, when she and Barney arrived home, the press was back and their phone was ringing nonstop. They fled the premises and sought privacy in a local restaurant but were soon besieged by autograph seekers. The Hills were amazed that anyone would want their signature. Two months earlier in a letter to Walter Webb, Betty had expressed the concern that "people would question my sanity and I would probably have to carry a certified statement from Dr. Simon testifying to the fact that I was safe enough to associate with the rest of the world's population!"

The following evening, Betty and Barney traveled to Kingston to ensure that the relatives knew and understood their position about publicity. They had decided that they would publicly discuss the UFO sighting, but refused to talk about their capture and hypnotic recall. It was such a long and complex story; they doubted that they could explain it adequately. Additionally, the sighting itself would have to be accepted before they could expect anyone to consider the possibility of an abduction.

That night at 9:45, as they were leaving Betty's parents' home, they saw a red-orange bouncing light directly in front of their vehicle, about 200 yards back from the highway. It traveled over a nearby pond, across an adjacent field, and south over the treetops. Its flight pattern was erratic. The craft seemed to follow the contours of the treetops, ascending over taller trees and descending over shorter ones, exactly as a similar craft had traveled in September of 1961. Barney braked the car and flashed the headlights to signal the craft; then he opened the door to light the car's interior. In response, the craft stopped and rocked back and forth as it descended behind a heavily forested area. The Hills turned their car around, picked up their relatives, and headed down a side road, attempting to approach the craft for a closer look. However, it had disappeared into an inaccessible area of deep swampland. They decided not to attempt to approach it on foot, but to return to the family home to study a topographical map of the area. This would be the first of many subsequent sightings, and the Hills wondered if their captors had somehow learned that their capture had been made public.

The public response to Luttrell's newspaper articles was overwhelmingly positive, and New Hampshire's citizens were clamoring for more information. The *Boston Traveler* sold the greatest number of newspaper copies in 84 years of publication, and there were 3,000 requests for reprints of the articles. Requests for additional information were beginning to snowball, so the Hills agreed to speak publicly, for the first time, at a forum at the Pierce Memorial Unitarian-Universalist Church in neighboring Dover, New Hampshire. Betty and Barney were anxious to mitigate some of the sensationalism perpetrated by Luttrell's newspaper columns. On Sunday evening, November 7, people from as far as 40 miles away stood in the frigid, penetrating rain only to be turned away from an overcrowded church. All 400 seats were filled and a loudspeaker was hastily improvised to accommodate an overflow crowd in the basement and hallways. Many of Betty and Barney's friends, including Captain Ben Swett and his wife Wyn, Walter Webb, Lauri D'Allessandro, Adele Darrah, Admiral Herbert Knowles, and his wife Helen were in the audience. Author, playwright, and distinguished columnist for *The Saturday Review*, John Fuller had driven up from Connecticut with an NBC cam-

Adele Fahey, Betty Hill, and Lauri D'Allesandro, July 4, 1971. Courtesy of Kathleen Marden.

eraman and radiomen. He introduced himself to Captain Swett in the church basement. After talking with him and liking what he said about his factual approach to such subjects, Swett led Fuller upstairs and introduced him to Barney.

Lieutenant Alan Brandt, the public information officer from Pease Air Force Base, in uniform, addressed the crowd from the podium. He reviewed the official Air Force policy on UFOs, indicating that UFO sightings were taken seriously and should be reported to the base, immediately. Next, the Hills spoke, in a way John Fuller described as "circumspectly" about their experience. They emphasized that they could only attest to the veracity of their conscious memory of a close encounter with an unconventional craft in New Hampshire's White Mountains. Barney explained that the publicity surrounding their case had been published without their consent or cooperation, that they had hoped to maintain confidentiality about their experience—particularly the hypnosis sessions. Further, although their hypnosis had revealed that they had been captured and taken onboard a UFO where they endured a physical examination, they did not know if this was the objective truth. However, neither they nor Dr. Simon could adequately explain the two hours of amnesia that followed the period when the craft hovered over their car's roof and emitted buzzing sounds that caused them to experience a strange tingling sensation. They refused to discuss the content of their hypnosis tapes, stating only that Dr. Simon's hypnotherapy had relieved their traumatic amnesia. So intense was the public interest that the question and answer session following the Hills' presentation lasted for more than an hour. Many participants spoke of their own UFO sightings.

In her diary Betty wrote:

After Lt. Brandt, Barney, and I had spoken, we opened up the session for questions. Barney told how the publicity about us had been published without our cooperation; we had hoped to maintain confidentiality about our experience, particularly the hypnosis sessions. The highlight of the evening was a question from the floor: "Tell me Mr. Hill, whether or not you are happy to be here." I could see Barney was ill at ease, for this question could not be answered satisfactorily. I tugged at his coat and said to tell him the answer was yes. Barney turned to this man and said, "My wife says to say I am happy to be here, so I guess I am happy." Everyone laughed heartily and the man left.

This statement seems to reflect Barney's attitude toward any publicity surrounding the event. Initially, he insisted that it remain a secret between husband and wife. At Betty's insistence, family and close friends became privy to the information. Then the Air Force, NICAP, physical scientists with an interest in UFOs, the Two-State UFO Study Group, and finally the media gained information about the encounter. Barney agreed to share information for the benefit of science and national security as long as it remained confidential. Despite Barney's concerns, he participated as a reluctant adjunct to Betty, but continued to focus his energies primarily on the poverty program and civil rights. He always expressed apprehension because he felt the occupants onboard the UFO had threatened him in some way. Therefore, he feared for his own personal safety.

In a letter to Walter Webb dated November 27, 1965, Betty wrote, "After the news article in the *Boston Traveler,* we got in touch with Richard Hall [NICAP's director], as you suggested. He said that he had never made those statements to the press in any way. He was going to publish some kind of statement about our sighting, but said that he would reconsider. Later, Admiral Knowles called him and he said that he had decided not to publish anything, at this time." She added, "We feel that this is a good decision on Dick Hall's part, for we would not want NICAP discredited in any way. Actually, we will always be very grateful to you and to NICAP for your help, encouragement and all. In a way, emotionally, this whole experience has been similar to a disaster, and we know that you have been there for us in piecing together the whole puzzle."

On the evening of the Dover presentation, John Fuller was in the area interviewing witnesses to the local UFO flap that seemed to be playing out nightly in Southern New Hampshire's towns. A local teenager and two Exeter police officers had observed a UFO at close range, and craft were seen hovering over power lines in Fremont and Exeter, and landing in the fields of area farms. Some sheared off the tops of trees, burned foliage, and left physical trace evidence on the ground. Average citizens going about their daily business observed landed craft and small beings that seemed to be collecting samples from vegetable gardens or water from local ponds. Fuller was exhilarated by the overwhelming public response to the UFO question, and wanted to interview the Hills for inclusion in *The Incident at Exeter* or perhaps another book about their experience. He and Walter Webb had coffee with Betty and Barney following their presentation, and he arranged to meet them for dinner to discuss their sighting and UFOs in general.

At dinner, Fuller presented the Hills with a cooperative book proposal that would satisfy the public's interest in their case and set the record straight. Betty and Barney were upset by the inaccuracies in John Luttrell's articles, and because confidentiality had already been violated on a grand scale, they decided to accept Fuller's proposal. Fuller's publicist, Ashley Famous Agency, Inc., drew up a contract between the Hills and Fuller stating that all would be named as joint authors in the publishing contract. The royalties would be divided with one third going to John Fuller and two thirds going to the Hills after the agent's commission was deducted, but the copyright would be credited to John Fuller. Apparently the Hills desired the inclusion of Dr. Simon in the contract and refused to sign the first draft.

In a letter to Walter Webb dated November 27, 1965, Betty wrote that Dr. Simon had agreed to work with them and John Fuller in the writing of a nonfiction book about the entire experience, with an emphasis on the hypnosis and its meaning. She stated that Dr. Simon had been consulting with many top psychiatrists about the matter, and had indicated that he planned to contribute information on hypnosis and its characteristic use in lifting traumatic amnesia. He was willing to state that the Hills underwent a highly traumatic experience with a "flying vehicle." But he would reserve judgment about the reality of their claim and leave "the explanations in the hands of the scientists."

Betty wrote a letter to Dr. Simon dated December 27, 1965 to explain her position with regard to the contract.

Dear Dr. Simon,

I am sending you a copy of our agreement with John Fuller to write the book, and a copy of the contract with Dial Press for the publication and exploitation of the book for your consideration.

As for the royalties in the contract, John Fuller will receive one-third for writing the book. Usually, the writer receives one half, but he has offered two-thirds because of all the details involved in the costs of these.

As we have always agreed, we are willing to share our two-thirds of the royalties with you on a one-third basis, i.e. 1/3 to you, 1/3 to Barney, and 1/3 to me; and the full terms of the contracts will be equally binding to the three of us.

The basis of the two-thirds royalty depends on our willingness to take a six- or 12-month leave of absence from our employment to exploit the sale of the book. If and when we sign the contract, we will legally be agreeing to do whatever Ashley Films and Dial Press ask in exploiting, as long as it is not illegal, immoral, or defamatory to us. We are not sure what all this will mean, but we will be expected to go on lecture tours with some TV and radio appearances, as well as autographing books in Macy's basement.

So, we are asking you to study these contracts as to whether or not they would be satisfactory to you. If not, we are wondering if some agreement could be reached where you would be willing to receive some percentage of the royalties, after deduction of expenses, on the basis that we attempt to arrange with the writer and publisher that you would retain some legal rights whereby you might be able to lecture at Medical Societies and retain their fees; also the right to publish your findings in scientific journals; also we would need to work out some kind of agreement as to TV, radio, and public appearances. I assume that if you are not included in these contracts, then you are free to make your own contracts in this matter.

If this book is to be published, the important thing involved is time. John must have it completed by June 1st. Barney and I are ambivalent about the whole thing, for we did not realize so much would be involved, such as the loss of our salaries during the exploitation period. We have no way of predicting the sales of the book, but we have been talking to writers and it is our understanding that books are not a way to "get rich in a hurry," but can be fine as a supplemental income.

We will meet with you on January 7th to discuss all of these things.

Sincerely,
Betty Hill

John Fuller had entered into a deal with Dial Press that awarded a $10,000 advance to be issued in thirds: one third upon signing the contract, one third upon delivery of a partial manuscript, and the final third upon completion of the manuscript. Throughout the next four months the lawyers and principals ironed out the minute details of the contractual agreement. The major disagreements centered on the sharing of royalties, the ownership and confidentiality of the hypnosis tapes, and the ideas and conclusions expressed by John Fuller. In fact, at one point before the contract was signed, Dr. Simon was nearly ousted from the project because his "proposed contract was entirely unsatisfactory to the Hills and that they simply would not accept it." The Hills' lawyers wrote, "They are more ready to withdraw from further negotiations with Dr. Simon because some of the terms of the proposed contract, which our clients consider to be vital, are terms that your client knew beforehand that our clients would not accept, because they definitely told him so on several prior occasions. Our clients are still desirous of working with your client, and for that reason, authorize us to make the following counter proposal. If it should turn out to be unacceptable to your client, then our clients, unless other terms can be agreed upon, are prepared to proceed without Dr. Simon's further help. This our clients would deeply regret, but at the present time, no alternative seems to be available."[1]

The task of writing *The Interrupted Journey* was lengthy and difficult for John Fuller. Dr. Simon's revisions, comments, and corrections to Fuller's work were even longer than the manuscript itself. He was forced to revise and rewrite the text to comply with Dr. Simon's professional opinion regarding hypnosis and the possibility of false memory production. This shattered many of Fuller's preconceptions regarding the characteristics of hypnosis. He also cautioned Fuller against the use of sensationalism, which put Fuller somewhere between a rock and a hard place. The publisher wanted a sensational book, but the psychiatrist, who had editing privileges, rejected this notion. With all of the haggling, it is a wonder that the book was ever completed. In the end, Fuller did not meet the June 1 deadline, and came under pressure from the publisher. But finally, after a copious amount of rewriting, the book was published.

Patient confidentiality was a major issue. Dr. Simon wanted the tape recordings to remain his exclusive property, but the Hills insisted that the ownership of the tapes should be held jointly. The Hills agreed to release Dr. Simon of the patient-physician relationship only where John Fuller was concerned for the purpose of publishing the book. However, Fuller was to take temporary control of the tape recordings for the purpose of completing a manuscript. Then, the original tapes and any copies made of them would be promptly returned to their owners at the completion of the manuscript.

Finally, the principals agreed that Dr. Simon had the sole right to approve or disapprove of all medical statements or conclusions contained in the manuscript. To further protect the rights of the principals, they agreed to refrain from individually writing, dramatizing, or collaborating with a third party to write or dramatize any material pertaining to the events or incidents in the manuscript without the prior written consent of the principals. Therefore, Fuller, the Hills, and Simon were prohibited from expressing their personal or professional opinions regarding the UFO encounter and the abduction in written form without the written consent of all surviving principals.

In all, the hardcover and paperback versions of *The Interrupted Journey* sold nearly 300,000 copies and made its way to the top of *The New York Times* best-seller list. Foreign rights for the publication of the book were sold in England, France, Holland, Spain, Portugal, Brazil, Yugoslavia, and Japan. Dial Press published the hardcover copy of the book, and later, Dell published the paperback version. Later still, Berkley bought the rights to the paperback, and in the mid-1980s, Dell purchased the rights again. In all, the book was available on the market from 1966 until approximately 1988. It is currently out of print.

In 1975, the movie rights were sold to Academy Award nominee James Earl Jones. He had read the book and wanted to play the dramatic part of Barney in the movie. In addition to Betty Hill, John Fuller and Dr. Simon took part in the negotiations for the production contract. The picture was based upon John Fuller's *The Interrupted Journey* and was supplemented through many hours of conversation between Betty and screenwriter Miss Hesper Anderson. Just before the production began, Betty flew to New York to meet the producer/director and Estelle Parson, the Academy Award-winning actress who would play Betty in the movie. Stanton served as the technical advisor for the film. *The UFO Incident*, a two-hour motion picture, was presented for the first time on NBC on October 20, 1975.

In August of 1983, Betty was invited to appear on the F. Lee Bailey *Lie Detector* show. At first, due to the controversy regarding the validity of lie detector testing, she was apprehensive. However, Bailey's representative explained that the controversy stemmed from the test results interpreted by inexperienced and untrained personnel. When she learned that the president of the American Polygraph Association planned to do the testing, she agreed. She was asked three questions: (1) Did you initially receive the star map information while onboard a UFO? (2) Did you obtain it from a source other than a UFO? (3) Do you believe your star map is a hoax? Betty passed with flying colors.

After the show, Ed Gault, who administered the test, informed Betty that he had received many letters from individuals who claimed they had been abducted, and wanted to prove it by taking a lie detector test. Everyone failed, except Betty.

Then in 1989, Harper and Row Publishers produced a three-hour audiotaped version of *The Interrupted Journey* read by Whitley Strieber, which included excerpts from the original recording of the Hills' hypnosis sessions. These are the only audiotapes of the Hills' hypnosis sessions that Betty approved to be released to the public.

In 1996 Betty Hill took possession of the tape recordings and turned them over to Kathy for transcription and analysis. Except as the transcripts appear in this book with expressed permission of Betty Hill, no copies of the hypnosis tapes will be available to the public. The raw emotion and sheer terror expressed by the Hills on the audiotaped sessions is difficult to listen to. Additionally, personal information of a sexual nature is discussed in confidence. The voyeuristic exploitation of these tapes would not only be cruel, but also unethical.

The opportunity to travel and meet a variety of interesting people, including television celebrities, added a new dimension to the Hills' lives. They lectured at schools, colleges, and pubic facilities throughout the United States. They didn't become wealthy, but their standard of living increased somewhat. They were able to purchase new living room furniture and upgraded from a Chevy to an Oldsmobile.

On the surface, Barney seemed more comfortable with the publicity than he previously had. On November 17, 1966, in his second televised interview, Barney recapped his and Betty's activities as social activists. Appearing on the Louis Lomax television program, Barney explained that he and Betty were promoting the agendas of the New Hampshire Archdiocese in the areas of civil rights and family structure. Additionally, he spoke of his activities as legal redress chairman for the Portsmouth chapter of the NAACP and Betty's position as the editor of their newsletter. He was most proud of his appointment to the U.S. Civil Rights Commission. The Hills gave a brief outline of their initial sighting, their close encounter, period of missing time, evidence, the investigation, their recovered memories of abduction, and the aftermath.

Barney described how Henry, a young sergeant at the air base, and his wife, along with the Hills, experimented with the compass over the silver-dollar-sized, highly polished circles on the trunk of their car. The ensuing conversations with investigators Walter Webb, Hohmann, and Jackson, according to Barney, were so long and involved that all forgot to look at the evidence on the car's trunk.

Then, Betty's friend Lei Stewart testified about her recall of the Hills' return of her cooler when they arrived home, and their detailed account of a UFO sighting.

Later, Barney discussed Dr. Simon's hypothesis that he had absorbed Betty's dreams, refuting this as being unbelievable:

> What is implied here is that Betty's dreams would become my reality. One theory is that I absorbed Betty's dreams as she talked in her sleep. She would have to talk in complete sentences and when I am asleep they would have gotten into my subconscious. But I commuted from Portsmouth to Boston where I was employed nights, so we didn't sleep together. Next, as she told her dreams

to Walter Webb and the other two scientists that visited with us and the many others that were involved in getting the evidence of this, I obviously would have been in the same room and I would have overheard these dreams. This is much like saying that if you were hypnotized, having talked to me or listened to me, that you would have gone off and relived the same experience that I am telling you. It's incredible...the dream theory [laughter].

Barney's closing remarks summed it up: "We're not defending UFOs. I couldn't really personally care less. What we were compelled to do as the result of a newspaper article that ran in one of the Boston papers for five days...we had not cooperated with this reporter, so he wrote a story much like we had talked to Lei and told her. All of this got around and in 1965 everyone was talking; although the place and the people were not put into proper perspective, he put the story together and wrote it without any cooperation from us. So we, after that, we were more or less compelled to put down the documentation. The tapes are part of the record. They are something that you can listen to, although we would never permit anyone, other than the scientists, with the doctor's obvious cooperation to listen to these tapes."

Next, a question and answer session ensued. One of the participants cited his curiosity of the Air Force's failure to investigate the UFO sighting and evidence, even though they could easily have driven to the Hills' home. He then mentioned that Dr. James MacDonald had recently discovered a CIA document that ordered the debunking of UFO reports.

At the end of the show, Barney expressed his desire to fight for civil rights and to become more involved in the struggle for human justice. The selling of his UFO story was a secondary issue to him, and one that had not changed him in a profound way. Betty concurred with Barney's statement, joking that she was still the same person who had to defend herself, because she couldn't expect Barney to do it for her.

The years 1966 and 1967 were busy for the Hills. They appeared on *The Mike Douglas Show*, *To Tell the Truth*, *Art Linkletter*, *The Merv Griffin Show*, and *The Alan Douglas Show*, to name a few. They traveled extensively, promoting the book at colleges, public meetings, and on radio and television programs.

In a telling 1967 letter to Walter Webb, Betty wrote:

We have been overwhelmed by the response to our book, and TV and radio programs. We have received letters by the basketful and we are answering every one of them, which is quite a chore. We wrote hundreds of letters before we decided to have a special form letter printed, which we sign and send out—so this is making the letter-writing easier. Most people want to know where they can buy the book, cost, name, etc.

We enjoyed our trip to California—we were doing about four TV and two to three radio programs a day, as well as autographing books at the sellers, and having meetings with the newspapers. It was a hectic time and we really enjoyed it. While in Denver, we were interviewed by Dr. David Saunders of the University of Colorado UFO Study Group. On our return, we did a science program which will be shown either this month or next as a 90-minute special. Dr. Carl Sagan, Cambridge; Dr. Fred (Leo) Sprinkle, psychologist at the University of Wyoming; Dr. James McDonald, physicist from the University of Arizona; as well as the science editors from *Time* and *New York Herald Tribune*; John Fuller; and we were the panelists. Dr. Sagan does not believe in UFOs, but we met him in Boston one night and he wants to visit us in Portsmouth to discuss UFOs, and our experience, so we invited him to visit any time.

Look Magazine *photographer at Kathleen Marden's high school graduation with*
Betty and Barney.
Courtesy of Kathleen Marden.

We feel that the scientific world is just beginning to take a look at UFOs; before this time all their reactions were emotional ones. In fact, those who still deny close contact with UFOs are still being emotional because of their own personal fears. They are closing their eyes and hoping they will go away. Also, the so-called scientific method of wanting to put one [UFO] in a box so they can feel, touch, and show it is an obsolete idea—a 17th century theory or practice which they are trying to apply to a 20th century fact. We feel that many of the top scientists who have been in contact with us—those who have had access to Air Force files (many of them have had Air Force files opened to them) have no doubt about our experience—to them it is an actuality.

To the public who have read the book there is also no doubt but the experience is a real one. If we should meet someone who says he does not believe it, we find that he has not read the book. Last week we spoke on WLOB, Portland, Maine. The newscaster told us that when he read our story in *LOOK* he canceled his subscription because he objected to their publishing science fiction, but after meeting us, and hearing us tell our story, he was renewing his subscription.

Did you see the *Air Force Times* book review? They recommended *Incident at Exeter* and *The Interrupted Journey* as the two books about UFOs worth reading, and gave excellent reviews.

Confidentially, we plan NOT to go to any meetings of any groups of UFO enthusiasts, but we are hopeful of doing this tactfully—refusing, that is. Also it is unfortunate that NICAP took the position they did in reviewing our book before it was published. In this area, people have lost confidence in them, and John Reynolds, who receives the reports in this area, does not receive any. No one gets in touch with NICAP. About two months ago, Exeter had an excellent sighting at 7:45 p.m., witnessed by approximately 40 people—and no one contacted NICAP. A UFO hovered directly over a house for 45 minutes—approximately 15 feet above the house. The windows were clearly visible. Occasionally I send a sighting along to John—particularly the close daylight sightings.

Also, we have found that other people have seen UFOs fairly close and have suffered amnesia, followed by dreams. Efforts are being made to have these people undergo hypnosis. One man [was] found while still in the trance [or hypnosis] and underwent hypnosis right away. So, it is some consolation to us to know that others have had similar experiences.

The publicity surrounding the Hills' UFO encounter increased the scientific community's interest in the topic. In addition to the scientists who explore the UFO dilemma publicly, such as J. Allen Hynek, James MacDonald, Leo Sprinkle, David Saunders, and Carl Sagan, others were doing so quietly and secretly. They were most often interested in the propulsion system used by the craft. Betty informed family members that visits were scheduled with researchers from many universities. Scientists from many disciplines came quietly and secretly to question the Hills. They all made it clear that confidentiality was imperative. Some revealed that they knew UFOs existed, but that nothing could be done until they became officially recognized. When they were asked why they did not take a public stand, they explained that their livelihood depended upon federal research grants. They stated that they were aware that prejudice existed. If their interest in UFOs became known, it would jeopardize their chances of securing the grants needed to conduct their research.

One scientist came for another purpose. He came quietly—so quietly that the Hills met him outside their home. He asked only one question: What did the aliens look like? When the Hills described their physical characteristics, he could barely control his excitement. Betty later re-called, "He stood there shaking his head. He said, 'My God, you really were captured!' We asked him how he could be so sure of this. He said that before such a tight censorship had been imposed, he had seen an official photo of the aliens, taken from a plane—a good clear picture of them. He did not know where the picture was now, but the aliens in the picture and the aliens that we had met were of the same description. Then, he left as quietly as he came." Betty maintained confidentiality and carried the scientist's name to her grave.

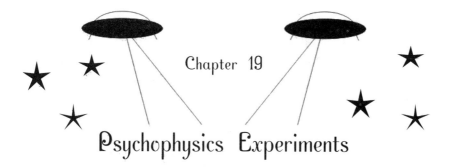

Chapter 19

Psychophysics Experiments

Three and a half years after their initial contact, Robert Hohmann, the second investigator to examine the Hill case, penned a letter to NICAP's original investigator, Walter Webb. Hohmann, a scientific writer, wrote that he had heard via NICAP Director Dick Hall that the Hills had successfully undergone professional hypnosis to remove the block that resulted from their extreme fright. He requested a tape or transcript of the information reported during the hypnotic state, along with Walter Webb's opinion. Apparently, Mr. Webb passed the information onto the Hills, because on July 15, 1965, Betty reestablished contact with Hohmann via a long and informative letter. Thise letter is significant and appears in full as follows:

Dear Mr. Hohmann,

I hope this letter reaches you successfully for both Barney and I wish to thank you for your suggestion back in 1961 that we undergo hypnosis. [USAF Major James MacDonald was the first to make this suggestion.]

Since it has been such a long time since there has been any contact between us, you may remember us as the couple who had the experience with the UFO on Route 3 in the White Mountains on Sept. 19–20, 1961. At the time that you and Mr. Jackson visited us, there were many puzzles about our sighting that were unexplained, such as Barney's "blackout" when he looked at the leader in the craft, loss of time on the trip, the orange moon on the ground, etc. In an attempt to clear up these aspects, you suggested hypnosis by a qualified psychiatrist.

Starting in January, 1964, Barney and I underwent hypnosis for a seven-month period of time with a highly qualified psychiatrist in

Boston, at quite an expense to us. Before starting these sessions, he assured us that it is impossible to fabricate under hypnosis. He hypnotized us separately, and caused us to forget our tapings so that we could not communicate [them] with each other.

The results of these sessions were amazing and very difficult to believe. They were particularly upsetting to the psychiatrist, who does not believe in UFOs, and is searching for an explanation.

As to my opinion, I believe that the information that was revealed during these sessions is valid. We do have copies of the tapes, which show the extent of our fears during the experience. They are filled with raw emotion where we scream, cry, become hysterical, etc.

During these sessions, it was revealed that Barney and I were followed by the spacecraft, [and] stopped on the highway. We watched it descend fairly close to us. At that point where Barney had the "blackout," it revealed that he was looking at the leader who was hypnotizing him and telling him to come closer, he was safe, he had nothing to be afraid of. As he was watching, he saw a ladder descending, and was able to break away and run to the safety of the car, although he was in somewhat of a trance.

Apparently, the first beeping sounds that we heard had somewhat of a hypnotizing effect on me, although I was more conscious of what was happening. We did turn off Route 3 to a secondary road, to a third road—very desolate. The orange glow (moon) on the ground was the spacecraft, and 11 men were standing in the road. Our car motor and electrical system died. The men came up to the car, opened the doors, and took us out. At this point we both went into deep trances, but mine lasted only about five to 10 minutes.

The men took us onboard the spacecraft and took Barney and me into separate rooms where they gave us physical exams. They were very puzzled over the fact that Barney had dentures and I did not. Barney did not communicate with them, but I was able to do this with the leader and the examiner, but not the crew members. This is puzzling, for we did not speak English, but were able to understand each other, particularly the leader and I.

At first they were going to permit us to remember the experience and the leader gave me a book, but then they decided against this and he took the book away from me.

My main purpose in this letter is to tell you about the map, for I remember that you were interested in planets where there may be life. I have asked the leader where he was from and he showed me a map. During the sessions, the doctor told me that I would remember the map exactly as I saw it. I was to go home, be perfectly relaxed, and then draw the map as I saw it. I did this and gave the map to the doctor, more or less forgetting about it, until I read *The New York Times* of 4/13/65. In this paper was an article about the Russian report of radio signals from this source CTA-102, with a map giving the location. This map looked vaguely familiar, so I wrote to the doctor and asked him for a copy of my map. I am sending you a copy of this map with the addition of the names of the stars, planets, or whatever they are, which I have added from the *Times* map, as well as the Russians' location of CTA-102.

On this map you will note a difference in the size of the planets as well as the lines drawn between them. This is the way I duplicate their map. The leader said they traded extensively with the planets near them, but the broken lines were expeditions.

I do not know the validity of this map, or the location of the planets, but the Russians said that it was the constellation of Pegasus. I do hope it will be of benefit to you for it is an amazing coincidence. [It was only a coincidence and does not correlate to the stars on Betty's map or to the Fish model.]

Another coincidence was some warts that Barney developed soon after our experience. They developed in a perfect circle. During the hypnosis he found that they had placed a cup-like object on his body in the spot where the warts later developed. During his sessions when he found out how he received them, they became infected and he went to a skin specialist and had all 21 warts removed. The first specialist refused to remove them as he had never seen any like them and referred Barney to another specialist, who removed them but did not identify them.

Incidentally, the leader made me feel very stupid, as I was not able to answer his questions. In my attempt to let him know that there were more intelligent people on this Earth than I am, I invited them to return and I would introduce them to people who could answer their questions. He said that it was not his decision to make, but if they decided to do this, they would get in contact with me. I chided him about this—how would he find me in all of the billions of people here? He told me that if this was their decision they would find me—that they always find the people that they want to find.

As a sidelight, since 1961 we have met many people who would be of interest and education to them and could discuss these things with them. In September 1961, we did not know anyone who would share their interests.

If you should have any questions, we will try to answer them for you now that we have more information from our hypnosis.

Sincerely,

Betty Hill

This renewed correspondence led to a meeting between Hohmann and the Hills in New Hampshire's White Mountains in early November of 1965. Hohmann, who traveled extensively on business, was scheduled to visit Plymouth State Teachers College during the weekend of November 5–6. Initially he requested a map and directions to the landing site along with a query regarding the assistance of a local guide. Betty and Barney, however, citing the fact that it would be difficult for him to locate the spots where the close encounter occurred, offered to give Hohmann a guided tour late in the afternoon of November 6. It was his intention to explore the Hills' UFO encounter area to test the hypothesis that the UFO phenomenon is related to the geology of a region. The Hills met with Mr. Hohmann and escorted him through the encounter area and to the site where they observed the orange moon on the ground. Additionally, they discussed with him the hypnotically retrieved information regarding their abduction memories and the highly controversial status of its validity.

Later that month, Hohmann wrote a note to thank the Hills for their generosity and assistance in escorting him to the site of their UFO experience. He stated that although there were several aspects of the case he did not understand, he found Barney's observation that his captors cloaked themselves in a conventional image to minimize the shock of seeing something so completely foreign, to be profound. Citing the fact that this could best be understood by a therapist, not a layman like himself, he added that he could only respect Barney's observation, not explain it.

His letter indicated that the Hills had, once again, discussed the possibility of reestablishing contact with the craft's occupants in order to obtain physical evidence to support the Hills' abduction claim. This evidence—possibly a piece of hardware, he assured Betty and Barney—would prevent their material from becoming tabloid news, a direction that they most certainly did not want to take.

This renewed contact led to ongoing communication throughout the next several years, and precipitated scientific interest in Betty's stated desire to attempt to reestablish contact with her captors. Betty's memoirs state that she and Barney entered into a series of experiments with two scientists in an attempt to contact the occupants of the craft that abducted them. In interviews with Kathy, Betty identified the "scientists" as Robert Hohmann and C.D. Jackson. Throughout her lifetime, it was not clear to Betty that Hohmann was a writer, not a scientist. However, C.D. Jackson was correctly identified as a senior engineer/scientist. Betty stated that the two agreed to work with her under the condition that she would disassociate herself from UFO groups and work quietly, without publicity, with them.

Betty's and Barney's 1965 meeting with Mr. Hohmann apparently aroused his interest in assembling a loosely structured team brave enough to pursue scientific investigation in attempted ET contact, even though it was a strange path to follow. This occurred prior to the series of UFO sightings by the Hills that convinced them their captors were continuing to monitor them. These proposed

Mr. Richards, C.D. Jackson, Robert Hohmann, and White, 6/10/67.
Courtesy of Kathleen Marden.

experiments would serve as Betty's opportunity to acquire physical evidence to prove the veracity of her belief that she had been abducted by aliens. Further, the fact that scientists had indicated interest in attempting contact with the Hills' captors leant a sense of respectability to the experiments.

The experiments involved what the team termed "psychophysical" communication between Betty and the ETs. Initially, Betty attempted to reestablish contact with her captors by placing the star map she had drawn under posthypnotic suggestion, as well as some of the materials that were present in her vehicle during the Hills' initial contact in September of 1961 in her car. Additionally, she and Barney were instructed to report to the team any and all unusual occurrences, regardless of how insignificant they seemed.

In a letter dated January 14, 1966, Betty described her family as hard-headed practical realists who were beginning to feel "on edge" over the intrusion of paranormal activities into their homes. She wrote, "These things are happening to Barney and me as well as to most of my relatives, but they have been witnessed by other people who were present. We do not believe in ghosts, but we do believe in space travel and life on other planets, so we wonder if these space travelers might have the ability to be unseen to us."

Next, Betty described numerous puzzling, intrusive events, including the December 10, 1965 appearance of a chunk of ice on her kitchen table. She wrote, "Barney and I returned home from work and found a chunk of ice on the kitchen table, under a newspaper. The newspaper was in the same spot I had left it in that morning. At the time there was no ice outdoors, only ice cubes in the refrigerator. It was oval-shaped and had some kind of imprint on it. We were so shocked about this that we hurriedly put it in the sink to melt so we could forget about it."

Betty wrote the following more detailed account in her diary:

I put the newspaper into the trash and we stood there, staring at this "ice," wondering. It looked as though it had been frozen in a bowl; it had some small pieces of leaves, twigs, and dirt in it. It appeared as though there were a pattern in the bowl-shaped chunk of ice, like the design one might find on the sides of a cut-glass dish. But this was inside the ice, not on its surface. I picked it up and the outsides edges were smooth. There was no wetness on the table and no traces that it had been there. It felt ice cold but it did not have the weight of a block of ice that size. Also, it did not have the solid hardness of ice, but had flexibility to it. We put it into the sink and ran hot water on it. As I was preparing for bed, I turned on the hot water and let it run until all traces of the ice were gone. Barney and I have more puzzles in our lives then we can handle without adding one more to them. So, we solved the puzzle by destroying it and deciding we would forget this one.

In her January 14 letter to Robert Hohmann, Betty also reported, "Recently Barney and I heard the front door open, someone stamp his feet and walk upstairs. We checked and found no one and the door was still locked. This happened in the middle of the night and it awoke both of us. All of our apartments are empty as the servicemen have been transferred elsewhere. As I sit here and write this, I can hear the sliding door on a closet in one apartment going back and forth; in another apartment we can hear the water running in one of the bathrooms. Also, on three occasions we found a light turned on in one of the apartments. On Christmas week as we were going into the apartment to turn the light off, and we were unlocking the door, it went off by itself."

Although the above intrusive acts may have been human in origin, paranormal events were beginning to manifest in Betty's and Barney's home. She reported that these strange occurrences were also taking place in the homes of her family members. One involved four witnesses who were astonished to observe the exterior storm door of a relative's home open out and an interior door open in, seemingly without human intervention. The family cat entered the house and both doors closed behind it, although no one was observed in the vicinity of the doors.

Then, in another inexplicable incident, a vehicle seemed to have entered a family driveway at night, and a man with indistinguishable features exited the car and seemingly lit a cigarette. When no one appeared at the door, the eight witnesses went to look for him. They could not locate the man or his car, but they observed a large ball of light traveling about 10 to 20 feet above the ground. They watched in bewilderment as the ball of light traveled across the street, through the adjacent yard, and disappeared behind a garage located approximately 100 feet from the witnesses. This was the first of many observations of anomalous balls of light by Betty's family members and their guests.

It seems more than a coincidence that, according to Betty, her Portsmouth home was entered and uncanny events transpired almost immediately after her contact attempts were initiated. Given the multiple-witness component to some of the paranormal events, one must place these reported phenomena in one's gray basket—that which cannot be proved or disproved. The possibility exists that some of the reports could be attributed to group hysteria or hyper imagination. However, where no logical explanation can be found, one must suspect psi activity or human intervention. We do not think that all of the events were purely psychological in nature. But we have not been able to identify a friend, relative, or tenant who had the means or motive to perpetrate a hoax against the Hills and their family in these particular events.

Later references to phone monitoring, overheard by objective witnesses, leads us to speculate about the source of these early "paranormal" events. But speculation leads nowhere, without evidence, and a formal investigation of this alleged psi phenomena was never carried out. One must, however, consider this alleged pattern of unusual events and intrusive acts in the context of the publicity surrounding the Hills' UFO encounter. In 1961, when Betty's leaf-encased earrings mysteriously appeared in the kitchen of her home, the U.S. Air force and NICAP were investigating the Hills' close encounter with an anomalous craft. In late November 1965, John Luttrell's series of articles about the Hills' UFO encounter, hypnosis, and alleged abduction had received widespread publicity. If an intelligence agency were perpetrating psychological warfare upon the Hills in an attempt to discredit them by portraying them as crackpots, it would have the motive to hoax these alleged paranormal events. The Hills were not crackpots. On the contrary, they were a levelheaded couple who were persistent in their attempts to understand an extremely bizarre experience.

On April 4, 1966, Betty replied to a letter from Robert Hohmann as follows:

Dear Mr. Hohmann,

We have delayed answering your letter because we have been giving it a lot of thought as to the prerequisites for contact. It is just impossible to know these. We have thought and thought, but cannot come up with an answer. We do not know.

We do know this. Barney and I go out frequently at night for one reason or another. Since last October, we have seen our "friends" on the average of eight or nine times out of every 10 trips, outside of Portsmouth. Last Tuesday night we spoke in Dover, N.H., and on Monday night two policemen witnessed one, and several people saw one on Tuesday night, including me.

One night six witnesses and I watched for 45 minutes while one came out over a lake and performed for us, by maneuvering at different heights, different flight patterns, different lighting effects, and then it met with a second one for a few minutes before they took off in different directions. Last Saturday Barney and I decided to retrace our trip in the White Mountains, as of September 1961, but this time my parents were with us. As we were returning through the Franconia Notch in the general area of the tramway and Cannon Mountain, one moved around the mountain about 50 feet from the ground, in front of us. Its lights dimmed out and we could see the row of windows before it became invisible. It just faded out of sight and then reappeared with different lighting behind us. It started to move closer to us when some cars came along and it again disappeared. On the opposite side of the highway was a second one, which also faded out.

At first we thought that all these were a coincidence, but I'm changing my mind, since many people still have not seen them; not even one. I have the feeling that they might be acquainting us with some of their techniques. Also, they seem to find me sometimes when I am alone at night, but not Barney. I go around asking myself, "What is it they want?" I wonder if they are trying to overcome any and all fears of them we might have, in preparation for another direct contact. If so, we will request some hardware and contact you. I am hoping that this is their purpose rather than our going on an unexpected trip with them.

We have not told anyone but my family about all of these contacts, with the exception of you: I wonder if anyone else has had experiences like these?

Sincerely,

Betty and Barney Hill

The multiple-witness lake sighting that Betty mentioned occurred on February 22, 1966. A young woman who lived a short distance from the Barrett family farm reported that she had been approached by a UFO at close range as she walked home at 9:10 p.m. the previous Tuesday. She testified that she had felt a "strong force" as the craft passed overhead that seemed to catch her, and she had to exert considerable strength to hold onto her purse. When it let go, she was unsteady on her feet, nearly losing her balance. She contacted Betty because she was beginning to become fearful of walking home alone, although she had routinely done this without concern for years.

Betty drove to her parents' farm a week later for the purpose of attempting a UFO observation. She, joined by her mother, sister, niece, nephew, and the young woman, departed in Betty's car at 9 p.m. for the location where the UFO had appeared the previous week. Betty documented the following details in two sighting reports, which we have merged together:

We stopped in the spot where Rosemary reported her sighting the previous week. We decided it was not a safe place to stop at night because of traffic, so we drove ahead about 100 yards.

As soon as we stopped, we all saw the UFO flying between the trees. It was a large, bright red flashing light. I flashed the car headlights and the interior light, and the UFO wobbled and went down. We wanted to go up to the UFO, but we knew we could not walk through the yard of that owner. (He raises mink, fox, etc. for their pelts, and might shoot at a prowler.) We were parked in front of the home and someone turned on the side light, lighting up the yard, so we decided to leave. We did wait about five minutes without seeing the UFO again. Since we were acquainted with the terrain, we decided that the UFO had landed on the knoll down by the lake. We knew that if we went down Country Pond Road to Country Pond, we could park the car, and cross the lake on the ice, to the spot where it had settled. We decided to do this.

As we arrived, the UFO was going up, as though from the knoll. We did not see it on the ground, but assume it was very close from our observation. This time I did not flash the car lights or use the interior lights, but as we were running down to the lake itself, Janet lit a cigarette. At this, the UFO seemed to hesitate and then started to swing around in our direction. It swayed back and forth in a pendulum motion and rose to the tops of the trees. It traveled slowly around us, following the shoreline and flying just above the treetops. We all observed its disk shape through the binoculars. Janet, Kathy, and Glenn saw windows when the UFO turned on its interior lights. When we flashed the flashlight in its direction, it put off its light, so we decided to point it only at the ground. It continued to travel around a projection of land where it was impossible to see it.

We returned to the car and drove out onto the projection, which leads to a bridge, which connects to an island. During the drive I was flashing the headlights, trying to imitate the sound (pattern) they had made on the trunk of the car in the White Mountains. We drove out to the end of the island. The craft stopped ahead of us and then went around the island in the direction of the bridge. We turned the car around and headed back. Suddenly we saw the UFO, and a second one was with it—the second one was very close to the ground while ours remained at treetop level. The UFO returned to this point and was headed for the knoll again. Again it reversed direction and gave us a demonstration of its abilities. It flew above the treetops with the red light flashing. Then, it climbed to airplane level and skipped along with red and green lights flashing. Then, it turned off all of its lights with the exception of a large yellow light, and moved across the sky at an angle where it looked just like a moving star. It reversed direction again and headed for the knoll, flying as though it was a plane. Then it flew in a step-by-step downward pattern, followed by a falling leaf motion. It wobbled and came close to the ground again. Suddenly we saw that a second one was with it, very close to the ground. The two of them stayed side by side just above the ice, about 25 feet apart. We were astonished at seeing this second one and somewhat unnerved. We watched for a moment debating what to do. One of these UFOs projected a telescoping funnel-like spotlight onto Janet. Our impulse was to get out of there as quickly as possible.

We decided to go back and park the car at our first location. We did this, wondering what to do next. At this point, a train came through the junction, about a quarter of a mile away. We saw the second UFO rise up and go over the treetops, and the last time we saw it, it was traveling along the top of a boxcar on the train, heading south towards Haverhill, Massachusetts.

The first UFO came up and stopped behind the car, just above the treetops. I started the car and headed back to the highway. It swung over on the right-hand side of the car; about 10 feet back from the road above the trees and traveled along beside us. It paced me at my speed. When I slowed down, it slowed down. When I increased my speed, it increased its speed. When we came to the highway, I stopped for the stop sign but it continued on. I made a left turn and went about a quarter of a mile, and turned right onto a side road to follow it. We followed it for about a mile but it was getting ahead of us, so we went home to my mother's. When we arrived, Barney complained that he should have gone with us, for the TV had so much interference that he and my father could not enjoy the program.

Betty suspected that her attempts to establish contact with her captors were slowly moving toward fruition. However, she felt somewhat ill-equipped to develop a methodology that would lead to direct contact. For this she required scientific input to steer her in the right direction.

In a letter dated April 27, 1966, Hohmann wrote that through the past several weeks he (representing the team) had been contemplating what details would be acceptable to all parties concerned if the Hills succeeded in their attempt to arrange direct contact with their abductors. Its top priority was to reassure the UFO occupants that every effort would be made to guarantee their personal safety and that of their vehicle. For that reason, the Hills or the occupants were to determine the time and location of the anticipated contact. Additionally, he added that the team comprised three individuals engaged in science and engineering activities, and a fourth person, an industrial electrician, who would serve as an unbiased spectator to the event. Hohmann stated that all three engineers considered UFOs to be a scientific possibility, and would participate in the contact experiment "without malice or intent to deceive or betray the purpose of the meeting," adding that they would not carry concealed weapons of any kind. Further, he informed the Hills that all three had access to the highest level of their company's organization. If the contact experiment yielded desirable results, Hohmann told the Hills that they would be able to personally deliver the physical evidence to its final destination, facilitated by the experimental team in the most "direct and expeditious manner." Apparently, the team of independent researchers planned to deliver the hardware to its employer if the Hills succeeded in their attempt to obtain a workable piece of hardware. Citing the team's desire to gain a better understanding and worldwide acceptance of the UFO phenomena, Hohmann offered to contribute its assistance to that objective. He cautioned, however, that for scientific acceptance, physical evidence was a prerequisite.

Encouraged that she was slowly and methodically heading in the right direction, Betty attempted another contact experiment. She elaborated on this experiment in a report in her memoirs. She stated, "It was suggested to me to try to contact a UFO by sending my thoughts to them, to set up a meeting. I did not think it was possible, but agreed that I would try it. Every night at 9 p.m., I would stand on by back porch and think: 'UFOs, where are you? Can you hear me? If so, go to Kingston; go to the Barrett's home; land in the field. Go to the house and knock on the door; you will be admitted and we can meet.' Every night I did this faithfully. I repeated, 'No harm will come to you,' three times."

Betty continued:

After several weeks my father called me and asked me to come home for he wanted to talk to me. He said that he had received a telephone call from his cousin's widow, also named Barrett [who lived a few hundred feet away from Betty's parents' farm], asking him to visit her, for she was extremely upset. She is 73, lives alone, and is strong and healthy and not senile in any way. She had sold her home to the Episcopal Church, and in turn they had built her a small home behind the parsonage and back from the street. She was awakened during the night by a knocking on her door. This was very unusual for anyone to pass through the minister's yard and go to her house. Besides, he had a light on and she did not. The knocking was very strange: knock...[delay] knock, knock, knock...knock. She became fearful and did not go to the door. Then she spotted a red flash of light and thought that a thunder shower was approaching and maybe the wind had been blowing something that made a knocking sound. Then, the flashing changed color and seemed to be on the opposite side of the house. So, she went over and looked out the window. There was a craft, with windows lighted, flashing all kinds of multicolored lights. At this point, she decided that she was losing her mind. She pulled down the window shades, jumped into bed and covered her head." [Mrs. Barrett had not been apprised of Betty's experiments.]

In a letter to Hohmann dated April 29, 1966, Betty indicated that her "psychophysics" experiments seemed to have reaped limited success. She wrote:

As you will remember, I suggested that they go to my parents' home in Kingston and knock on the door, but instead my cousin, who has the same last name, had the knock and saw a UFO. Since that time I have been saying that they had the wrong home and giving directions to my parents' home. Last Saturday night, or should I say Sunday morning, at 1 a.m., my mother was awakened by a slow methodical knock on her front door (Just like the one mentioned above), but she panicked and did not dare to answer it. The next day a pilot who lives two houses from her said that he saw a UFO hovering in her back yard.

Betty's memoirs provide a more detailed description of this event. She wrote:

My mother was awakened by a knock-knock-knock on the front door, which is directly under her bedroom. These were measured knocks, in that there was one knock, followed by a waiting period; then a second knock and a wait, etc. This knocking continued for several minutes. My mother became terrified, so much so that she could not move to awaken my father. Then the knocking ceased, and she regained some of her courage and woke him up. She did not turn on any lights. Then, they heard a roaring sound, followed by an explosion. The whole house shook. Thinking that the furnace had exploded, they ran downstairs to investigate. The furnace was fine. Needless to say, they were not able to sleep for the rest of the night.

The next day, a neighbor said that he was returning from his job at about 2 a.m. and he had seen a UFO landed or going down in the woods near their home. Family members started to search to find any evidence of a landing. They crossed the lawn, went over the stone wall, into a wooded area. They had gone only a short distance when they found the area. In the midst of the trees was a small clearing, ringed with pines and birches.

The family phoned Betty and she drove to Kingston to investigate.

Betty Hill took a picture of this craft as it hovered silently above her auto. Look to the right of the craft for what has an uncanny resemblance to an alien bust.

Courtesy of Kathleen Marden.

In her letter to Robert Hohmann, Betty described the physical trace evidence that her family discovered when they investigated the suspected landing site. This was investigated by Betty and a NICAP investigator. She wrote, "In a clump of trees nearest the home, they found all trees in a circular pattern were broken, bent, or the bark badly scraped at a height 12 feet from the ground. In the center was a triangular mark of slight indentation, measuring 36 inches on each side. The ground, dried grasses, etc. were burned in this area, as well as some of the branches of the trees. In the midst of this triangle was a piece of burned birch bark, which I am sending to you."

Betty elaborated further in her memoirs:

In a small clearing they found what appeared to be many markings of a landing, as though the craft had difficulty in getting down.

From the evidence, we determined that the craft was approximately 15 to 18 feet in diameter. We determined this by measuring the distances between the trees where the bark had been scraped off on the facing sides. Also, three birch trees had been sheared off at the exact same height, which was the same point where the scrapings stopped—10 feet from the ground. A small tree had been bent over as though a weight had rested on it, and it never stood up again, but later died. There were three slight indentations in the ground of three triangle-shaped markings. In the middle of the triangle-shaped markings was a slightly burned area, or to be more precise, a dark soot-like substance. It covered the branches of the small tree which died.

Betty mailed the 14-by-5 1/2-inch bark sample to Robert Hohmann, who coordinated radiation testing on it. An engineer who was one of Hohmann's colleagues completed the photographic, microscopic, chemical, ultraviolet, infrared, and curl examination on the sample, and wrote the technical report. The report revealed that the bark was from a tree of the Betulaceae family, and most probably a genus of Betula, species paprifera. These trees, which mature to 60 to 80 feet, are indigenous to Canada, the northern United States, and the Southern Appalachians. The sample was tightly rolled from both ends and had obviously been submitted to a short-duration blast of an extremely hot flame, which had heavily scorched one end of the rolled bark, but had not been sufficient to kindle it. Chemical analysis revealed that the fuel for the flame that scorched the sample was a petroleum product. It was determined that exposure of the sample to a five-minute blast of 275-degree heat would be sufficient to curl it. The engineer hypothesized that the blast of heat to which the sample was subjected was sufficient to curl it in a very short period of time. He concluded that there was insufficient data to draw significant conclusions.

Betty monitored the site and reported back to Hohmann in a letter dated May 18, 1966. She stated, "We went to my mother's home last night and questioned her as the possibility of any fire in the area, which has definitely been ruled out. Also, no one has used a blow torch or fuel oil in any way, with the exception that about five years ago, my father dumped some crankcase oil on an ant hill about 200 yards away." Betty did not know that a youthful neighbor visited the alleged UFO landing site prior to her arrival and perpetrated a hoax to elicit excitement from her. The burned bark evidence that she submitted for testing had been removed from a neighborhood tree, doused with lighter fluid, and set on fire briefly. It is unfortunate that the one sample she submitted for testing was, in reality, a hoax.

Betty's May 18 letter to Robert Hohmann continued:

> We are still watching the spot and find the small trees that were bent over are slowly beginning to straighten themselves up—while the trees that were bent from the winter snows have not done this, because our weather has not been warm enough. From the markings on the trees, we would estimate the craft to be 15 to 18 feet in diameter, so it was much smaller than the one we had contact with in 1961. Incidentally, my mother did say that she remembered that sometime during that night she heard a noise— a loud boom that sounded as if someone had slammed shut a heavy door, which caused her house to vibrate. This noise awoke both of my parents and they checked the doors and windows to try to find the source of the noise, without success.

During the summer of 1966, the experimental team suggested a more scientific approach to Betty's and Barney's attempts to contact the UFO occupants. It suggested a specific methodology for a psychophysical contact experiment Betty agreed to carry out. As a precursor to the experiment, Betty attempted verbal and telepathic communication with the ETs from the back porch of her Portsmouth home each day. In the interest of advancing scientific knowledge, she asked the "UFO people" to appear at her parents' farm on the night of August 20–21. The experiment produced less than the desired results, but she complied with the team's request for a detailed description of anything that might seem out of the ordinary. In a letter dated August 23, 1966, she reported that she and Barney had observed a bright light that traveled north to south and then appeared to descend toward her parents' back yard. Suddenly, it stopped, and its lights dimmed and extinguished as conventional aircraft entered the area. They waited for the light to reappear, but when it did not, she and Barney retired to her parents' travel trailer to camp out for the night. They were listening to a radio, which was to serve as a technical appliance for contact, when suddenly the music stopped and they heard a series of notes, followed by a 10-second pause. This pattern repeated approximately 15 times and then stopped. Betty wondered if this might be the signal she was looking for, so she watched from the window, but could not see anything unusual. A few moments later, Betty's parents' dog, which was tied in the yard, started to jump and howl. In response, Delsey, the Hills' dog, walked to the door and gave several deep, threatening howls. Later, Barney observed a few flashes of light from their window, but could not identify its source. Betty wondered if any of these seemingly mundane events could have been signals that she and Barney failed to comprehend, and asked for Hohmann's opinion.

In an August 29 letter, Robert Hohmann, on behalf of the team, suggested that perhaps the Hills had failed to comprehend details given to them by the ETs prior to the 20th that might have prepared them for the events. He informed the Hills that if indeed they had received radio signals from the UFO occupants, the next step would be to acknowledge the radio signals. This could be accomplished by answering with an exact repetition of the same signals or pattern of signals they had received. He suggested that the Hills could respond by flashing lights, electrical switches, or headlights off and on. As an alternative, they could reproduce the pattern of the signals through percussion, such as clapping metal objects together. Or, he suggested that the combined use of a portable radio and flashlight would be adequate, adding the comment that perhaps the UFO occupants expected a special response from the Hills. When this response was not forthcoming, the communication attempt failed to produce a response in kind, and all hopes of securing a workable piece of hardware failed. Hohmann added the comment that one cannot expect to reach a conclusion without a minimum of working data. Speculating that the Hills had not received an adequate preparation for the events of August 20, he reasoned that the disadvantages, which handicapped the Hills' desire to cooperate, were sufficient to assume there was no basis to expect a meeting or quantitative proof.

When the Hills' experiment failed to produce a clear signal, they concluded that they had entered the experiment at a disadvantage, and that additional time or effort could not be justified to produce the desired result. Likewise, Hohmann was not able to offer concrete suggestions to the Hills or further assistance in their effort to secure a workable piece of hardware. It seemed that there was no point in continuing the contact experiments.

In a letter dated April 3, 1967, Hohmann speculated that, following the publication of *The Interrupted Journey* and the widespread public interest in UFOs, the Hills might enter a new phase of their experience. His intuition told him that this new phase would run through a variety of "shades and tones of curious phenomena," and offered his assistance if the Hills encountered circumstances that were seemingly without logical interpretation or explanation. In response, the Hills sought technical assistance from him and his scientific team to test the hypothesis that the human capability for extraordinary sensory communication is entirely possible with the science of psychophysics.

This led to a discussion of psychophysics with Dr. J. Allen Hynek, which stimulated interest in the scientific community. Dr. Hynek and John Fuller had discussed the extraordinary sensory communication hypothesis and expressed an interest in participating in a contact experiment. Fuller offered to inquire about the Hills' interest in participating in the proposed test.

The team discussed the advisability of entering into a formal contract with the study group at the University of Colorado, headed by Dr. Condon. However, Dr. Hynek suggested that, in the interests of sound planning, it was advisable for the group to plan the project on a local or regional level, rather than wait for a formal contract. For this plan to be implemented, all expenses would be paid locally.

Hohmann advised the Hills, at the suggestion of Allen Hynek, that he would coordinate the procedural steps to convert the hypothesis into a specific program. Additionally, he would assemble an unbiased group of technical observers as soon as the funding for the project had been established. Additionally, he asked for the Hills' thoughts pertaining to a date and a suitable location convenient to Betty and Barney for the contact experiment.

Once the prerequisite steps had been achieved, Hohmann planned to coordinate all information with the scientific team to set in motion a step-by-step procedural prospectus involving the hypothesis. The scientific team would manage the quantitative data required by the scientific community. During this process, Hohmann agreed to consult with the Hills at each step of the planning to update them on the team's progress.

Thus, with the Hills' full cooperation, the plan to conduct a psychophysics experiment was set into motion. Through the next several weeks, Hohmann's communication with the Hills was primarily through the telephone. However, as we will see in the next chapter, he also informed the Hills of the detailed instructions pertaining to the upcoming contact experiment.

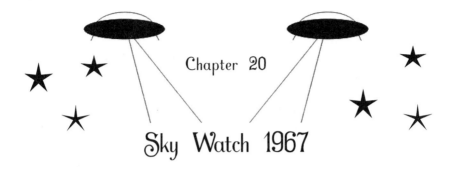

Chapter 20

Sky Watch 1967

The Hills' spirit of scientific cooperation led to a plan, coordinated for the experimental team by Robert Hohmann, to again attempt contact with the ETs on June 10, 1967. Betty's parents agreed to host the experimental team at their Kingston, N.H. farm, while Robert Hohmann worked to assemble what he assured the Hills would be a "friendly, cooperative, cordial, and truly scientific group." This team would be made up of IBM personnel (mentioned earlier) and the UFO encounter investigation team, including C.D. Jackson, J. Allen Hynek's personal representative, Jacques Vallee, John Fuller, and Dr. Benjamin Simon. The photographer was under contract to photograph exclusively the phenomena itself, should it appear. He guaranteed that there would be no publicity before, during, or after the test. This was an extremely important element to the project if the team were to rule out a hoax and avoid media publicity.

Jacques Vallee documented the experiment in his book, *Forbidden Science.* His journal states that on May 31, 1967, Allen Hynek asked him to act as an observer in a contact experiment that Betty Hill wanted to conduct with John Fuller, Dr. Simon, and IBM engineer Robert Hohmann. (Again we see Hohmann misidentified as an engineer. This trend seems persistent.) Hynek told Vallee that Betty believed she had become a "transducer"—able to vector in a flying saucer and cause it to land.[1] It does not mention the fact that this "psychophysics" experiment was planned by the experimental team in cooperation with Betty Hill or that Hynek took part in the initial phase of the planning. Although Betty hoped to contact her abductors and to secure a piece of hardware as evidence, in this case, she merely served as a "subject" following the scientific team's precise instructions. Hohmann's letter to Vallee included the following quote from a letter written by Betty: "I followed your suggestions regarding the message and I hope that the next manifestation will take place closer than that of Saturday evening in Kingston, very close, very clear, and just above the trees." Again, Betty is referring to her desire to elicit positive results from her attempt to communicate the experimental team's message to the extraterrestrials. Apparently, her attempt the previous Saturday night had once again failed to produce the desired result.

Betty wrote in her memoirs that from the inception of the experiment, she doubted that her attempts to communicate with the ETs would be successful. However, she continued, "We were contacted by a scientist, asking our cooperation in an experiment that they would like to attempt. We agreed to work with them."

In preparation for the event, the experimental team instructed Betty to communicate a message to the extraterrestrials beginning on Friday, June 2, and continuing until the day of the experiment. Betty had previously communicated to Hohmann that, in her opinion, from the first day of her attempted communication it had taken four months to produce the desired result. She attempted this experiment at a disadvantage. In accordance with her original methodology, Betty stood on the back porch of her home at 9 each evening and delivered the following message:

Today is (Friday, June 2), the (153rd) day of the year.

In eight more days go to my parents' farm in Kingston, New Hampshire.

Best science men are there.

Come close to science men.

All is safe.

A week later, on Friday evening, June 9, Robert Hohmann and his colleague, the industrial electrician, arrived at the Kingston farm to examine the general land area and set up tents and sleeping equipment. They were met by Betty and Barney who had arrived earlier that evening. On Saturday morning the group worked diligently to have facilities, food, sleeping bags, two tents, a portable stove, utensils, plates, and so on, ready to accommodate the nine participants. Additionally, Hohmann and his colleague set up the test layout, according to his sketch of a ground plan in preparation for extraterrestrial contact. The plan consisted of a central white circle containing a table, clock, compass, cameras, and a thermometer. All participants were instructed to enter the white circle if alien contact was made. Also, 500- and 1,000-foot distance markers extending north, south, east, and west were assembled in preparation for the anticipated contact.

By late afternoon on Saturday, the remainder of the team had arrived. John Fuller drove up from Connecticut, stopping to pick up the Vallees and C.D. Jackson at Boston's Logan Airport. From there they drove to Dr. Simon's home in Arlington, Massachusetts, before heading north for Kingston, New Hampshire.

According to Betty, one of the scientists, the astronomer, had an audiotape of strange beeping sounds that he played for the Hills. Betty wrote that it had been recorded in a very desolate area, and the military had constructed roads to access this area for testing. She reported that the strange beeping sounds seemed to affect all of the wildlife, driving it out of the area. The Hills listened to the sounds on the signal tape and determined that they did not resemble the mechanical buzzing sounds that bounced off the trunk of their car on September 19–20, 1961.

That night the team scanned the skies for an unconventional flying object, but observed only conventional aircraft and satellites. Betty sat with Jacques Vallee, observing satellites crisscrossing the night sky through his telescope. But not one UFO was sighted. Betty wrote in disappointment, "All we attracted was mosquitoes!"

On June 14, 1967, Robert Hohmann informed the Hills that no one was disappointed that the expected phenomenon did not appear on schedule. The team reassured Betty and Barney that the fact that they had made an active attempt to establish contact was more important. The transition from passive interest to an active effort had established a beginning point from which to refine their later steps.

On June 26, 1967, Hohmann told the Hills that three members of the original team planned to return to Kingston on Saturday, September 9, to repeat the experiment. This would allow Betty nearly three months to communicate the message to the UFO occupants—short of her four-month requirement, but greater than the brief time period she was allowed for the June 10 sky watch. In the interim, he asked Betty to inform him of any detail, no matter how seemingly insignificant, that could confirm that the original message had been received. Again, he assured her that all information she provided would remain confidential.

The September 9 experiment failed to produce the desired result, but the experimental team remained undeterred. According to Betty, Hohmann phoned Barney and her to ask them to check around to see if anyone in the area had reported a UFO sighting that weekend. Betty learned that a family who lived in Newton, New Hampshire, "a short distance" from the experimental site, had conducted a UFO contact experiment on the evening of September 8. This family's land bordered a farm located approximately two air miles from the Barrett farm. The family informed Betty that shortly after dusk, they signaled a silent, red-orange light that appeared to be bobbing slowly along the top of the ridge behind their home. The family: a husband, wife, their children, and the wife's brother, a NICAP investigator, flashed their flashlights and waved at the object. In response, the UFO also turned its lights off and on. To their amazement, the UFO left the top of the hill and crossed the field to within close proximity of where they were standing. They said it sat in midair, not more than 20 feet off the ground, rocking back and forth. The disk-shaped craft had white flashing lights on its rim and a red light on top of its dome. The wife became frightened and retreated to the house with her children in tow, but the two men remained outside, observing the craft. Next, a jet appeared on the scene and the UFO turned its lights off. After the conventional craft left the area, the UFO turned its lights on and drifted back over the ridge of the hill, and was lost from sight.

This was one of four sightings reported by the family between July 27 and October 30, 1967. The NICAP investigator filed a preliminary report, but to Betty's disappointment, no formal investigation ensued. Without a formal investigation, one cannot make assumptions regarding the validity of the report. However, Betty seemed to believe that she had reaped limited success. The UFOs allegedly appeared within close proximity to her requested contact site. However, they seemed to appear at the wrong time or in the wrong location.

The experimental team tentatively interpreted the nearby sightings as a logical sequence of events: July 27, the preparatory stage; September 8, the principal phenomenon; September 30 and October 30, the follow-up stages. However, it stated in a letter that the greatest difficulty was in not knowing more about the UFO mission. Without more exact knowledge, the team of scientists/engineers was unable to understand fully how to interpret the meaning of the preparatory, principal phenomenon, or follow-up phases of the experiment. But it expressed the optimistic message that perhaps in time they would be able to get clearer answers.

Hohmann's next letter, dated September 14, 1967, informed the Hills that the requirement seemed to be one of watching and waiting for some kind of advance signs or notice of some kind from the UFO occupants prior to the awaited contact event. The team's challenge was to be able to recognize and understand what might be extremely subtle signs. He informed the Hills that they should remain continuously alert to things seen, as well as unseen, in order to prepare themselves for contact.

The experimental team seems to have given Betty an impossible order—to report even the most inconsequential anomalous event, assuming that it might be a sign from the ETs. Without a point of reference, Betty attempted to comply with the team's request.

In a letter dated October 16, 1967, Hohmann updated the Hills on the results of an October 14 experiment conducted at a Lake Desolation, New York retreat. The retreat, best described by its name, "Desolation," bordered thousands of acres of state forest in upstate New York. This was the first of a two-stage contact experiment. The experimental location was completely isolated with the exception of a house trailer, which the experimental subject planned to occupy, and his vehicle. On October 2, the experimental team had instructed Betty to attempt to communicate specific instructions to the ETs regarding the subject's exact location on a composite map, including geographic, topographic, and aerial locations. In addition to the team's specific instructions, they planned to introduce a severe discontinuity factor, completely unrelated to the other words in Betty's communication. This would make the communication nearly impossible to comply with, but if compliance did take place, it would nearly eliminate the possibility of coincidence. In return, Betty was instructed to request specific instructions from the UFO occupants.

On the evening of October 14, the experimental subject placed a 4- by 5-inch file card bearing the message "Huntsville, Alabama—East to West" face-down in a clip-holder and attached the clip-holder to the dashboard of his car, which was parked approximately 15 feet from the window of the house trailer at Lake Desolation. He stationed himself at the window of the house trailer to watch for any unusual activity. At approximately 12:15 he observed the car door open, which switched on the interior dome light. Approximately three minutes later, when he went outside to check for a communicated message, he found that everything was intact and undisturbed. The card, face-down, was still in the clip-holder, just as he had left it. He anticipated that if the opening of the car door had any experimental significance, at some future, unspecified date, there would be an east-to-west phenomenon over Huntsville, Alabama.

A prior experiment, conducted on June 26, 1967 attempted to communicate instructions for a UFO to appear in an east-to-west line over the Mt. Montesano landmark in Huntsville, Alabama. It failed to produce the desired result. However, perhaps coincidentally, a UFO phenomenon did occur in an east–west line over Montesano, Washington on July 5, 1967. In an attempt to eliminate the element of coincidence, the team revised its experiment.

The revision introduced a severe discontinuity factor in an attempt to eliminate the possibility of coincidence. The experimental team was attempting to find language or phonetic factors for an outgoing message that could be easily complied with. If this added element were successful it would increase the possibility of a response from the UFO occupants.

The phonetic message, "reply by new moccasins" according to the Hohmann's letter, represented a "discontinuity factor" unrelated to other words in the communication. This discontinuity factor would eliminate the possibility of coincidence by being nearly impossible to comply with. If compliance did take place, according to the experimental team, it would nearly eliminate the possibility of coincidence. Therefore, if a UFO appeared in a location named "moccasin," a correlation could be drawn between Betty's communication with the ETs and the event. Additionally, Betty was instructed to send a UFO in an east-to-west line in view of Montesano—a mountain in Huntsville, Alabama, topped with a large illuminated cross.

The team strove to examine the psychophysical communication's capability, and to construct an experiment designed to produce no coincidental results. It wanted to continue the experiment using language/phonetic factors that were usable in an outgoing message, thus the "new moccasins" explanation.

At 3:45 a.m. on November 18, 1967, a team member, who served as an uninformed control subject, and five additional witnesses, observed a UFO near East Fishkill, New York. The team member pinpointed the exact location in the immediate proximity of Moccasin View Street. This first phase of the moccasin discontinuity experiment seemed to have reaped success. However, the team would have to watch and wait for results in the Montesano experiment.

Then, at 7:30 p.m. on December 1, 1967, the 12-year-old son of a team member observed a "phenomenon" on an east–west route over Huntsville, Alabama. Two nights later, it reappeared in the sky, traveling in a west–east direction.

When these experimental results came under scientific scrutiny, it became evident that coincidence rather than correlation had to be factored into the equation. The experimental team learned that a UFO sighting that involved the keyword "new moccasin" had also occurred in New Zealand. Additionally, a 1965 New York sighting also listed the word "moccasin." The experimental team seemed confounded by this apparent coincidence.

The repeated failure of the "psychophysics" experiments to produce solid, correlating evidence seems to have soured some of the team's enthusiasm. Team members, who had previously expressed commitment toward the series of experiments, lost their enthusiasm when the experiments failed to produce scientifically verifiable results. The drudgery of months of personal commitment and extraneous work ended the cooperative effort between the experimental team and Betty Hill to vector in a UFO.

This marked the end of formal experimentation by a courageous team of scientists and observers who quietly, without publicity, attempted to contact intelligent life forms who were allegedly visiting our planet. Betty, however, with resolute determination, continued the contact experiments, without the benefit of scientific design and supervision.

On Friday evening, July 13, 1973, Betty and 35 observers, mostly members of UFO study groups, assembled at a quiet location in the Kingston area. Shortly before midnight they assembled their vehicles in a circle and switched their headlights off and on in an attempt to signal the occupants of a UFO. The experiment failed to produce the desired result, but a member of the media reported the event in the *Boston Globe.* Thereafter, the formerly respectable, conservative scientific nature of Betty's contact experiments was replaced by a new tabloid news quality.

Sky watch 1967.
Courtesy of Kathleen Marden.

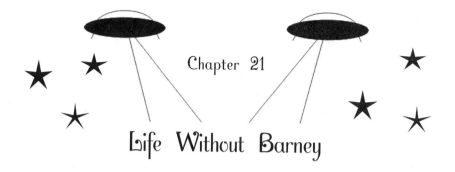

Chapter 21

Life Without Barney

During the promotion of the book, the Hills were besieged with a variety of health problems. In 1967, Betty's health had declined to the degree that she requested a transition from full-time to part-time employment at the Welfare Department. In a letter dated October 6, 1967, the bureau chief wrote, "We are all very concerned that so many physical ailments seem to have descended upon you." This letter recommended that she take a leave of absence, rather than transfer to part-time employment.

Betty was suffering from polyps on her vocal chords that required surgical removal in January 1968, followed by a second surgery in February. The surgery left Betty unable to speak above a whisper. Eventually she regained her voice, but the surgery had permanently altered the tonal quality of her speech. Thereafter, she spoke in a raspy voice that observers often thought was caused by years of cigarette smoking.

In June, she was hospitalized with a pericarditis, an infection in the lining of her heart. When she returned home, her now-widowed mother nursed her back to health during the daytime, while Barney worked. She was physically incapacitated, unable to perform even light household duties for several weeks. This forced her to take an unpaid leave of absence from her job as a social worker. By November, she was able to return to her employment on a part-time basis and to resume lecturing about her UFO experience.

Mysteriously, all of Betty's records pertaining to her UFO encounter disappeared from her medical file. This claim has been substantiated by a former employee at the clinic under a guarantee of anonymity. This individual stated, "Betty was such a nice, down-to-earth person. It's really too bad—what happened to her. She didn't deserve that kind of treatment."

Barney's health problems receded briefly, but came back with a vengeance in 1968. It was during a 50-mile drive to a scheduled appearance that Barney experienced a health crisis. As he motored his way to the lecture hall, Barney began to experience vertigo so severe that he could no longer drive. Betty, assuming that the dizziness would pass, assumed a position behind the wheel and drove to their scheduled appointment. By the time the Hills arrived at the meeting, Barney was unable to walk without assistance. Undeterred, he addressed the group while he leaned against a chair for support. On the return trip, Betty stopped at the hospital and Barney was examined, but the doctor was not able to diagnose Barney's condition as more than transient dizziness.

A genetic predisposition, a lifetime of poor dietary habits, a cigarette-smoking habit, and stress had taken its toll on Barney. He had successfully refocused his energy to take leadership positions in the civil rights movement and the poverty program. Serving as legal redress for his local chapter of the NAACP and on the Governor's Council of the U.S. Civil Rights Commission, he fought for African-American equality. He worked side by side with Betty and community leaders to found the Rockingham County Community Action Program, and served as its first executive director. Barney pushed himself nearly beyond the limits of human capacity while he retained full-time employment as a city carrier with the U.S. Post Office. After the publication of *The Interrupted Journey*, he and Betty appeared on radio and television programs and spoke on college campuses across the nation. Barney was an uneasy participant, preferring to focus on his social and political activities. Being a UFO abductee never came easy for Barney. He would have preferred to erase the entire incident from his memory. Although he became health conscious, exercising regularly, quitting smoking, and dieting, Barney could not ward off the impending cerebral hemorrhage that would soon take him at age 46.

December 24, 1968, brought the first period of grief to the Hills. Their precious companion and fellow UFO experiencer, Delsey, died. Her death was unexpected, and followed a bladder infection and brief period of dehydration that did not respond to veterinary treatment.

Then on February 25, during a raging blizzard, Barney was stricken. Betty documented the day in this poignant excerpt:

> Barney and I had both gone into our work, not realizing that we were heading into one of the worst snowstorms in our history. Soon all businesses and offices were closed, and all travelers were warned to stay off the highways. We came home, a day of unexpected

holiday. Barney was elated, for all the years he had worked for the Post Office, this was the first time it had closed because of the weather.

After a leisurely breakfast, we fed the birds in the back yard, which were flying around in the swirling snow looking for food. We tossed our bread out to them and the birds came in large numbers. We watched them from the kitchen window.

Barney challenged me to a game of pool, proclaiming that he could beat me with one hand tied behind his back. Barney and I went downstairs and he built a fire in the fireplace. Then, he beat me at two games of pool. He was teasing me about his winning and was showing his prowess in hitting his trick shots. What a happy frame of mind he was in—laughing and joking. Suddenly he put his hand to the back of his neck and said he felt as though a hornet had stung him. A hornet in February in a snow storm—"impossible," I said. Then he felt a second sting and began to hurry upstairs. I saw him stumble on the stairs and continue his ascent as if he were crawling on his hands and feet.

He sat on the couch, and then he slipped onto the floor. He was very puzzled, and told me that something was very wrong. A moment later he asked me to call the ambulance. I put through an emergency call and then sat on the floor, holding him until they arrived.

Barney knew the ambulance crew and they immediately started to kid him. 'What's the matter, Barney? Is the snow storm too severe for you to drive yourself?' Barney was clearheaded and remarked, 'Why should I drive myself when I have you to do it for me?' The attendant began to reach for the oxygen but, after reading Barney's blood pressure, he put it away. He told Barney not to worry—he was going to be alright. I seconded that thought.

The admitting doctor at the hospital had known me for many, many years, for we had been college students together. He asked Barney his birth date, and he gave the wrong date. Then, his blood pressure was taken and he was admitted. He was beginning to become incoherent.

Barney's doctor was unable to get into town, because of the storm, so he called a friend of his who lived close to the hospital. This doctor called me and said that he was walking there. When he arrived, he did a few tests, and told me what I already knew—

that Barney had suffered a stroke. How severe? He gave me a suggestion—if I had never prayed in my life, now was the time to do this—to pray that Barney would not survive. He said that the survival rate for this type of stroke [a cerebral hemorrhage] was three percent, but if he survived, he could live in a vegetative state, possibly for several years. This was one of Barney's worst fears. [Though much older than Barney, his father had suffered a stroke, which left him in a permanent vegetative state.]

The doctor said there was no point in my remaining at the hospital, for Barney was in a deep coma and he would not come out of it. In fact, the death process had already begun, and the hospital would call me when he died. I kissed Barney goodbye and left.

Betty returned home and began the process of informing relatives and friends of Barney's impending death. Her best friend drove through the blizzard to be by Betty's side, and her minister had just arrived when the phone rang. A voice on the other end conveyed the tragic news that Barney had died. It was 7:20 p.m.

Betty reminisced, "I turned on the TV, and sat on the living room couch, with the wind blowing and the snow swirling. What a strange twist to a day that had started out to be an unexpected holiday for us! This morning I was married, and now I was not. I thought that in any marriage one wonders how it will end. Now I knew."

Next, Betty phoned her sister Janet, Barney's brother in Virginia, his sisters in Philadelphia, and the Red Cross. Arrangements had to be made for family members from as far away as Panama to travel to Portsmouth for the funeral. Next, she called John Fuller, who planned to leave his Connecticut home immediately to rush to Betty's side. In a twist of fate, John called back a few minutes later to inform Betty that his friend, the cameraman who accompanied him to the Hills' first lecture at the Dover, N.H. Unitarian Church, had died suddenly from a heart attack. He was needed there. Dr. Simon was next on her list.

Soon, Betty's phone began to ring incessantly. Television and radio programs had been interrupted to announce Barney's untimely death, and the media wanted more information. Finally, at 4 a.m., Betty dropped into bed, confused and completely exhausted, for a three-hour nap.

Friends and the community joined together in an outpouring of support for Betty. The people of Portsmouth opened their hearts and their homes, providing rooms and meals for out-of-town guests and transportation to and from the airport. Betty found food and gifts left in her car and on the porches of her home, so much that they filled her freezer.

On Saturday, March 1, family, friends, and large delegations from the Portsmouth Post Office and the NAACP filled the Unitarian-Universalist Church of Portsmouth. City, county, and state politicians and community leaders were in attendance. After the service, the local branch of the NAACP provided food for the guests on the church's basement level. Following Barney's burial in nearby Kingston, Betty returned home alone with a severe case of the flu that left her bedridden for nearly a week.

On March 8, 1969, Betty ventured out for the first time since Barney's funeral to her mother's home in Kingston. As she drove north on Route 125 at 9 p.m., she noticed two red lights, one on each side of a pole at the power lines. At first she thought that tower lights had been installed within the previous two weeks, but quickly changed her mind when they started to travel in her direction. Betty slowed her car and the lighted object moved over the highway and stopped directly in front of her. As her curiosity piqued, she pulled to the side of the road and stopped her vehicle. Then, the object shifted back over the power lines and Betty was able to scrutinize its shape. It was a disk with a double row of windows the same as the one she had seen in New Hampshire's White Mountains in September of 1961. Peering into the dimly lighted interior, she could see shadowy figures. She opened the car doors to light the interior, exited the vehicle, and stood almost under the craft, wondering what to do next. Reasoning that the occupants were curious about Barney's death, she told them that Barney was in a nearby cemetery and pointed in the general direction of his grave. The craft rocked back and forth three or four times, crossed over the highway, and headed in the general direction of the cemetery. Betty returned to her car and made a quick exit toward Portsmouth.

The tragic loss of Barney caused unspeakable grief for Betty, which was amplified by the fact that her father had died only 10 months earlier. Her own health was in jeopardy resulting from a pericardial infection and bouts of pneumonia. Additionally, several acquaintances were openly speculating about Betty's impending death. They suspected that the sudden loss of Delsey, followed by Barney's untimely death two months later, was a direct consequence of the UFO abduction. Many expected Betty to drop dead later that spring, and naturally this created some anxiety within Betty.

Then on May 3, 1969, Betty was suddenly stricken outside her veterinarian's closed North Hampton office. She felt what resembled a sudden blow to the back of her head and saw a quick flash of light before she felt a paralyzing numbness that took her to the ground. She lay there for several minutes before the veterinarian's wife, a registered nurse, and her child came and assisted Betty to the house. Unable to sit or stand, Betty was put to bed while the group waited for the doctor to return home. When he arrived, they transported Betty to her home and waited while she phoned family members. Her sister Janet rushed Betty to the Exeter Hospital where she was treated and released, but spent the next two days under her mother's care.

Betty's health problems were compounded by continued harassment in her own home. Most notably, she had just finished preparing her tax documents and planned to deliver them to her accountant. To her chagrin, the materials disappeared from her home, forcing her to apply to the Internal Revenue Service for an extension. Then, several weeks later, Betty returned home from her office to find her tax documents on the floor, scattered throughout her apartment.

On other occasions, Betty experienced the shock of finding her kitchen chairs grouped in a circle in her living room. Clothing from her closets was piled in the middle of her room and her clock radio was reset, causing it to sound an alarm in the middle of the night. Not knowing what to do, Betty enlisted the assistance of an elderly retired gentleman who lived in an adjacent apartment building. On several occasions he observed two men dressed in dark suits enter Betty's apartment by unlocking her door with a key. Once again Betty had the locks changed, but the men continued to enter undeterred.

At the time of these incidents, Kathy was a college student at the University of New Hampshire, a short drive from Betty's home in Portsmouth. To protect Betty and give her a sense of safety and security, she and her husband took up residence in an apartment in Betty's building. They installed an intercom system between their apartments and listened for intruders during the daytime when Betty was at work. One day, as Kathy sat studying, she distinctly heard her apartment door open and the sound of footsteps in her residence. Thinking that Betty had decided to have her lunch at home, Kathy rushed upstairs to visit with her. To her astonishment, Betty wasn't there, and she realized that someone had entered her apartment and might be hiding inside. She apprehensively opened a closet door and peered under Betty's bed, before reason prevailed, and sensing impending danger, she quickly returned to her apartment. Then, moments later, a loud crash jolted her, followed by hurried footsteps and the slamming of the front door. Again she rushed to Betty's apartment, threw open the front door, and raced down the hall. A short, stocky man was rapidly exiting Betty's yard. He quickly sped away in his waiting vehicle. Returning to Betty's apartment, she found a closet door standing open. A baseball bat that had been stored in the closet had fallen to the floor. Perhaps she would have been assaulted if she had opened the door moments earlier.

Betty suspected that someone was attempting to prod her into making a police report. Reasoning that a concerted effort was being made to cause her to "freak out," she decided against creating a paper trail or risking publicity. She once again had her locks changed and checked regularly by a locksmith. She also enlisted the assistance of NICAP members who pledged to assist her in identifying the source behind the harassment. But when her home continued to be entered, she had an alarm system installed. Thereafter, the alarm sounded once, the police responded, the culprit escaped, and the harassment ceased.

Kathleen Marden with Aunt Betty Hill.
Courtesy of N.H. MUFON State Director Peter Geremia.

Betty's life returned to normal and she developed an interest in organic gardening. That summer she planted a large vegetable garden on her mother's Kingston, N.H. farm. Nearly every weekend, she and her granddaughter, who had come to spend the summer with Betty, camped out on the farm and tended the vegetable crop. It was an enjoyable, relaxing summer spent by the pool with close family members. During the week, Betty performed her professional duties as a child welfare worker, while Tammy attended summer camp. The slower pace, interrupted only by an occasional interview, facilitated Betty's healing process and her cardiac problems receded.

Just as life was taking on a more leisurely pace, Betty received a letter from Lakeside, Ohio. It was from Marjorie Fish, an unmarried elementary school teacher and member of Mensa, who received a B.S. degree in sociology with a minor in science from Juniata College in Huntingdon, Pennsylvania in 1954. She graduated with distinction. In 1962, she returned to college at Bowling Green State University in Bowling Green, Ohio, to pursue graduate studies in elementary education. Her intense interest in UFOs had developed in 1966 when she read Dr. Jacques Vallee's *Anatomy of a Phenomenon.* Fish informed Betty that she had developed an interest in attempting to identify the astronomical location of the stars on the map that she was allegedly shown during her abduction. This gave Fish the chance to verify scientifically whether or not the star cluster Betty drew represented a real set of stars, suitable for planets, that could have developed life.

Excited by another scientific interest in her UFO encounter, Betty agreed to meet with Fish in her Portsmouth, N.H., home on August 4–5, 1969. It would be the beginning of a long, cordial relationship between the two women, culminating in Fish's discovery of correlating data that seemed to substantiate the validity of Betty's star map.

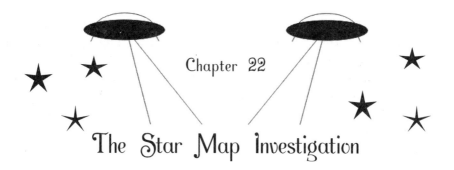

Chapter 22

The Star Map Investigation

Stanton Friedman met Marjorie Fish in 1971 through a referral from Coral Lorenzen, cofounder of the Aerial Phenomena Research Organization. During a subsequent visit to Fish's home, he was impressed by her intellectual curiosity and precise attention to detail. Additionally, her membership in Mensa verified that her intelligence level was in the top two percentile. When he agreed to attempt to verify her star map work, she sent him copies of much of her work tabulating the spatial coordinates of the local stars. The most troubling aspect was the big variation on various star lists of the distances from the sun to the various stars. The angular coordinates (in what direction to look) were in general agreement from list to list, but the distances were not easy to measure at the time, and there could be several light-years' difference from one catalog to another.

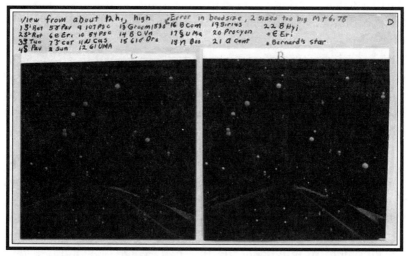

Star map models by Marjorie Fish (lines and numbers traced in white by editor for visibility). Courtesy of Kathleen Marden.

The models of our local galactic neighborhood that she built were three-dimensional. Beads of different colors, depending on the type of star, were strung in their correct 3-D locations on nylon fish line. Her original model was completed in December, 1968, but more of the pattern was not found until the summer of 1969. In December of that year, *Gliese's 1969 Near Star Catalog* was published. Fish used this to recheck her work, but three stars on Betty's map did not appear in the catalog. It was not until the fall of 1972 that the last three stars were found in an updated *Gliese Catalog*.[1]

Astronomers in the 1960s and early 1970s were certainly not talking of traveling to the stars. As a matter of fact, most of them are *still* very resistant to that idea. It didn't matter, when observing a star with a telescope, how far away it was, but trying to model the pattern meant that distances were crucial. The objective was to try to find a three-dimensional pattern (arrangement of stars) that matched the two-dimensional one that Betty had drawn—with the admonition of if, and only if, she could remember what she saw accurately. Betty described the map that she observed on the craft as having a three-dimensional appearance. The 3-foot-long by 2-foot-wide map was similar to a reflective hologram. The stars were tinted and glowed as if she were looking into the heavens. However, there was no concentration of stars like we might observe when stargazing. The star map that Betty viewed had to be limited to only local stars or selected stars.

Fish, who did not have access to a computer at the time, had to copy all the coordinates by hand at the OSU library, as it would not allow the catalogs to be borrowed.

She found that there were about 1,000 stars within about 55 light years of the sun in all directions. Obviously what Betty saw seemed to point to only about 16 stars as being connected with the lines denoting heavy trade routes, light trade routes, and occasional expeditions. Fish had initially expected to find many patterns that matched what Betty had drawn. She was looking at each model from many different directions. Fish used color-coded beads to stand for each star, depending on the type of star it was. Many of the stars in our local neighborhood were small red dwarf stars, which seemed very unlikely as the site of an inhabited solar system. The stars would have to have planets with environments conducive to the development of life. Further, the conditions would have to be right for the development of intelligent life that had evolved beyond our level of technological knowledge. Because the energy levels from the star reaching the planets would be quite low, red dwarfs were ruled out.

Fish also realized that there are many stars whose energy output varies in time. Most scientists feel that the development of life on a planet requires long-term temperature stability: Alternate freezing and frying would not be good for the development of life. Furthermore, many stars are also part of a closely associated pair of stars, or even a triplet. It would appear that, because of the complicated gravitational field of two stars quite close to each other, stable planetary orbits, on a cosmic time scale, would not exist near a double or triple star system.

Fish had expected, by looking at the models from many different directions, to find many patterns that were close to Betty's. Initially, she found none. She kept eliminating certain categories of stars (variable, small dwarf stars, and so on) as a matching pattern failed to turn up. It was only after she had data from the newly published 1972 *Catalog of Nearby Stars* by Wilhelm Gliese, and built yet another model using this new data, that she found one—and only one—three-dimensional pattern that fit, angle for angle, line length for line length, what Betty had drawn...a real eureka moment.

Northwestern University astronomer Dr. J Allan Hynek arranged a meeting in Chicago with Marjorie Fish and Stanton. She brought one of her smaller models to the Adler Planetarium. Dr. David Saunders, who wrote *UFOs? Yes! Where the Condon Committee Went Wrong,* a negative book about the University of Colorado study (Directed by Dr. Edward U. Condon, a well-known physicist) with which he had been connected, was also able to make it for that meeting. Fish discussed the catalogs she had checked and the standards she had used to select the stars in her model, and responded to the scientists' questions.

Dr. George Mitchell of the astronomy department at Ohio State University in Columbus, Ohio, used one of Fish's models as a teaching tool in his department. He assured us that her work was very accurate, and that he could find no problems with it. Saunders obtained a computerized version of the Gliese *Catalog of Nearby Stars*, which had the most recent stellar distance data, and checked on Fish's work as well. He also found it very accurate. Mitchell and Fish (who was now working at the Oak Ridge National Laboratory in Oak Ridge, Tennessee), and Betty Hill were all interviewed by Stanton in 1978 for the documentary film *UFOs ARE Real.*

Stanton sent an article that he had cowritten (with Ann Slate Gironda, which appeared in *Saga Magazine*) to astronomy writer Terence Dickinson. He was working at the Strassenburg Planetarium and had attended a college lecture that Stanton had given in Rochester, New York. By now he was editor of *Astronomy Magazine*. They met again when Stanton was lecturing at a college in Milwaukee, where the magazine was then headquartered. He suggested Dickinson do an article about Fish's work. Prior to writing the article, Dickinson talked to a number of people, including Miss Fish and Drs. Mitchell, Saunders, and Hynek. Showing great courage in view of the negative attitude of the astronomical community toward UFOs, he published "The Zeta Reticuli Incident" in *Astronomy*'s December 1974 issue. The article drew more response than any article ever published by *Astronomy*, to date. Dickinson published many letters and pieces about it over the next year. There were, as might be expected, several attacks, including one from Sagan and his Cornell associate, Dr. Steven Soter. Some of Hynek's students, whom he had asked to look at the work after the Chicago meeting, also joined in the discussion to cover such topics as the age of Zeta 1 and Zeta 2 Reticuli. These are the stars that Fish concluded were the ETs' base stars, quite close to each other, with heavy trade routes between them. These are in the southern sky constellation of Reticulum, "The Net." Because of the great interest, *Astronomy* published a 32-page full-color-on-coated-paper booklet, "The Zeta Reticuli Incident" (Astromedia Corporation, 1976). It included the original article and the subsequent publications, which included detailed responses from Fish and others. Amazingly, 10,000 copies were sold within a very short time. The booklet on the cover page included a list of authors of related commentary, including Sagan. Sagan's attorneys threatened to sue the publisher because his name was listed, even though he was just one of several contributors named. Somewhat to Dickinson's surprise, his young and courageous publisher, Steve Walther, who also had been behaving strangely for some months, caved in. The reason became obvious when Walther died of a brain tumor less than a year later. Because of the legal threats, and because Stanton had instigated the article, Astromedia made Stanton an offer he couldn't refuse, and he wound up distributing almost 18,000 copies of the booklet.

Fish's work was a splendid example of persistence and objectivity. She had to copy out all the coordinates, convert the data to useful angles and distances, string the beads, and hang them. Subsequently, she had to scan the results from many different directions, seeking a 3-D pattern that matched what Betty had drawn. Obviously there were limits, such as doorways, to the size of the model. Finally, in what was a relief to her, the Wilhelm Gliese *Catalog of Nearby Stars* provided the best set of distance data. Decisions had to be made as to the maximum star distances to include. Obviously it was farther to the corners than to the nearest frame pieces if the sun is in the center. She was studying quite carefully the work of various authors as to which stars would be more or less likely to have planets.

We have found that it comes as a surprise to many people that stars vary much more than do people as to age, intensity, size, nearness to other stars, and so on. Some stars are so huge that if placed at the center of the solar system, the Earth would still be inside the star. For example, the giant star Betelgeuse in the constellation of Orion is so huge that if it were in the middle of our solar system, it would reach out almost as far as Jupiter. Sources differ, but most say that it is about 600 times bigger in diameter than the sun. The orbits of Mercury, Venus, Mars, and Earth, which is 92 million miles from the sun, would fit inside the star. In contrast, some stars are not much bigger than the Earth. Some "burn" their nuclear fuel (nuclear fusion is the primary energy-production mechanism of the stars) in only millions of years. Others last for many billions of years, "burning" at an almost constant rate. To give a sense of perspective, Pluto is about 3.66 billion miles from the sun. The sun is about 800,000 miles in diameter, while the Earth is only 8,000 miles in diameter, and mighty Jupiter is 88,736 miles in diameter. It takes light from the sun only 8 minutes to reach Earth, only 43 minutes to reach Jupiter, and 320 minutes to reach Pluto. The speed of light, which physicists often quote as 186,000 miles per second, in more useful units is about 670,000,000 miles per hour. The distance to the nearest star is about 4.3 light years.

Thus our solar system, with our star, Sol, at the middle, is *much* smaller than the distance to our nearest solar neighbor. Our galaxy, the Milky Way, is about 100,000 light years in diameter, and is a flattened spiral pancake containing a few hundred billion stars. The sun is about 28,000 light-years from the center. Two small galaxies, the small and larger Magellanic clouds are a few hundred thousand light-years from us. The next big galaxy, similar to ours, the Andromeda Galaxy, is about 2.2 million light-years away. The universe with its billions of galaxies is about 13 billion light-years across.

It is important to stress this information, because we have found that many people don't know the difference between a solar system (such as our sun with its retinue of eight planets and dozens of moons, lots of asteroids, comets, and so on) and a galaxy. The universe is a very impressive place, but it is more important to focus on our local galactic neighborhood. Within only 54 light-years of the sun there are about a thousand stars. New ones are being found as we develop better observing techniques, especially space-based systems. About 46 of the thousand are quite similar to the sun, and were listed by Dickinson in his article. It seems absurd that some people will use terms such as intergalactic (between galaxies) to describe possible visitors and conclude it would take too long and too much energy to get here from somewhere else. *Intra*galactic and neighborhood travel make far more sense. It only takes a minute to walk to the neighbor's to borrow a cup of sugar. A Bostonian would hardly walk to a friend's house in Australia for the same purpose.

It is useful to focus on Fish's fascinating results:

1. All the pattern stars (connected with lines) are the right kind for planets and life, even though less than 5 percent of the stars in the local neighborhood qualify.

2. All the sun-like stars in the volume of space taken up by the 3-D model are part of the pattern. Just a little smaller, and many would be missed. A bit larger and many more would be included.

There have been many estimates made of the probability that #1 and #2 are just a coincidence: From one in a thousand to one in a million, depending on the assumptions. In short, this is a very unlikely coincidence.

3. All the pattern stars are, roughly speaking, in a plane—similar to thin slices of pepperoni on a thin pizza, as opposed to being raisins in a big fat loaf of raisin bread. This was not known until Fish's work. It matters, because it is much easier to travel within a plane. The planets of our solar system are also pretty much in a plane rather than scattered in all directions from the sun.

4. Nobody doing what Fish did before 1961, when the Hill encounter took place, or before the book was published in 1966, or before the Gliese catalog was published in 1968, could have achieved the same results, because science didn't have the right distance data. So how could Betty, who knew nothing about astronomy, have conjured up such a pattern?

5. The three-dimensional pattern of the travel routes makes sense from nearest star to nearest star to nearest star, rather than out and back, out and back. Furthermore, it seems reasonable to expect that if the stars visited are the same kind of stars, then other similar nearby stars should also be visited.

6. Finally, Fish's work determined that the base stars, between which there were very heavy trade routes, were Zeta 1 Reticuli and Zeta 2 Reticuli, in the southern sky constellation of Reticulum: "The Net."

As it turns out, for our neighborhood, this is a unique pair of stars. They are the closest (to each other) pair of sun-like stars in the neighborhood, being (as we now know because of the wonderful recent measurements of star distances made by the European satellite, Hipparchus) only 1/8 of a light-year apart from each other and only 39.2 light-years from the sun. Our star, the sun, is out in the boondocks; the nearest star to it is 4.25 light-years away. Zeta 1 and Zeta 2 Reticuli are next-door neighbors. They are 34 times closer to each other than the next star over (Alpha Centauri—a triple star) is from the sun. Of great importance is that they are far enough apart so that each could have a stable planetary orbit around it, unlike the situation for a close double or triple star. An important additional fact is that Zeta 1 and Zeta 2 are about a billion years older than the sun.

The implications of the special situation are fairly clear. Beings on a planet around either star could directly observe the other star all day long. It would be more than 20 times brighter than Venus is in our sky. One would, within hundreds of years of developing telescopes, be able to directly observe planets around the other star and would soon know which of those planets had biological systems because of the composition of the planetary atmospheres. The composition of our atmosphere is to a large extent dependent on the creation of various gases, such as oxygen, by biological processes. If none did, there would still be room for "terraforming," as has been proposed for us to do to Mars. This would mean artificially changing the planet in such a way as to make it suitable for colonization. Finally, there would obviously be a far greater incentive to develop interstellar travel when there is a neighboring star system only an eighth of a light-year away. At a quarter of the speed of light it would only take six months to make the trip.

Anyone studying the development of advanced technology would recognize that technological progress comes from doing things differently, in an unpredictable fashion. Lasers aren't just better light bulbs; they require entirely new physics. The nuclear fission rockets Stanton worked on are not just better chemical rockets; they require entirely different physics. The fusion rockets are, again, not just better chemical rockets. As a matter of fact, every advanced civilization would determine that fusion is the process that produces the energy of its star. With a billion-year head start on us, it seems reasonable that Zeta Reticulans would have developed entirely new (to us) techniques for energy production, transportation, communication, computers, biological activities—that we can't even imagine. They would presumably study biology, aging, and reproduction, and be able to more or less control these as well.

Furthermore, it seems reasonable to expect that a special location, with two older sun-like stars in relatively close proximity to each other, would become the hub of the local neighborhood. They might well be expected to colonize and migrate and patrol the neighborhood. It is also reasonable to expect them to be concerned about their own security and survival. This means that we would expect them to check much more closely on the primitive societies in the neighborhood who show signs of soon developing the technology for interstellar travel, but no signs of developing the sociology of learning to live at peace with their neighbors. From their viewpoint, we would surely appear to be a primitive society whose major activity is tribal warfare, resulting every so often in the slaughter of millions of people. It is estimated that the First World War cost 16 million lives. World War II cost about 50 million lives and the destruction of 1,700 cities as well as the development of weapons of mass destruction that have indeed been used for killing. Of course they would want to monitor the third rock from the sun...and monitor us much more closely after the spies in the neighborhood became aware of our development of rockets such as the V-2 used by Germany to attack England, fancy electronics such as manifested by high-power radar, and nuclear weapons. Putting these observations together would strongly suggest that primitive Earthlings, though previously confined to Earth, would be able to leave for the stars within perhaps 100 years, providing they don't destroy themselves first. It is interesting that the only location in the world in July of 1947, at the time of the Roswell Incident, where one could study all three of these technologies, was southeastern New Mexico. Man's first atomic bomb was tested at Trinity Site on the White Sands Missile Range, New Mexico, on July 16, 1945. White Sands is also where we were testing dozens of captured German V-2 Rockets, and where we had some of our best radar systems to track the rockets, which often didn't go where they were expected to go.

It should be noted that there is no reason to assume that the aliens who abducted Betty and Barney popped over from Zeta 1 or 2 Reticuli just before the abduction. In the first place, there are many excellent reports of huge "space carriers" or mother ships running from 0.5 to 1.2 miles long and capable of carrying many much smaller "Earth Excursion Modules" (analogous to the Lunar Excursion Module, which was small, but launched from the Earth on the huge Saturn 5 rocket) such as the one into which Betty and Barney were brought. In the second place, there is no reason to say there haven't been local monitoring, refueling, or rest and relaxation systems within the solar system. Some would like to believe that we are the Crown of Creation and there is nobody else nearby. It is much more likely that we, with a technological history of only thousands of years in a multibillion-year-old neighborhood, are as ignorant of our surroundings, outside our local solar system, as are the gorillas in a nature preserve in Africa.

Some critics have been quite upset because they can't find any reason for aliens to come to Earth and certainly no evidence of "trade routes." Who is trading with whom? In a paper Stanton wrote many years ago, he suggested 26 reasons for aliens to come to Earth. Is there anything about Earth that is unique? We are clearly the only planet in the solar system having most of its surface covered with water. We are the only planet in the solar system that has an atmosphere clearly indicating much biological life, cities, construction, and developed "civilization." As it happens, Earth is also the densest planet in the solar system: A typical cubic foot of Earth weighs more than a cubic foot of any other planet in the system. It should be noted that the density implies more dense elements here than on any of the other planets. These include such metals as gold, uranium, tungsten, rhenium, osmium, and platinum. These are not only very heavy elements per unit volume, but they have very special properties: some with very high melting points, some with great strength at high temperature, some are very corrosion-resistant, and some have very special electrical and nuclear properties.

Just 100 years ago the primary use for uranium was to provide yellow glazes for china plates. Now it is, of course, the basis for a major nuclear power and weapon industry. We also have a number of so-called rare earths such as dysprosium, gadolinium, erbium, europium, neodymium, cesium, and so on, which many people have never heard of, but have very special properties of use in the electronics and nuclear industry. There are titanium and zirconium, which were hardly used at all a century ago, but zirconium and hafnium, a chemically similar element, are very important in the nuclear industry. The piping and cladding in the Navy nuclear reactors are almost all made of zirconium alloys because of its very low neutron absorption cross-section and excellent corrosion resistance. Hafnium has a very high neutron absorption cross-section, and is used for control elements.

We also know, from studies of the composition of the stars using systems for analyzing their composition, that heavy elements are rare in the universe. We are all aware that there were many migrations on Earth to obtain gold and other precious elements. Much commerce in the world many hundreds of years ago was to trade spices and silk. Look at the cost per pound of antibiotics and other biological substances such as Vitamin B-12, and poisons and products made from creatures of the sea and from soil microbes. There have been many reports of "unidentified submerged objects" seen rising from the ocean; perhaps they have been mining the oceans for both minerals and substances from sea creatures. More than a million carats of diamonds were recovered from the ocean near Namibia in Africa. There are loads of metallic nodules at the bottom of the ocean with high concentrations of manganese, copper, and cobalt.

It is also of interest to note that our solar system has many mineral-laden asteroids with relatively high levels of expensive metallic elements. Serious thought is being given to mining them. We may not be the first. As we move into space, we may be considered a threat to "their" mining claims.

We now know enough about genetics, recognizing how little we knew even 50 years ago, to know that many diseases have a genetic basis, and that there is a huge variety in genetic material from different races. It would take a great deal of sampling to get any idea regarding the frequency of various genetic diseases (or special beneficial genes) in Earthlings. About one in 10,000 males, for example, has hemophilia, one of many genetic diseases.

This is noted because it is not unreasonable to expect an advanced civilization, where beings live very much longer than we do, to control reproduction. What if a supernova exploded not too far away and damaged a great deal of our genetic material? It should not be surprising that sperm was taken from Barney and that a "pregnancy" test was done on Betty. Many other abduction reports indicate that this extraction of genetic material is going on. As we do more and more to destroy Earth's environment, and therefore our natural habitat, perhaps these extraterrestrial biological crews are harvesting our genetic material to protect it from extinction.

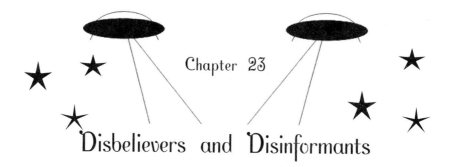

Chapter 23

Disbelievers and Disinformants

It should be no surprise to anybody that the Hill case in general, and the star map work in particular, have been attacked, sometimes viciously and almost always irrationally, by the small group of nasty, noisy, negativists making up the UFO debunker community. Generally, debunkers use the four basic rules of debunkdom:

1. What the public doesn't know, I am not going to tell them.

2. Don't bother me with the facts, my mind is made up.

3. If one can't attack the data, ignore it, and attack the people instead.

4. Do one's research by proclamation; investigation is too much trouble and most scientists and journalists won't know the difference anyway.

Clearly, if there is reasonable evidence that the Hills were abducted by aliens, then Earth is indeed being visited. Not only is Man not alone, but we are not at the top of the heap as we yearn to believe we are. Aliens finish the job that Polish astronomer Nicolaus Copernicus started in 1543 when he concluded that the Earth wasn't the center of the universe, the sun was. His book was banned by the Catholic Church for 300 years and Giordano Bruno was burned at the stake for later agreeing with him. Furthermore, if Earthlings have been abducted by aliens, the government must certainly know about it because of all their radar and satellite monitoring of the planet. Most of this data is classified and inaccessible to most scientists.

The general complaints about UFOs are that there is no evidence (as long as we are willing to ignore all the large-scale scientific studies, the multiple witness radar visual cases, the thousands of physical trace cases, the pilot sightings, and the highly censored government UFO documents), that you can't get here from there, it would take too much energy and too much time, and the speed of light limitation means we will forever be on our own. The SETI specialists, of course, must insist that no one is coming here, but there is intelligent life sending radio signals using technology so much like ours that we can receive and "translate" them, but we will never visit each other. There are, of course, some very respectable ancient academics and fossilized physicists who were convinced that man would never fly except with a balloon, that there is no way to put anything in orbit around the Earth because it would take far too much energy, that a rocket to the moon would have to weigh a million, million tons, and so on, ad nauseum. Some academics think they are so smart that they know what to expect in the actions of visiting aliens. In the case of astronomers, they seem to believe that visitors would want to speak with them. Frankly, if one was looking for insight into the behavior and motivation of aliens, astronomers would hardly be at the top of the heap with regard to motivation and behavior: perhaps psychiatrists such as Dr. Simon, or psychologists or social workers (such as Betty), lawyers, doctors...people whose profession deals with thinking beings, no matter how different. Astronomers certainly cannot be expected to have such expertise, dealing as they do, with activities that involve Mother Nature, but hardly involve intelligent beings.

Some professionals still tell Stanton, "Look, you are a physicist, don't you know that Einstein said that nothing can go faster than the speed of light? Therefore, just to go to Zeta Reticuli, even at the speed of light, would take at least 39.2 years, if you ignore the large amount of time during which one would accelerate to the speed of light." These people want to pick and choose about Einstein. He also showed us that as one gets close to the speed of light, time slows down for the things moving that fast. It would take a little more than 20 months, pilot time, to go a distance of 39 light-years at 99.9 percent of the speed of light, and about six months at 99.99 percent of the speed of light. Yes, we physicists, using huge accelerators, make particles that go that fast. Mother Nature produces cosmic ray particles that go that fast and faster. Furthermore, at 1 G acceleration (21 miles per hour per second), it only takes about a year to get close to the speed of light.

It is almost funny to look at the absurd reasoning of the negativists. Dr. John William Campbell, professor of mathematics and astronomy at the University of Alberta, "proved" in 1941 that the required initial launch weight of a chemical rocket able to get a man to the moon and back would have to be a million, million tons. He assumed a single stage rocket limited to 1 G acceleration, required that the rocket provide all the energy, and that the only way to slow down upon return to Earth would be with a retro rocket. The Saturn V rocket that launched the Apollo spacecraft weighed only 3,000 tons. It was, of course, multi-stage, and not limited to 1 G acceleration. It used the Earth's atmosphere to slow it down on return, as well as using the moon's gravitational field to provide some of the energy to get it there. We launch to the east, from near the equator, to take advantage of the Earth's rotation (almost 1,000 miles per hour), and always use cosmic freeloading for our deep space probes. Because Campbell didn't know anything about aeronautics or astronautics, his conclusion as to the required initial launch weight was too high by a factor of 300,000,000. Obviously, ignorance can lead to very wrong conclusions, despite having a Ph.D.

In 1926, Dr. A.W. Bickerton, professor of physics and chemistry at Canterbury College in New Zealand, had "scientifically" shown to the British Association for the Advancement of Science that it would be impossible to give anything sufficient energy to get it into orbit around the Earth. He noted that the best explosives can only release one tenth as much energy per pound as an object in orbit needs. He made two seriously wrong assumptions. First, there are chemicals that can be combined, such as hydrogen and oxygen, that provide more energy per pound of propellant than any explosive, and can release their energy out the back of the rocket, using a nozzle, rather than in all directions. Second, what he had shown was, roughly speaking, that it takes the energy of 10 pounds of propellant to orbit one pound of payload. There is little benefit from placing the propellant in orbit. Furthermore, if one uses staged rockets, the second one starts at the velocity produced by the first, and the third one begins at the final velocity of the second.

Equally wrong, and for much the same reason (false assumptions about the process), Dr. Simon Newcomb, one of the top American astronomers of the 19th century, had shown in a "scientific" paper published on October 22, 1903, that it would be impossible for man to fly in a vehicle other than with a balloon. This was just two months before the first flight of the Wright brothers. Newcomb, when so informed, supposedly remarked, "Perhaps a pilot, but never a passenger." The Wright brothers were two bicycle mechanics who conducted loads of experiments to evaluate lift and drag and the effects of changing many different parameters.

Based upon all of these cases, it should not be surprising that astronomers have been so reluctant to accept the notion of alien visitors, interstellar travel, and alien abductions. Throughout the years, they have made many false claims about various aspects of astronomy, no less ufology. Astronomy, by its very nature, doesn't involve intelligent behavior of other beings. For example, astronomers claimed that the sun was less than 50 million years old because they had no idea how it could produce the energy it does. Nuclear fusion wasn't really understood as the energy production process of the stars until about 1938. We now know that the sun is at least 4.5 billion years old. Astronomers claimed that there was only one galaxy, until a big debate in the 1920s. It turns out that the visible universe is about 13 billion light-years across—vastly greater than they had assumed. They claimed that rocketry and manned rockets were impossible. They were flat out wrong about the atmosphere of Venus (supposedly a tropical paradise), now known to have a sulfuric acid atmosphere hot enough to melt lead. They were also wrong about the surface of Mars having always been dry as a desert.

The problem actually goes much deeper. Many astronomers have claimed that there is no evidence for UFOs. Looking more carefully, one finds no basis for these claims. These astronomers never refer to the large-scale scientific studies that present the evidence they claim doesn't exist. The largest study ever done for the United States Air Force, "Project Blue Book Special Report 14," has 240 charts, tables, maps, graphs of data, and so on, for about 3,201 sightings. The work was done by engineers and scientists at the highly respected Battelle Memorial Institute in Columbus, Ohio, under contract to Project Blue Book (the Air Force's unclassified study of UFOs), which was closed in 1969. There are quality evaluations, categorizations, and statistical analyses of **unknowns** vs. **knowns**. Briefly, it was found that 21 percent of the sightings could not be explained. These were completely separate from the 9.5 percent listed as "Insufficient Information." They found that the better the quality of the sighting the more likely it was to be listed as an unknown. Furthermore, they found that the probability that the unknowns were just missed knowns was less than 1 percent based on six different observables, such as apparent color, size, shape, speed, and so on.[1]

In 13 books by UFO debunkers (three of these by astronomers), there isn't even a mention of this vital source, even though all the authors were aware of it. Dr. Carl Sagan claimed that there are interesting sightings that aren't reliable, and reliable sightings that aren't interesting, but no sightings that are reliable *and* interesting...exactly the opposite of the facts. Dr. Donald Menzel, a Harvard astronomer, claimed "All unexplained sightings are by poor observers"; this despite the fact that he had, according to his correspondence, a copy of Project Blue Book Special Report 14.[2] Of course, he might have been influenced by the fact that he had done highly classified work for the CIA, NSA, and 30 companies, and was probably a member of the Majestic 12 Group controlling classified UFO research.

The late Philip J. Klass, who was for many years the noisiest of the anti-UFO negativists, had, of course, attacked the Hill case. He often almost ludicrously claimed that there were no UFO sightings for which he couldn't find a prosaic explanation. The claim was even quoted in his obituary. He ignored all the sightings (more than 600) that couldn't be explained in the Air Force's Project Blue Book Special Report 14 and the more than 35 cases that couldn't be explained by the University of Colorado in the Condon Report.[3] And he neglected to explain the 41 investigated in detail by Dr. James E. McDonald in his 1968 Congressional testimony,[4] and the more than 700 unknowns of *The UFO* Evidence.[5] Of course, Klass didn't mention Blue Book Special Report 14 in any of his five anti-UFO books, though he was well aware of it from Stanton's Congressional testimony in 1968 and at lectures Klass had attended. In his 1966 book, *UFOs Identified*, he explained the Hill case away as a plasma phenomenon related somehow to ball lightning. In his book *UFO Abductions: A Dangerous Game*, he explained the Hill case away as only a shared fantasy stemming from Betty's dreams that she recounted over and over again while Barney read newspapers or watched television. He cited tape recordings of Betty's abduction that Dr. Simon had played for him. In comparison to Barney's terror, he stated that Betty's voice was calm, as if she were describing a trip to the local supermarket.[6] He apparently had not read John Fuller's description of Betty's terror in *The Interrupted Journey*, or listened to Betty's intense emotional outbursts as she relived the abduction on the hypnosis tapes. Instead, he added, "The ETs were familiar enough with earthly gadgets to know how to operate the zipper on Betty's dress. But they were completely baffled by the fact that Barney's teeth were removed, while Betty's were firmly anchored." He apparently did not know that the Betty's zipper was badly torn and discolored in the area where her captor's hands had come in contact with it. Or, that the dress has undergone several scientific analyses in an attempt to determine the cause of its degradation and ruin by a pink powdery substance (see Chapter 24).

He certainly provided one of the silliest star map challenges at a debate he and Stanton had on the stage in an auditorium at Trinity University in San Antonio, Texas. On stage he walked over to Stanton's table and flashed a sheet of paper with a bunch of dots on it saying he wanted to do a scientific experiment that would undoubtedly show that Betty Hill could not have accurately remembered the star map. He wanted the coauthor to look at it for a few minutes and then draw it later on. Stanton refused, pointing out how this was not a scientific experiment. One Website promoter claimed that he refused the test for unknown reasons. The reasons were simple and straightforward:

* Stanton Friedman is not Betty Hill. They have different perceptions, memories, and learning styles.

* Betty had been carefully conditioned, under controlled circumstances, by a world-class hypnotist/psychiatrist to remember accurately whatever happened onboard the craft, and then to draw the map after the session if, and only if, she could remember it accurately. Stanton had no instructions from a hypnotist and was in front of hundreds of observers.

* Betty recalled the map as having a three-dimensional appearance, certainly not true for a sheet of paper.

* Betty recalled the different lines on the map as being heavy trade routes, light trade routes, and occasional visits. There were no lines on what Klass handed Stanton.

One of the most unexpected attacks on Fish's work came from a surprising source: Allan Hendry. Hendry was, for a number of years, the primary field investigator for Dr. J. Allan Hynek's Center for UFO Studies. His primary education was as an artist with a strong interest in astronomy. His wife was an astronomer. He authored the book *The UFO Handbook: A Guide to Investigating and Reporting UFO Sightings* in 1979, and he published an article in *Fate Magazine*, later picked up and changed a lot by *OMNI Magazine*, which was slicker and had a much larger circulation. His basic contention was that an article in an astronomy journal by French astronomer Dr. David Bonneau, had shown that Zeta 2 Reticuli was a double star! But Fish had supposedly shown that all the pattern stars were single stars and amenable to stable planetary orbits. If Zeta 2 Reticuli was a double, that called into question all of Fish's work. Stanton contacted Hendry and determined that he was referring to a footnoted reference indicating "unpublished data." Unpublished work, after all, has not been subjected to peer review. When asked if he had contacted Bonneau about this reference, he indicated that he had not. Later, Bonneau indicated that neither star had been shown to be a binary or double! The original thought that one might be was the result of an artifact of the newly developed instrumental technique for determining duplicity, "speckle interferometry." They had even given it a name: "Mickey's ears." It took a while to breathe a sigh of relief, especially because *Omni Magazine* had claimed that Hendry had used the term "hoax" about Fish's work and the Hill case. He hadn't, and made that clear in a statement he later released. But the damage was done, and some uninformed people still point to Hendry's early work as proving that the Zeta Reticuli explanation was bunk.

It is of some interest that Dr. Carl Sagan, who has probably done more than any other scientist to interest the public in extraterrestrial intelligence, has attacked UFOs in several venues. In the outstandingly successful television series, *Cosmos*, he briefly discussed UFOs and the star map. The series has now been seen in 60 countries by more than 600 million people. It was a nine-minute segment in episode 12 of *Encyclopedia Galactica*, first broadcast on December 14, 1980. Speaking of the Hill case, Sagan said:

> They had observed, so they said, an unidentified flying object. It seemed to follow them for miles. After a time the lighting patterns on the UFO changed. It appeared to land. It blocked the road, preventing them from driving on. They said they saw mouthless creatures approaching who were not exactly human....At this point the story becomes still stranger. They lost all recollection of what happened in the next few hours. But weeks later, they recalled some details and discussed the experience with others. Just 26 months later, under hypnosis, they reported that a UFO had landed and that the crew had emerged. They were captured, they said, and then taken aboard the craft. That was the story.

This neglects the report to Pease Air Force Base the day after the experience, the report to NICAP, numerous discussions about the many details recalled without hypnosis, and the simple fact that there were many months of separate, weekly sessions of hypnosis—not the one session implied by Sagan. They had both used binoculars; there were the scuffed shoes, the damaged dress, the spots on the car, and the two rows of windows....Though the night was clear, *Cosmos* reported that the windshield wipers were running. Sagan depicted the Hills as staggering out of the car like absolute fools beckoned by a light, but with no beings around. Not only did he get the basic story wrong, but he misrepresented the star map, not surprising in view of his earlier letters to *Astronomy*.

Sagan held up a drawing in which a number of points were connected by single, straight, solid lines, and said, "She was shown a strange window through which she could see a glowing pattern of dots connected with lines. It was, they told her, a star map displaying the routes of interstellar travel. Here is what Betty said it looked like." What he held up is *not* what Betty said it looked like. Her drawing had two large circles with five curved solid lines between them. Sagan then brought another point and line drawing into view, noting that it "had been widely publicized by UFO enthusiasts." He didn't note that some were scientists, such as Stanton, and that the attacks came from UFO un-enthusiasts. Then he got rid of the lines. They were irrelevant because "These particular stars are selected from a large catalog. Our vantage point in space is also selected to make the best possible fit. If you can pick and choose from a large number of stars viewed from any vantage point in space you want, you can always find something resembling the pattern you are looking for." This is total nonsense, as Dickinson pointed out in an overview, *Zeta Reticuli Update*, published in 1980 when he was editor of *Star and Sky Magazine*. Space is three dimensional, and the stars are where they are—not where one would like them to be. And there was nothing arbitrary about the choice. Sagan, as might be expected, made no mention at all of the work of Marjorie Fish, though he was well aware of it, nor of the huge effort that went into building a host of models and reviewing them from different directions.

Stanton Friedman and Marjorie Fish (holding an alien bust she sculpted).
Courtesy of Stanton Friedman.

Sagan took another swipe at UFO abductions in general, and the Hill case in particular, in a very widely read article in *Parade Magazine* on March 7, 1993. Because Stanton had visited him at his home on December 1, 1992, prior to his lecturing at Cornell University, Sagan sent him an advance draft of the article. The two had been classmates at the University of

Chicago for three years, and had been infrequently in contact since then. Stanton responded to the draft with a 10-page single-spaced critique noting that Sagan's description of abductions in general and the Hill case in particular were way off the mark.

In an earlier letter he had noted that Sagan's insistence in the discussion of "reproducibility as the essence of science" was also way off the mark. Stanton pointed out that yes, reproducible, controllable experiments and observations—the first type of scientific activity—are certainly important to science, because they can be published and then presumably duplicated by others. However, the second type is also science: when one can't reproduce, but can only predict certain events to be scientifically observed (such as eclipses). They can be predicted, but not arbitrarily reproduced. The third kind involves events that can neither be controlled nor predicted, but scientific measurements *can* be triggered by such stimuli as noting a major solar storm with a radiation detector and then launching a prepared balloon with a block of nuclear emulsion to measure the energy and number of charged particles emitted during the storm. (This was done at the University of Chicago when Sagan and Stanton were there.) Seismographs can be deployed and readings taken after an earthquake to determine the magnitude, location of the epicenter, acceleration at the surface, and displacement of roads and buildings. The fourth type of scientific activity is the most relevant. These are events involving unexpected observations by untrained personnel of events involving intelligence (such as automobile accidents, airplane crashes, bank robberies, rapes, and so on). Here, eyewitness testimony can be crucial, and scientific methodology may be used to measure skid marks, blood alcohol levels, DNA samples, brake lining thicknesses, and so on. We can be certain that about 40,000 Americans will be killed in automobile accidents each year, even if we can't determine what will happen to which car, where, or when. We can use science, after the fact, to provide much useful data. Obviously UFO sightings fit into this last category of events.

Courts have long since had to learn how to evaluate testimony whether by experts on fingerprints or blunt trauma, or by just plain witnesses. That is why there are prosecutors and defense attorneys. One must be far more accurate in describing a bank robber (height and weight to 20 percent just isn't good enough), but estimates of velocity including zero miles per hour, vertical soundless flight, right angle turns without exhaust or visible external engines don't have to be either reproducible or terribly accurate to separate the wheat from the chaff. The statistical cross comparison between unknowns and knowns in Project Blue Book Special Report 14 is of particular interest here. The fact that, based on six different characteristics, the probability that the unknowns were just missed knowns was less than 1 percent, is of special importance.

The star map was also the focus of an attack from The Amazing Randi, a noted magician and busy member of the Committee for the Scientific Investigation of the Paranormal (CSICOP)—now known as the Committee for Skeptical Inquiry). Sagan was also a member, along with Klass, science fiction writer Isaac Asimov (also a UFO debunker), and other skeptics. Randi discussed the Hill experience in his aptly named book *Flim Flam*. He writes, "It was immortalized in John Fuller's book *Incident at Exeter*." Hardly! There are all of 6.5 pages about the Hill case in *Incident at Exeter* but 350 in Fuller's *Interrupted Journey*. Randi says, "It seems evident that Mrs. Hill saw the planet Jupiter, talked her husband into believing it was a UFO, and then imagined she had been taken aboard and made to forget the experiences, which she remembered only after a dream of the supposed event kept recurring. But when she had her story in full bloom, Betty Hill was able to suddenly recall—three years after the event—that she had seen a navigation map in the control room and she sketched it for posterity. This map is one of several said to support the Hill claims."[7]

The reader will recognize that this is a totally inaccurate, false, and misleading description of the Hill case. Both Betty and Barney observed the UFO through binoculars. Sketches of what they saw are in *The Interrupted Journey*. A report of the sightings was made very soon after it took place. The sessions with Dr. Simon lasted a period of several months—suddenly recalled? Betty didn't use the term "navigation map," and who says she was in a control room as opposed to medical examination room? After all, there are many kinds of maps. We travel a great deal and use city maps, state maps, country maps, and even a globe. The latter wouldn't be of any help in finding a street address in a big city. But it could, for example, be very helpful in trying to plan a trip to Hong Kong and then Dalian, China.

Now Randi did admit to the existence of Marjorie Fish, but surely doesn't get the story straight. He says, "She somewhat rearranged the viewpoint and redrew a section of the constellation Reticulum to conform." Everybody who has examined the models and the publications should recognize that she did an enormous amount of work building more than 25 accurate 3-D models of our local galactic neighborhood, some with as many as 250 stars. Although the base stars are indeed in the constellation Reticulum, the others are not. Randi doesn't seem to know that a constellation is a relatively small region of the sky whose stars are at nearly the same angular direction from the Earth, but in most instances, not close to each other at all. Randi, as did Sagan, shows totally misleading sketches with points and single-dashed, straight lines. There are no curved lines or solid lines.

There have been many claims by interested readers attempting to refute Fish's explanation. One Charles Atterberg wrote many letters and worked on coming up with another set of stars, but without having the solid basis found by Fish. His claims were discussed by Dickinson in "Zeta Reticuli Update." A Soviet astronomer claimed that the base star had to be Alpha Centauri; no adequate basis was given. A German researcher, Mr. Joachim Koch, has been insisting that the alien actually showed Betty a map of the solar system and that several of the points of light were asteroids. This more or less ignores the fact that asteroids change their locations very rapidly compared to stars. Also of course the aliens were on planet Earth and not on one of the asteroids. No good basis is provided for why certain asteroids were chosen and others ignored. It is interesting indeed that nobody built detailed 3-D models; none provided new scientific information or a solid basis for their conclusions as did Marjorie Fish.

One of the most recent and least scientific attacks on UFOs in general and abductions in particular can be found in the 2005 book *Abducted: How People Come to Believe They Were Kidnapped by Aliens* by Dr. Susan Clancy, Harvard University Press. She is a psychologist with a Ph.D. from Harvard and had been involved in other published papers, such as "Memory Distortion in People Reporting Abductions by Aliens" and "Psychophysiological Responding During Script-Driven Imagery in People Reporting Alien Abduction," as well as appearing in the Peter Jennings ABC UFO show on February 24, 2005, and on a Larry King UFO show on July 6, 2005. She seemed, on TV, to be claiming that all abductions could be explained away as sleep paralysis, and seemed ignorant of the contrary evidence, such as people who report that they have been abducted from many locations outside their bedrooms and while driving, working, walking, and so on. In the book, she explains that she had been working on false memory syndrome in people who may have been sexually abused as children. There was a serious problem of determining whether or not they really had been abused. She thought UFO abductions would be much easier because: "Here was a group that had repressed memories, but the memories would be much less painful to hear about than memories of childhood sexual abuse."[8] She provides no data to substantiate this claim. Dr. Simon had noted to Dr. James E. McDonald that the intensity of emotion in some of the hypnosis sessions of Betty and Barney Hill exceeded that of any soldiers with whom he had worked. Clancy goes on: "Even better, alien abductees were people who had developed memories of a traumatic event that I could be fairly certain had never occurred.... I needed to repeat the [false memory] study with a population that I could be sure had recovered false memories. Alien abduction seemed to fit the bill." She would use the same techniques as with the sexual abuse people, and addressed the "corroboration issue since it was certain the event hadn't happened." Surely a scientific study about UFO abductions can't start with the presumption that such events have never happened. She got her study population by advertising in newspapers, "seeking 'subjects': Have you been abducted by aliens?" Considering that the late Dr. John Mack (1929–2004), a psychiatrist, who as a full professor at Harvard, had worked with more than 200 abductees (some of whose experiences are discussed in detail in his books, *Abduction* and *Passport to the Cosmos: Human Transformation and Alien Encounters*), one might have thought she would, if not investigating any abductions herself (she did not), have dealt with nearby people whose cases had been investigated by an outstanding professional. They would have, in general, been much closer to Boston than most of the subjects helped by Budd Hopkins of New York or Dr. David Jacobs of Philadelphia as discussed in their books. She makes the truly incredible claim that "I believe I have read every account of alien abduction ever published and just about everything that social psychologists, psychoanalysts, postmodernists, journalists, physicists, biologists, and ex-military personal [sic] have to say about them. I've watched nearly every American movie and TV show ever made about aliens." Her text clearly indicates that this claim is nonsense.

Here is a typical example of her inaccuracy. Speaking of a meeting with a number of abductees, she says: "Highlight of Saturday evening was a conversation with two brothers from Manchester, New Hampshire. These men were relatively well known abductees who had written a book about their experiences. One night in the late 1960s they had been canoeing on a lake in Maine and had seen weird lights across the water. A few years later one had fallen down an elevator shaft at work; he'd suffered brain damage, developed epilepsy, and became severely depressed." The simple fact of the matter is there were four people involved, not two; the event took place in August of 1976, not in the 1960s. The book *The Allagash Abductions* was written by an experienced abduction investigator, engineer Raymond Fowler, and not by the brothers. It was based on data obtained independently from each of the four. The book is not even referenced, though there are 146 items on the reference list.

She apparently feels she has exhaustively studied the UFO phenomena as well as abductions: "So far as we know, there is no evidence that aliens exist. You can't disprove alien abductions. All you can do is to argue they're improbable." No argument is given. She herself supplies a good reason for her disregard of facts and data: "The confirmatory bias—the tendency to seek or interpret evidence favorable to existing belief or reinterpret unfavorable evidence is ubiquitous, even among scientists." She certainly provides ample evidence of her own such bias. In a holier-than-thou fashion she states, "We don't accept the alien abduction explanation because there is no external evidence to support it." Strangely, she never discusses the several thousand physical trace cases that Ted Philips has collected from more than 70 countries. He has visited several hundred such sites. About 16 percent of these cases involve reports of strange beings. There is no mention of the missing time cases wherein other people confirmed the missing time. She never mentions Marjorie Fish's star map work, though she does mention the Hill case.

She says, "Betty had spotted a bright star that seemed to be pursuing them. Nervous, they had turned off the main highway onto narrow mountain roads, arriving home two hours later than expected." If she had read *The Interrupted Journey*, she would have known this was simply false. It does sound similar to the *Parade Magazine* article by Carl Sagan, which makes a similar false claim. The fact is that they had both observed the large object at close range with binoculars. They had observed its strange motions, certainly not star-like. It crossed in front of the moon. There was a double row of windows through which Barney recalled seeing strange beings, without hypnosis. We have never heard of stars that look and act that way. She says, "Betty was a long time believer. Betty was a fan of science fiction movies featuring aliens (she had seen *Aliens from Mars*), and had already read Donald Keyhoe's *Flying Saucers Are* Real." These comments are not only not backed up by any evidence, but are total fiction. Betty read the book *after* the experience, had *not* been a sci-fi fan, nor seen that movie. Clancy says "Betty and Barney were advised to undergo hypnosis in order to determine whether, as she firmly suspected, they had been abducted." Their purpose was to see if Dr. Simon could get rid of Barney's ulcers and to find out what had happened during the missing time. Clancy claims, again falsely, that Barney had watched "The Bellero Shield," a science fiction story on *The Outer Limits* television program, and that his drawing of the alien is based on what he saw. But he and Betty were far too busy to watch science fiction movies. An artist we know watched "The Bellero Shield" and indicated that the alien's features did not match drawings done in response to Barney's description, and was also much taller. Obviously Clancy had not done her homework. She clearly hadn't examined John Fuller's papers at the Boston University archives not far from Harvard. These contain many comments from Dr. Simon.

Further demonstration of Clancy's "confirmatory bias" and her ignorance is given by her claim, "Betty and Barney Hill—the mom and pop of abductees...became famous in abduction history in the 1960s because, in the words of Seth Shostak, an astronomer associated with the SETI Institute 'They were more or less Mr. and Mrs. Front porch.'" They were the *first* abductees; there was no real history before them. Furthermore, an interracial couple in New England in 1961 could hardly be considered Mr. and Mrs. Front Porch, whatever that is supposed to mean. In addition, no reasonable person could consider Seth Shostak an expert on any aspect of ufology, much less abduction. His books and papers do maintain that there is nothing to UFOs—without any references to the many large-scale scientific studies published by scientists who, unlike Shostak, have done in-depth investigations.

Clancy also never mentions the large-scale scientific studies either. She almost discusses the Condon Report with this strange comment: "In 1969 the National Academy of Sciences sponsored a study of all the available evidence on UFOs. The Conclusion 'On the basis of present knowledge the least likely explanation of unidentified flying objects is the hypothesis of extraterrestrial visitations by intelligent beings.'" These comments are from a brief summary by the NAS at the beginning of the 965-page Condon Report. The NAS did *not* sponsor the study. The U.S. Air Force did. The NAS Review Committee did no investigation itself—not one single case. Buried in the volume is the simple fact that, according to a UFO subcommittee of the American Institute of Aeronautics and Astronautics, 30 percent of the 117 cases studied by Condon's people could not be identified.

Clancy also misrepresents the facts of the Travis Walton abduction case as reported in *Fire in the Sky* and discussed by him in *UFOs ARE*

Real. She claims that Kenneth Arnold in his very well-known June 24, 1947 observation of nine UFOs, was flying his own private jet, even though it has always been correctly described as a propeller-driven airplane. She really blows a fuse about Roswell, getting dates and events wrong with this proclamation: "The evidence for a crashed spaceship and dead extraterrestrials was entirely anecdotal, consisting of first-hand reports from people who wished to remain anonymous, and even more tenuous second- and third-hand reports (so-and-so told what's-his-name who told me that such-and-such really happened 30 years ago)." For one who claims to have read just about every book ever written about UFOs and seen every movie, this is pure nonsense. Stanton's book *Crash at Corona: The Definitive Study of the Roswell Incident* (with Don Berliner) and numerous other books name loads of witnesses. The Fund for UFO Research assembled a 105-minute documentary *Recollections of Roswell* with first-hand testimony from 27 Roswell witnesses, all of whom are named.

It is not at all surprising that a blurb on the back cover of the book, by Elizabeth Loftus, one of the leaders of the false memory syndrome group, says "*Abducted* is an enormously brave, smart, original book." It is indeed brave and original to spout so much false information.

Dr. Michael Shermer, editor of *Skeptic Magazine*, as might be expected, truly admired Clancy's book. He is quoted on Amazon.com with "Clancy offers a superb contribution to our understanding of human memory, mental anomalies, and how the mind works." This qualifies as another example of confirmatory bias. Shermer, in a TV documentary on Roswell, said he would believe in aliens when he was shown an alien body. Nobody else's personal testimony that they have seen aliens would be good enough for him.

Another fairly new book, focused almost entirely on the Hill star map, is *Interpretations of an Alien Star Map* by William McBride, published in 2005, by PublishAmerica (Baltimore). It is small, having only 131 pages. There is no bibliography and no index. There are a host of stars noted, a primer on astronomy and star names, constellations, and discussions about Marjorie Fish's work on Joachim Koch's solar system explanation, the James Randi map, Charles Atterberg's study, and McBride's own interpretation. McBride seems to think Betty and Barney were abducted, but that Marjorie Fish's work is badly flawed. Unfortunately, he starts from the premise that because, according to Einstein, things can't go faster than the speed of light, 39 light-years is much too far away, and he looks for other stars much nearer, with the very bright star Sirius (only 8.6 light-years away) as the base star. He seems to be unaware that as one gets closer to the speed of light, time slows down so that from a pilot's point of view, long distances don't take very long. Also, the fact that the base is 39 light-years away doesn't mean that the aliens had to come here directly from there. Stanton once lectured at 25 colleges in 35 days in 15 states without being home at all between the time he left and finally returned. McBride also ignores the fact the Fish's pattern of stars are all in a plane, that Zeta 1 and Zeta 2 Reticuli are the closest (to each other) pair of sun-like stars in the neighborhood, and that they are a billion years older than the sun. He acts as if she limited her attention to sun-like stars, ignores or is unaware of Dr. George Mitchell's comments about the accuracy of her work, and uncritically cites some of Sagan's objections. He tries to make the size of the circles on the map for the base stars an indication of the size of the star. Because stars, even the largest, are so much smaller than the distances between them, there is no way size and distance can be represented to the same scale.

McBride used star catalogs on the Internet, but doesn't reference his specific sources. He does note that there are many different star catalogs. Past history tells us that, until the Hipparcos satellite distance data was available, most distance data was not very accurate at all. But McBride gives distances to three decimal places, such as 8.163 light-years. He seems to think that aliens would live on planets near any type of star: old, new, hot, or cold. He points out, as if it mattered, that planets have not yet been found around many of the pattern stars, implying that there are none there. The fact of the matter is that with our current very crude extra-solar planetary detection techniques, planets the size of Earth cannot yet be detected; only quite large gaseous giants usually orbiting very close to a star can. Absence of evidence is not evidence for absence. Microscopes couldn't observe viruses until recently either, yet they were there.

A distant object on the ground or in the sky doesn't represent much of a threat, but abductions imply a loss of control, something which some people *can't* handle.

Many persons willing to allow for the possibility that some UFOs are alien spacecraft are still unwilling to accept the notion that Betty and

Barney or anybody else has been temporarily abducted and returned, often with a missing time experience. Perhaps anybody who accepts that some Earthlings have been abducted also has to admit that he, or somebody he knows, may be abducted, which makes it a very personal and threatening. If a signal is received from a transmitter in a solar system 1,000 light-years away, there is hardly a threat. If, on the other hand, aliens are abducting Earthlings from down the street, that is another matter entirely. Denial is a very common response to threatening situations: "No, my teenagers can't be taking drugs," and such.

Clearly the zealous attacks on UFOs in general, and abductions in particular, seem to be based on bias, ignorance, laziness, and unwillingness to look at all the evidence. Perhaps a graduate student at Harvard in the psychology department could do a study on "The Resistance Amongst Certain Academics to Alien Visitations and the Notion of Abductions by Aliens." There is certainly plenty to work with, not the least of which were the very nasty and irrational attempts to get Dr. Mack stripped of his tenured professorship at Harvard. Mack fought and won that battle, though his interview with the Peter Jennings TV people remained on the cutting room floor.

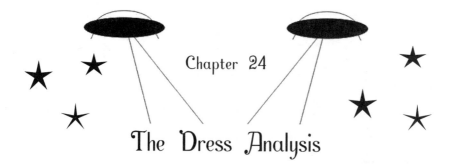

Chapter 24

The Dress Analysis

On the morning of September 20, 1961, Betty removed the blue acetate sheath dress that she had worn on the drive home from Canada, folded it, and placed it in the back of her closet. It was a new dress that had never been laundered, and she had worn it only one other day during the trip. She recalled that she had handled the dress in this manner because it was torn and required mending before she could wear it again. For some unknown reason, Betty then forgot about her dress, and did not retrieve it from her closet until the spring of 1964 (her accounts vary from "a few days later" to "during the hypnosis"; her memoirs indicate that the dress was recovered in 1964). She explained that she remembered the dress only after her amnesia had been lifted by Dr. Simon. She returned home and retrieved it from her closet. It was then that she noticed that it was coated with a pink, powdery substance. Puzzled, she examined the rest of her clothing, but found that only the blue dress had been damaged.

Betty initially placed the dress in her trash receptacle, but then rethought her action and decided to hang it on her clothesline. The pink powdery substance blew away, but the dress was badly stained, especially along the hem, around the sleeves, and along the top of the bodice. As Betty examined the dress, she noticed that a section of the stitching in the hem had ripped, causing it to hang down, and the lining on the right side of the dress was torn from waist to hemline. Additionally, the dress lining was torn from the bottom of the center back zipper to just above the hem stitching. She remembered the difficulty that her captor experienced as he attempted to open her zipper, and found a 2-inch tear in the stitching along the top right side. On the left side of the upper zipper was a 1-inch tear in the thick zipper fabric, separating the metal teeth from the fabric. This fabric is extremely durable and almost impossible to tear

Betty's dress, showing torn lining and zipper.
Courtesy of Kathleen Marden.

through human strength. Betty thought that the dress evidence might be significant to her case, so she decided to hang the dress in her closet.

In 1977 Betty met Leonard Stringfield, director of public relations at Dubois Chemicals in Cincinnati, Ohio. He offered to have an elemental analysis done on samples from the dress by the chemistry department at the University of Cincinnati (the university had not been apprised of the dress's history or ownership). Betty received a letter from Stringfield dated August 30, 1977 regarding the elemental analysis of the powder. It stated that the x-ray fluorescence test revealed sulfur, sodium, chlorides (possible trace evidence), and silicon (possible trace evidence). The spectroscopic emission test discovered large amounts of sodium, aluminum, iron, and magnesium on the fabric. There were also small amounts of manganese, calcium, and silicon. He commented, "The powder substance is strange in relation to its inorganic elemental content. It appears to be high in undetermined organic hydrocarbons."

On May 11, 1978, the chemist wrote the following report regarding additional testing that he had conducted on Betty's dress swatches:

1. Direct analysis by x-ray fluorescence shows no difference in elemental composition of the front and back samples.

2. One-inch squares, from each the front and back, were digested with a concentrated nitric acid-sulfuric acid mixture. The resulting solutions were analyzed by emission spectroscopy (a much more sensitive test than test 1). Traces of copper, calcium, silicon, magnesium, and iron were found, but were essentially the same on both front and back samples.

3. Several methods, which normally bleach or discolor cloth dyes, were tried in an attempt to duplicate the color change observed on the dress. These were (a) chlorine bleach (both wet and dry), (b) acid treatment, (c) base treatment, (d) ultraviolet light (one day exposure), and (e) sunlamp (one day exposure). None of these produced any effect similar to the color change observed. The closest was acid treatment, which bleached it white, but not red. This is interesting, even though it is not a negative result. It shows that whatever the reaction was, it was not the usual discoloration reactions that I know. It is too bad that the white [actually pink] powder was not saved because it had to fall into certain chemical classifications and we probably could have found out what it was.

In 1980, a mainstream scientist whose identity must remain anonymous obtained an analysis on Betty's dress. He reported that "the dress fragment was absolutely clean, containing no pollen or spore microorganic material." Other researchers agree that the material is most likely biological.

BP-Amoco analytical chemist Phyllis Budinger, M.S., became interested in Betty's dress after she read articles about the Hill abduction in the September 2001 issue of the MUFON journal. She has 35 years industrial experience in chemical analysis, specializing in troubleshooting and problem-solving. She contacted Kathy regarding the possibility of obtaining dress samples for chemical analysis. Betty, who was initially reluctant to part with additional dress swaths, accepted Budinger's proposal and eventually contributed five fabric swaths for analysis. Budinger conducted extensive tests on the dress from November of 2001 through October of 2003. Numerous surface infrared spectra were acquired from every square centimeter of the front and back surfaces of all fabric swaths and on particulate materials on two swaths. Solvent extraction using hexane followed by water was also conducted, as well as microscopic analysis. Budinger concluded that the stained areas were coated with a biologically derived material of mostly protein and a small amount of natural oil. This protein biologically attacked the fiber and dye in the stained samples of Betty's dress, resulting in discoloration and a looser fiber structure. The evidence shows that this did not derive from Betty's bodily emissions, but came from an external source. The stained area's pH level revealed a higher acid content than did the control fabric sample. She also found microscopic debris materials such as house dust, pet hair, and assorted clothing fibers that one would expect to find on a dress that had hung in a closet for nearly 40 years. There is indication that the biological substance originally contained moisture. This moisture, Budinger speculates, served as a nutrient for a natural biological growth.[1]

Infrared spectral analysis provided evidence for the presence of foreign materials on the swaths consistent with protein-type materials. These materials apparently permeated the exterior surface of the stained swaths, but caused less damage to the interior surface of the dress fabric, indicating that it originated from an outside source.

Phyllis Budinger conducted an analysis of the hexane and water extracts from three stained dress swaths and one control swath. Compared to the hexane extracts, the stained materials produced significantly more water soluble material than the control. Also, for both solvent extractions, less material was extracted from the control sample compared to the stained samples. The trace levels of hexane extracts contained natural oil. The more abundant water extracts were most interesting; they primarily contained low molecular weight protein degradation products. When agitated, the discolored swaths produced foam, which suggested the presence of substances with detergent-type properties (not soap). The degraded protein products with highly polar functional groups would do this. The control sample did not foam—the small amount of material extracted from the control was probably not enough to generate foaming. All four extracts fluoresced under ultraviolet light. Although the dry dress fabric did not emit an odor, a "putrid" odor was noted in the water used for the soluble extracts of the stained samples. This odor reminded the researcher of the odor resulting from a bacterial attack on water bottoms from fuel service tanks. In all, the chemical analysis supported Betty's account of the event.

Budinger has offered several speculations regarding the origin of the pink powdery substance and discoloration on Betty's dress. Betty noted a foul odor in the craft's interior that she could not identify, although it somewhat resembled marigolds. It is possible that the captor's respiratory emissions and natural oily eliminations were deposited on Betty's dress upon contact. Betty recalled that her captors grasped her tightly around the sleeves of her dress as they escorted her to the craft. This would account for the heavy pink discoloration on the dress sleeves and the upper portion of the bodice. The dress fabric at the top of the zipper is also stained where an occupant struggled to remove Betty's dress, causing tearing. There is also discoloration on the hem area of the dress that could have resulted from contact with the occupants when Betty violently resisted being taken aboard the craft. The right dress sleeve was totally permeated with the biological material on the side where the dress lining was torn from waist to hem, indicating that her captor may have affected a tighter grip around Betty's arm during her struggle. As an alternate explanation, Budinger speculated that some of the material may have transferred from the top of the dress to the skirt when Betty folded it and placed it in her closet. She further speculates that the slightly acidic moist substance on the dress, deposited by the captors, served as a nutrient for a natural biological growth of bacteria, mold, or mildew. This natural biological growth left a pink powdery residue and discolored the dress.

Phyllis Budinger enlisted the expertise of noted biochemists who conducted DNA analysis on the fabric samples. Additionally, a blood sample was obtained from Betty. The analysis found three DNA deposits of note: The first was alpha-proteobacterium from the upper left sleeve of Betty's dress. This is bacteria found in soils and water, and could have been deposited on the dress sleeve when it was thrown in a heap on the craft's floor during Betty's physical examination. The second DNA sample was taken from the dress front and could have been a human, mouse, or cow fragment, but not from Betty. The third, taken from the upper sleeve underarm was human, and of probable African extract. It seems logical to speculate that Barney had escorted Betty at sometime during the weekend and his DNA became deposited on her dress. No unidentifiable DNA samples were found on the stained swaths. Therefore, the researchers could not confirm DNA evidence from other than Earthly sources.

Additional bioassay tests were conducted by the Pinelandia Biophysics Laboratory of Michigan. Preliminary experiments were conducted to determine whether or not the pink-stained dress fabric would induce a higher degree of energy in water than the blue unstained sample. It did. Next, the water in which the dress samples had been soaked was applied to wheat seed on moist paper disks in petri dishes. The researchers observed that the water from the stained sample germinated the wheat seed at an unusually fast rate. At the end of seven days they were significantly larger than the control sample from Betty's blue dress swath. An additional experiment used three samples: a plain water control sample, water obtained by soaking the pink-stained fabric, and water obtained by soaking the blue control fabric. The seeds germinated at the same rate in the plain water and the blue water. However, the pink-stained fabric water caused the seedlings to develop at a significantly faster rate than the controls. The researchers noted that it is extremely difficult to alter seedling development in plants.[2]

The scientific analyses on the pink discolored and blue control swaths taken from the dress that Betty Hill wore on the evening of September 19–20, 1961, have produced some very interesting results. They seem to point to the presence of an anomalous biological substance that has permanently altered the physical characteristics of Betty's dress. Considering the dress's history, there is no valid reason for it to be covered with biological material. It seems to be an indirect result of her UFO encounter. Additionally, the extensive damage to the zipper, hem, and lining indicate that Betty's dress underwent extreme stress during a period of missing time following a close encounter with an anomalous craft and its occupants. Betty reported that her abductors touched her on the sleeve area and zipper area where there is the greatest concentration of pink discoloration. This fact lends credence to her account. It could not have been caused by perspiration because it was concentrated on the outside of the dress. These factors, taken together, also indicate that Betty could not have intentionally damaged the dress for testing. Some of these later tests were not even in existence when the dress was originally analyzed.

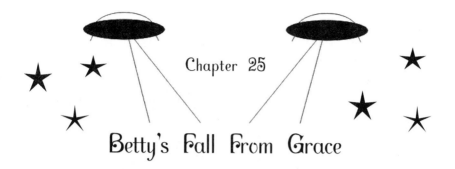

Chapter 25

Betty's Fall From Grace

Marjorie Fish's star map investigation brought renewed scientific interest to the Hill abduction. For many people in the scientific community it represented tangible, measurable evidence that the abduction hypothesis was highly probable. This gave new life to Betty's commitment to solving the UFO mystery. She began to conduct her own experiments and even found a possible UFO "window" in East Kingston, a small farming community that she passed through on her travel between Portsmouth and Kingston. It is topographically an area of rolling hills, swamps, three lakes, and a river. Two sets of power lines traverse from east to west through the north and south ends of town. About 10 miles south of town lays the Clinton-Newburg geological fault zone, and there is a small geological fault line 2 miles south of her observation area. A large quartz deposit lies beneath the surface and extends northeast of the adjacent town of Exeter, N.H. In the 1970s it was a very rural area, spotted with dairy, horse, chicken, and turkey farms. The side roads were narrow and winding, and some had not yet been paved.

East Kingston had developed a reputation as a hot spot for UFO sightings. Many residents had observed anomalous craft hovering over the railroad tracks that cut through the center of town. Residents reported that disks had landed on the railroad tracks and in several fields throughout town. Two well-educated, conservative, highly reliable neighbors had observed landed UFOs in their pastures. One night in 1975 when Betty was passing through East Kingston on her way home from her mother's farm, she was buzzed at close range. The UFO rose up from the ground and approached her vehicle, hitting it with beams of light that blistered the paint and punctured small holes through two layers of metal. She observed a lit row of windows and figures looking out at her as the craft hovered above her vehicle. Quickly, she grabbed her camera and snapped a picture of the disk-shaped craft and its humanoid occupant. The photograph reveals a shadowy figure at the window and a possible stereotypical gray alien emerging from the right side of the disk (see page 214).

Kathleen Marden, former MUFON International Director John Schuessler, and Betty Hill at a MUFON symposium.
Courtesy of MUFON and Kathleen Marden.

Betty suffered a long history of failing health following her 1961 UFO encounter. By 1975 she was experiencing crippling episodes of chest, back, and head pain accompanied by tremors, profuse sweating, and loss of balance. Her physician referred her to an oncologist, suspecting that she had cancer, but the test results were negative. However, she was not able to return to her position as the supervisor of intake and referral for the New Hampshire Division of Welfare, and was forced to retire at age 56.

Betty's retirement gave her the opportunity to focus primarily on UFO studies. She became easily accessible to the public, who were reporting their own sightings to her. At times, she went out with them to areas where they were observing unconventional lights in the sky, and she began to document their reports. This resulted in an extensive database, but the sightings, often without directional data, estimated size, time reference, or detailed description, were never investigated. Betty was beginning to accept the mere description of lights in the sky as evidence that a UFO had been observed, without the careful, sometimes tedious investigation and documentation required as acceptable standards of evidence. Many of her witnesses were reporting multiple sightings, and she too had observed more than one UFO. She was growing frustrated with NICAP's cautious stance regarding multiple sightings and its refusal to take these reports seriously. Out of her frustration, she formed a loosely structured group of sky watchers who reported directly to her, which she named her "silent network." She lowered her standards of evidence from scientific investigation to the subjective reporting of observational data, and she began to publicize her findings that large numbers of UFOs were flying in squadrons through New Hampshire's skies.

The UFO community that had previously given Betty support began to publish highly critical reports about her observations. The media, on the other hand, became fascinated by Betty's fantastic, highly credulous reports, and this became the focus of their coverage. John Fuller wrote several cautionary letters to Betty in an attempt to dissuade her from disseminating subjective information to the public. In one message he wrote, "I just want to emphasize that, for your own credibility, that anything that cannot be documented or substantiated by others can do severe harm to your reputation, regardless of whether or not you believe it to be true. *The Interrupted Journey* would not have been widely read at all without the restraint placed in writing it. It is also important for you to realize that even if you believed something subjectively, that is not good enough—we all can deceive ourselves at times."

In a lengthier letter Dated January 8, 1979 he wrote the following excerpts:

> As you know, Betty, I am very cautious about the whole UFO situation, and always have been. Your story with Barney interested me and the editors of *LOOK* because of the cautious approach that you and Barney took to the subject, and your careful analysis of your own experience. You let the facts speak for themselves and were careful not to extrapolate beyond them.
>
> As you know, any conclusions drawn from observations of this type of phenomenon must be drawn only on data that can be confirmed by careful observation and supportive verification, and then only on a tentative basis because there is no hardware at hand. Even photographs have to be examined with a grain of salt.

Regardless of the intensity of your belief, it must still be backed up by cautious and competent witnesses or it works against you very seriously. You may be right. But if you are, you've got to seek better confirmation than the type we encountered that evening.

Because your first encounter was so well documented, it served as very good evidence of the existence of UFOs. Unless you can back up any current happenings with equal caution, you can seriously harm your position, and that of those who found your original evidence so interesting because of your reserve and caution. Betty, it is very important to do so, if only for protecting your own reputation.

Seemingly undaunted by Fuller's cautionary letters, Betty surged ahead, enlisting the help of friends, military observers, and UFO enthusiasts in her undying effort to prove the existence of UFOs. She carried a movie camera and shot footage of anything that appeared to be unconventional. Later the footage was analyzed, but the results were inconclusive. She had the movie film frames made into slides and did numerous presentations, which engendered additional criticism toward her within the UFO field. Betty's slides showed discoids with unconventional, often blue lights, and spheroids of various colors. One slide showed an orange-white spheroid projecting a red beam upwards. Another appeared as a huge maraschino cherry with a white stem-like structure protruding from an area of gaseous discharge (see page 148). In other photos, balls of light seem to descend along a blue beam and part in various directions. Another photo, taken at dusk, shows a glowing landed disk on legs in a triangular arrangement silhouetted against adjacent trees. Another photo showed landing trace marks made by the alleged UFO.

In response to the lambasting that Betty was taking from observers who had witnessed her misidentification of conventional aircraft and lights as UFOs, witnesses were writing in support of her sightings. One wrote as follows:

On October 23, 1979, [name deleted], who is producer of my television series, went up to Portsmouth, N.H. to do a preshow interview with Betty Hill and later accompanied her to a railroad track site in East Kingston. He reported seeing a large saucer-shaped "mother ship" on the tracks, saw it lift off to let a train pass underneath, heard it "beep," and claims that it directed a red beam of light at the car, causing Betty to floor the accelerator and take off down the road.

On the evening of January 3, 1980, I and my son, while riding with Betty, saw a faint pink glow down between the tracks. We also observed a railroad signal at one of the nearby intersections change repeatedly, even though no train was approaching. On the same evening, we also watched strobe-lit flying objects that moved across the sky, hovered, converged on one another, and periodically vanished—yet did not exhibit the telltale characteristics of helicopters, weather balloons, or any other aerial objects with which I'm familiar.

On February 18, 1980, [name deleted] and I, while riding around the area with Betty Hill after dark, first saw two small "headlight-sized" objects down between the tracks. On the next pass across the tracks, we saw a large pyramid of lights (actually large circles of what looked like backlit, smoked Plexiglas) that appeared on the tracks minutes after a train had passed by, and which blinked on and off in random sequences for close to an hour.

On the night of April 5, 1980, while Betty stayed behind in her car with a couple visiting from Massachusetts, three of us walked down to the railroad crossing and observed flickering (strobe-like) white and red lights and a white glowing area, and a brightly lit red ball which rolled across the tracks, up along the trees on the right, and off into the sky.

Regards,
Thomas Elliott

An opposing opinion was expressed by a prominent UFO investigator who is not mentioned in Betty's memoirs as having accompanied her to her UFO observation area. He expressed the following opinion:

My own feelings regarding your "UFO" sightings remains unchanged based upon my personal conversations with those who have accompanied you on UFO hunts. Aircraft lights, street lights, and lighted trailers, etc., but UFO to you only because you are not able to identify them as such. Perhaps they are wrong, but I have a very high regard for their judgment. The recent articles in the newspapers about the "UFOs" sighted at your secret site further support their reports to me. I personally think that you're going out of your way to get publicity for such "sightings" gives the whole subject a bad look and I have asked those who have witnessed phenomena which you call UFOs to write a full report of just what is going on in order that your sightings are dealt with in a more objective way. The reputation that you have acquired from a possible initial experience may give undue weight to additional claims by you.

In retrospect, it seems that Robert Hohmann's recruitment of Betty to participate in psi experiments precipitated a feeling of confidence in her ability to contact UFOs. Her participation in continuing psi experiments under the observation of an experimental psychiatrist and a college professor cemented her faith in her ability to do so. To some observers, she seemed to have the ability to sense when a UFO would appear in the sky. One observer who accompanied her to the East Kingston UFO observation site hinted of a possible abduction. Betty had also reported this incident to Kathy during an interview session. He wrote:

> We were coming back from watching the saucer on the railroad tracks. I was driving on the road to Exeter, it was dark. We were going up a slight short rise in the road, and where the rise peaked and we should naturally have nosed down, we were suddenly airborne, floating, drifting, sort of, a very eerie feeling, not like you see in a car chase in the movies, but a slow-motion drift in space. It was such a sudden and drastic change, a dislocation really, that I lost my sense of balance and sense of time. The closest I can come to describing it is an earthquake. There is an instant, utter dislocation. That night on the Exeter Road, I don't know how long it lasted, but quite a while. Long enough where Betty and I exchanged a long, puzzled look. It felt as if time had slowed, or expanded. We did touch down, yes, after that long, weird drift. And we didn't like, hit the road hard, with sparks flying, but gently, gradually, like a very light aircraft landing, not bumping as would be expected when a heavy car hits the road after being airborne.

Betty recalled that they became airborne in Kensington, approximately 2 miles from Exeter, and touched down at the outskirts of Exeter. This occurred within 3 miles of the *Incident at Exeter* sighting by Norman Muscarello and Police Officers Eugene Bertrand and David Hunt on September 3, 1965. The 18-year-old Muscarello was hitchhiking along route 150 in Kensington when he spotted a round or oval-shaped silent object approach an adjacent farmhouse and hover a few feet above it. The anomalous object was lighted with four or five bright red lights and was approximately 80 to 90 feet in diameter. When the teenager was unable to gain entry into the farmhouse, he flagged down a passing car and was whisked to the Exeter Police Station. He was pale, shaken, and barely able to talk. The station notified Officer Bertrand, who had taken an earlier report from a woman who was paced by a UFO only a few feet above her car. He and Muscarello returned to the Kensington field, but the UFO was not in sight. However, as they entered the field to investigate the incident, the craft slowly rose from behind some nearby trees and approached the two, coming within 100 feet of them. They fled for the cruiser and Bertrand called for backup. Soon Hunt arrived on the scene and the three watched the silent craft drift away over the trees (see *Incident at Exeter* by John G. Fuller).

Betty's fall from grace ultimately transpired because she surrounded herself with UFO enthusiasts who looked to her for guidance. Many were not trained observers or UFO investigators, but friends who supported her belief that they were observing extraterrestrial craft, even when they were misidentifying conventional aircraft. Some of their descriptions seem to support the conjecture that at least a few of their observations were anomalous. Additionally, some of these observations were made by trained military observers and UFO investigators who confirmed that they had observed unconventional craft. Betty publicized this information because she thought she was contributing valuable information to the scientific community. What we must remember though, is Betty was not a scientist or a trained observer. After Barney's death, she turned away from careful, objective evaluation, and with subjective enthusiasm began to identify any lights in the sky as UFOs. In the end, it destroyed her credibility, not because she didn't observe or photograph UFOs, but because she failed to heed John Fuller's warnings.

By the mid-1970s, several alleged UFO abductions had been reported throughout the United States. Betty was instrumental in lending emotional support to several of the traumatized victims through phone calls, letters, and face-to-face visits. Nearly all of the abductions occurred at night, and several involved multiple witnesses. The director of investigations for the Aerial Phenomena Research Organization, Dr. James Harder, assisted Betty in the investigation of some of these cases, one of which took place near Manchester, New Hampshire, less than 60 miles from Betty's home.

Lydia (pseudonym), the young wife and mother of a 3-year-old son, was returning to her Goffstown home from her job in Manchester, N.H., at 2:45 a.m. on November 2, 1973. She had just met a coworker for a cup of coffee, gassed up her car, and started the drive home, usually less than 30 minutes away. As she passed through Pinardville on the outskirts of Manchester, she spotted a large, bright, star-like object in the sky that flashed red-, green-, and blue-colored lights. In Goffstown, she drove through the center of town and took a left, continuing along Route 114. At this point, the object, which had been traveling on her left, shifted to a position directly ahead of her over the highway. A brilliant light blinded her temporarily, forcing her to use her forearm to shield her eyes. When she lowered her arm she could see a humanoid figure through the craft's window. She experienced a tingling sensation throughout her body and she soon realized that she was becoming unable to move. She heard a soft, reassuring voice tell her not to be afraid, that she would not be harmed.

Approximately 1 1/4 miles beyond this point, she saw a cemetery and two houses on her right. The UFO swooped down in front of her car again and she felt dizzy, as though she was being pulled toward the craft. Suddenly, her car began moving at a high rate of speed apparently under the control of the UFO, and she heard a high-pitched sound that hurt her ears. Through the window she could see the humanoid's large, grayish, elephant-skinned head and two large, dark, slanted eyes peering down at her. She did not notice ear flaps or a nose but observed a slit-like mouth that turned down at the corners. Her description was remarkably similar to Betty's and Barney's, although she could not have known about the elephant-like texture of the occupant's skin or its down-turned mouth.

In her attempt to escape from the craft, she made a sharp left turn into a driveway and ran from the car toward the house. When the residents opened the door, Lydia fell onto the floor, holding her hands over her ears, and screaming uncontrollably. When she had regained her composure, she asked the homeowners to phone the police. This call was logged at 4:31 a.m. Within minutes, Goffstown Police Patrolman Jubinville arrived and the four exited the house in an attempt to observe the UFO. They saw a light behind the house above the treetops, but could not confirm that it was the object that Lydia had observed. The residents photographed it using a Polaroid camera, but the picture showed only a spot of light in the sky. They phoned a tracking station on the other side of the mountain, but they could not see it. Lydia believed that it was too low in the sky at this point to be visible.

Later, Lydia underwent hypnotic regression to reconstruct what had occurred during the apparent period of missing time. She recalled the face of the craft's occupant peering through the driver's side window of her vehicle. She was parked on a gravel road and recalled a pond, a bubbling brook with a rocky bottom and grass along its edges. There was a pile of cord wood and a gravel pit. She was abducted and underwent a physical examination immediately after her first occupant sighting and had been released moments prior to her second sighting.

Coincidently, she was wearing a blue dress similar to the one that Betty wore on the night of her abduction. Immediately afterward, she laundered it and left it at her mother's house, never to be worn again. Betty noted that Lydia's dress was damaged by a pattern of seven small holes just above the waist. This pattern was repeated on the lower back portion of the dress, reminding Betty of the type of degradation that had ruined her own dress.

Betty and Lydia had a cordial relationship, visiting and communicating via telephone and letters for the next several years. When Lydia's case drew local media attention, she and her husband moved to another state to escape recognition. Her family has successfully avoided the media circus, the intrusive investigations, and the dissemination of skeptical misinformation that Betty and Barney were forced to endure. Betty believed that, as was she, Lydia had been abducted, and the similarities between their experiences were remarkably similar. She had passed Betty's litmus test by providing the secret information about the occupants that had not been made public.

Another alleged abduction investigation that Betty participated in occurred on October 27, 1975, in Oxford, Maine. Two young men, David and Glenn, were relaxing in the trailer that they shared at approximately 3 a.m. when they were startled by a loud crashing sound. They rushed outside and observed a police car and a fire truck racing by without lights. Moments later, they traveled by in the opposite direction. For reasons unknown, the two men decided to drive to a nearby lake. Along the route, the car suddenly seemed to ascend and traveled to the right, although the steering wheel was being held straight. Although their car should have bumped along the rough road, their ride was remarkably smooth. They observed a blinding light that began to pulsate with green, blue, and red colors. A silent craft that appeared to be the size of a football field hovered only 20 to 30 feet above them. Their car was pulled sideward and they lost consciousness. When they awoke, their previously locked doors were unlocked, and their windows had been rolled down. They observed three more UFOs before they arrived at David's parents' home at 6:35 a.m. They were dazed and unable to regain their equilibrium or to speak fluently. Their hands and feet were red, swollen, and tingling, and their teeth were loose and sore. Both had orange circles around their eyes that later faded to a pale amber. Glenn's tongue was coated with a brown substance and there was a brown ring around David's neck. Two days later, David reported that a tall man in business attire knocked on his door. When he opened it, the man threatened him, "If you know what's good for you, you'll keep your mouth shut."

David was referred to a nearby medical doctor who was trained in the use of hypnosis. Under hypnotic regression he told of being abducted and given a physical examination in a circular gray room. His captors were approximately 4 1/2 feet tall with hairless, pale-white skin and large slanting eyes, a very small nose, and no visible ear flaps. He could not remember the appearance of their mouths. They had three webbed fingers and a thumb. A bright light was shining on him, and although he attempted to strike out at his captors, he was completely under their control. A large, square, lighted machine on a movable extension arm was placed over his chest. Then, his body was examined from head to toe and samples were extracted, similar to Barney Hill's exam.

Nearly a year later, Betty received a letter from Shirley Fickett from the International UFO Bureau, the primary investigator, informing her that on September 11, 1976, David's doctor had received a frightening visit from a man in black. Betty visited him at his home and subsequently wrote the following report:

> I called Dr. H and visited at his home regarding his contact with the MIB on September 11, 1976. Dr. H said that his family had all gone out to a drive-in movie. He was not interested so he stayed at home. About 8 p.m. his phone rang and a man's voice said he was vice president of a UFO research group in New Jersey and understood that he was the one who worked with David, and he would like to discuss this case. The doctor invited him to visit. He put down the phone and went to the porch to turn on the light. The man was standing there, ringing the bell. [This is before the invention of the cell phone.]
>
> He invited him in and the man sat on the couch while the doctor sat on a chair across the room. He verified that the doctor had done the hypnosis, had the tapes of this, letters, and other materials about UFOs.

Then he said that he knew the doctor had two coins in his pocket—correct. He told him to take out one of them and to hold it in his outstretched hand. He told him to watch the coin, not him. He did this and saw the penny change to a silver color, then to a blue color, become hazy, indistinct, and vanish. The doctor said that this was a good trick, and now he asked him to bring it back. The man said that no one on this plane would ever see that coin again.

Next, he asked the doctor if he knew how Barney Hill died. The doctor said he had heard that he had a heart attack. The man said that this is right; they had taken his heart just as he had taken the coin. Then he said that Barney knew too much. [This information is incorrect. Barney died from a cerebral hemorrhage.]

Then, he told the doctor to get rid of all his materials about UFOs—the tapes, letters, and all books—to forget about UFOs. He went on to say that the information he had received about David was correct.

The man said, "My energies are getting low and I must leave." He had difficulty getting off the couch, walking to the door, and was staggering as he went down the stairs. He turned the corner, and was gone.

The doctor ran to the window to see where he had gone—no car. He saw a bright white flash of light beside the corner of the house, and the man was not there.

The man was described as about 5 feet, 6 inches tall. He was dressed as a funeral director—black suit, tie, shoes, white shirt, derby hat, and wearing dark gray kidskin gloves. He removed his hat, and his head was completely bald. His eyes were normal, although the doctor could not tell the color of them. He had no eyelashes or eyebrows and no facial hair. His skin color was a pasty white—very pale. His ears were small and were set lower on his head than ours. His mouth was a thin slit and he was wearing red lipstick. At one time, he rubbed his glove across his mouth and the lipstick came off on his glove. His nose was a small bubble type—no ridge or bone. His body structure seemed different. His clothing hung on him—his pants had a razor-sharp crease, and his legs did not fill them out when he sat down. His shoes were the same as we wear. He did not remove his gloves.

His voice was monotone. He used perfect, precise English, but he apparently did not understand the fine meaning of words. When he came to the end of sentence, his voice did not drop down—he just stopped talking.

I had taken the French publication *Ceux Venus S'Ailleurs* with me and the doctor pinpointed my alien as looking the most like the one he saw. Of course, this drawing is not very much like the actual ones that I saw, but it does have similarities.

We talked about Barney's death and the doctor knows now that he died of a stroke—he was relieved about this and relaxed some. He was very uptight about his experience.

He erased the tapes and then burned them, burned or got rid of all letters, books, etc. about UFOs.

During the mid-1970s through the 1980s Betty became thoroughly engrossed in the UFO field. She joined the UFO lecture circuit, traveling from conference to conference, spoke in regional lecture halls and at colleges, and was a frequent guest speaker at Pease Air Force Base. It was during these engagements that she met several individuals who told her of their own close encounters. Three of these contacts suspected that they had been abducted and agreed to permit Betty to investigate their claims. She arranged for a UFO investigator who was qualified to hypnotize them, studied their life histories, met their families, and maintained a close relationship with them. Simultaneously, she was confidentially discussing their cases with a psychiatrist who was cooperating in the investigation. As it turned out, each was afflicted by a major mental illness with accompanying psychotic delusions.

Then, as UFO abduction came to the forefront of popular culture through best-selling books and docudramas, hundreds of alleged abductees sought help from the well-known abduction investigators. Betty's past experiences with mentally ill alleged abductees were difficult for her. The hypnosis sessions that she had arranged were damaging to those whom she sought to help. The trauma inflicted by the recovered memories may have precipitated destabilizing episodes that required psychiatric intervention in some of her alleged abductees. Perhaps they would have suffered a psychotic episode without her intervention, but there is documented evidence that each was committed to a psychiatric hospital within months of undergoing hypnotic regression. These regressions were not conducted by a hypnotherapist with a background in psychology or psychiatry. Amnesia was not imposed, and Dr. Simon's professional methods were not adhered to. Information was the main focus, and there was little regard for the victim's emotional well-being, except by Betty. It seems that Betty not only blamed the hypnotist, but also took personal responsibility for the misuse of hypnosis and her failure to identify the symptoms of mental illness in her subjects prior to their hypnosis. This failure brought about a diametrically opposite shift in her investigation of abductees: Thereafter, she reassured suspected abductees that they had *not* been abducted, and dissuaded them from undergoing hypnotic regression.

In the early 1990s Betty was agonizing over the direction that the UFO field was taking in abduction investigations. She was outraged by what she perceived to be the misuse of hypnosis for the economic gain of a few at the expense of many. She argued that Dr. Simon's greatest fear was being realized. Prior to the publication of *The Interrupted Journey,* he had voiced his apprehension about the possible misuse of hypnosis in UFO abduction investigations. He feared that this extremely useful tool in the treatment of traumatic amnesia would ultimately be discredited, not because it was ineffective, but because it was employed by individuals less qualified than he. The ethical and psychological implications were profound.

In 1991, Betty had become so disillusioned by what she perceived to be the misuse of hypnosis that she publicly announced she was retiring from the field. When Kathy asked why she decided to drop out of public life, Betty responded:

Because there are too many kooks in the UFO field. Today's UFO investigators know too little about the UFO field. They accept fantasy as if it were reality and distort information to fit their purposes. In the old days, events of high strangeness were dismissed as pure fantasy or delusional thinking. Most of today's investigators are too willing to believe these high strangeness events. I have a name for them—psychological abductions. When someone tells me that they were abducted right through the roof of their house, I tell them, "Oh my God, how much was the cost of the repair?" People don't walk through roofs or walls or windows. People take bits and pieces of what they see on TV and incorporate them into UFO experiences. Of all of the abductions that I have personally investigated, in my opinion, only nine were true abductions. I think that many of the others [psychological abductees] have a feeling of complete powerlessness. A lot of them have undergone severe child abuse, but others are affected by the sick society that we live in. People are scared. They have lost their sense of security. They know that they have been told lies all of their lives—we're the biggest; we're the brightest; we're the greatest; we're the most powerful...and they're reacting to this. They are looking for a better world. They're hoping that the ETs are going to save the world, or save them.

Then, there is another group that I have worked with over the past 10 or 15 years; 50 percent of these people are mentally ill. Their mental illness begins with the delusion of a capture. I got involved in this area when medical doctors began to refer patients to me. They know me and know that I am a retired social worker. I have put parents and children into the state hospital, and have had to distinguish between mental illness and emotional problems. I had all of those years working with doctors, psychiatrists, and mental health people. After you get to know these people, you learn that they are having delusions about other things too. I had one woman who came to my house wearing a winter coat in the middle of the summer, complaining about how terrible the snowstorm was—how she had all she could do to get here. These people go into psychiatric treatment for 30 days, they get put on the right medication, and they bring me the arts and crafts they made while they were there.

Of the hundred or so people that I have investigated, some were mentally ill and having delusions, some had the wrong UFO investigators, some were hypnotized by the wrong people—the misuse of hypnosis—and some were just highly suggestible. They were part of the "me too" group. Then, there were the few who had real abductions.

Several UFO researchers have asked Betty if she later suspected that she and Barney were tracked through alien implants. She scoffed at the notion, stating that she would believe in alien implants when there was scientific proof that they existed. In her feistiest voice, she told Kathy, "I find tracking devices difficult to believe. Only psychological abductions have implants. No real abduction has ever had an implant. When people are abducted it has nothing to do with the person; they simply want to do some kind of test. So, they grab someone, get the results, and that's it. They can find us because they followed us home in 1961."

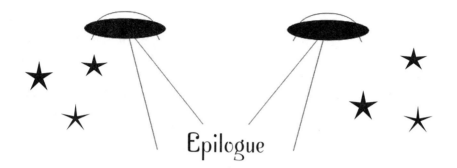

Epilogue

After Betty's retirement from the UFO field, she devoted more of her time to intellectual pursuits in the areas of archeology, social justice, genealogy, social psychology, ufology, and politics. Her thirst for intellectual stimulation and the acquisition of knowledge was lifelong. She researched and wrote her family's genealogical history, continued to write her memoirs, and became a frequent contributor of editorial comments to local newspapers. She expressed a liberal political agenda under the pseudonym "Feisty." Her solid ego, sharp intellect, and a terrific sense of humor served Betty well.

When Pease Air Force Base closed in 1991, many of Betty's closest friends were transferred to other bases. This closure marked a significant loss for Betty, who had participated in an active social life with her military friends. Suddenly, her Sunday morning brunches abruptly ceased, and her weekend excursions to the mountains or the seashore with close military associates halted. Life slowed down and Betty devoted more time to nurturing the lush English gardens that she had planted around her home. She was a nature lover who sought to care for her neighborhood's forest animals and to preserve their habitat in the city. Her pet fancy chickens drew the attention of neighborhood children, as did the abandoned felines that she fed and rescued.

She maintained warm relationships with many friends throughout the New England region, and always looked forward to their visits. She and her closest companion, Elaine Freiday, traveled to Europe together, and they were frequent visitors to New Hampshire's Indian Head Resort. Lanie, as she was called, operated a convalescent home for disabled veterans near Cape Cod, caring for soldiers who had never recovered from the psychological horrors of their war experiences. Although she outlived most of her contemporaries, Betty enjoyed the company of a wide array of younger friends. Those who loved, admired, and respected her often sought her advice on a variety of issues. She could converse intelligently on nearly any subject and loved to argue her social and political agenda with those of opposing viewpoints.

In 1993 Betty experienced another health crisis. Her long-standing abdominal complaints had developed into stomach cancer. A last-minute diagnosis saved her life but took 80 percent of her stomach. Fortunately there was no metastasis, and Betty made a full recovery.

In 1995, with the assistance of a close friend and Kathy, Betty wrote and self-published *A Common Sense Approach to UFOs*. She was no longer bound by the terms of her contract with Dr. Benjamin Simon and John Fuller, as they were deceased, so this gave her the opportunity to finally express her views in literary form. Because Betty was concerned about declining educational standards in America, she wrote to a 10th-grade audience. Her book was simply stated in "common" language, giving the reader the impression that they were seated in her living room listening to a monologue by Betty. Although the language and sentence structure were uncomplicated, she expressed a detailed journey through her 30 years of research in ufology, including her views on hypnosis, abductions, her silent network, her sightings, and her life.

At the turn of the century Betty's health began to decline again and she underwent surgery for a second cancerous tumor, unrelated to the first. Additionally, her long-term two-pack-a-day cigarette habit was having a deleterious impact upon her health. Those who expressed concern were subject to a lengthy defense of the benefits of cigarettes. By the time her lung cancer was diagnosed, her prognosis was poor. She endured chemotherapy and radiation treatment, briefly earning a remission status, but the malignancy was tenacious. By early 2004, it had metastasized to her brain and adrenals, generating a rapid decline in her condition.

With family and friends by her side she courageously awaited her fate. Often acquaintances half-joked, half-wished for extraterrestrial intervention. Although Betty insisted that she had been abducted only once and a deathbed visit was unlikely, a bizarre occurrence seems to have transpired in mid-June. Betty's daughter reported that Betty had retired on the living room sofa, the only comfortable location considering the fact that she had sustained a fracture to her upper humerus and a hairline fracture of her right wrist that afternoon. She was not able to recline without enduring excruciating pain from her cancerous tumor, so she slept in an upright position. Her daughter, an extremely light sleeper, who normally awoke whenever she heard Betty stir, retired to the adjacent bedroom with the door open, so she had direct sight of Betty. Without an apparent explanation, Betty's daughter slept soundly throughout the night, rising 1 1/2 half hours later than usual. The first thing she noticed when she checked on Betty was the absence of her splint and sling. The previous night the splint, held in place by an Ace bandage, had been tightly wrapped around Betty's forearm and hand. Now they were neatly placed on a chair 10 feet away from Betty's position on the sofa—an impossible task for Betty to have accomplished. The Ace bandage was still intact around the splint, as if they had been removed from Betty's arm without being unwrapped. The sling was neatly folded and placed on top of the splint.

At this point in the progression of Betty's disease, she was paraplegic with additional paralysis in her right arm. It would have been physically impossible for Betty to have removed, rewrapped, and folded her devices. Additionally, had either woman attempted to remove these applications, Betty would have screamed in agony. Neither individual remembered anything from the night in question.

Perplexed, Betty's daughter went about her morning routine of opening windows and unlocking doors. She was astonished to discover that the rear door, which she had deadbolted the previous evening, stood wide open. She was certain that she had closed and locked it. Then she noticed that the bolt was protruding from the door in a locked position. Could Betty have accomplished an impossible task in her sleep? Or could her daughter, who had never before sleepwalked, have carried out these uncanny occurrences?

But there was more. Betty's constant feline companion, the giver and taker of unbridled affection, suddenly feared Betty. She seemed unusually timid and skirted the perimeter of the living room, suspiciously eyeing Betty as she passed to her food bowl. The remainder of her day was spent in hiding, and this lasted for nine days.

Although this was not a good time for full investigation, Kathy attempted to find an earthly explanation. Both the interior and exterior environment of Betty's house failed to reveal observable evidence of alien intrusion. There were no landing traces, footprints, or odors to suggest UFO activity. Nor did neighbors observe unusual activity during the night. However, Betty's appearance and strength seemed to improve during the days following the uncertain event. This was witnessed by medical personnel, family, and friends, and recorded by Kathy. Betty's gray pallor suddenly became rosy, her mind clearer, and her pain level was significantly reduced. Her dull, glazed eyes took on their former sparkle, and she regained some strength and endurance. Possibly, this rapid improvement could be explained as a psychological effect or as a characteristic of the waxing and waning of cancer symptoms. However, that does not explain the sudden, uncharacteristic timidity in Betty's cat.

Whatever occurred, it did not effect a long-term change in Betty's health status. Within weeks she entered a rapid decline, and four months later she succumbed to metastatic lung cancer.

Her large funeral was attended by family, friends, hospice staff, and admirers. Two longtime friends reminisced to the mourners at the funeral service about their fond memories of Betty. The hospice chaplain, a Unitarian minister, spoke about Betty's wonderful sense of humor, her optimistic outlook on life, her genuine sense of caring, and her spiritual strength. Others mentioned that fame had not distorted Betty's sense of self. She was down to earth and unassuming. She was a fascinating conversationalist and extremely bright for her age.

Newspapers throughout the country carried Betty's obituary and articles about her UFO encounter, missing time, hypnotic retrieval, book, and movie. She had become a legend.

Following the funeral service, Betty was laid to rest next to her husband, mother, and father in Kingston, New Hampshire. An invitation-only reception was held at the Pond View Restaurant in Kingston near Betty's childhood home.

Betty lived her life by a lesson conveyed to her by a grade-school teacher: She said that each of us is like a speck of sand on a beach. Some are born closer to the water's edge, and others are born on the upper side of the beach, farther away from the tide. With each high tide, grains of sand are swept away into the ocean. Those at the water's edge are sometimes carried to the top, and those at the on the upper side of the beach are sometimes swept into the current by winds and storms. However, some of these grains of sand, whether carried by the tide or originating on the upper beach, escape being swept into the turbulent sea. It is those who go down in history. If Betty could have had her wish, she would have gone down in history as a groundbreaking social worker and a social and political activist. It was never her wish to go down in history as a UFO abductee. However, she was carried among those grains of sand that rose to the top, and unintentionally, she met her fate.

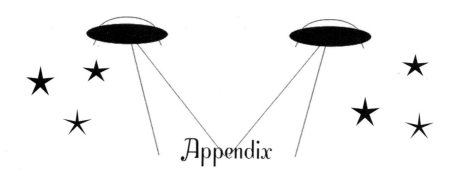

Appendix

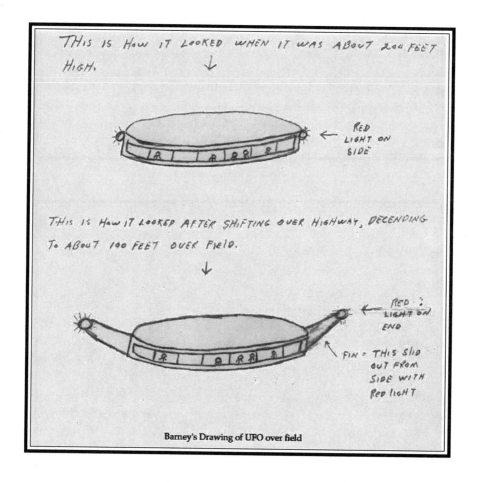

THIS IS HOW IT LOOKED WHEN IT WAS ABOUT 200 FEET HIGH. ↓

RED LIGHT ON SIDE ←

THIS IS HOW IT LOOKED AFTER SHIFTING OVER HIGHWAY, DECENDING TO ABOUT 100 FEET OVER FIELD. ↓

RED LIGHT ON END ←

FIN = THIS SLID OUT FROM SIDE WITH RED LIGHT ↖

Barney's Drawing of UFO over field

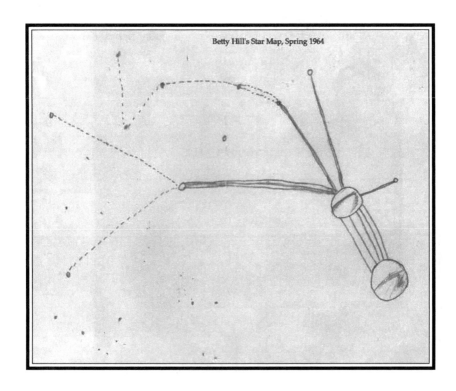

Betty Hill's Star Map, Spring 1964

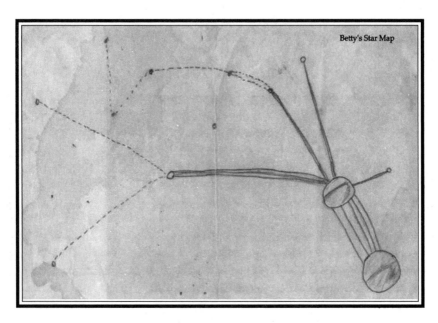

Betty's Star Map

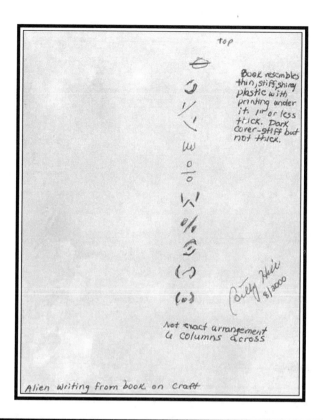

top

Book resembles thin, stiff, shiny plastic with printing under it. 1" or less thick. Dark cover-stiff but not thick.

Betty Hill 8/2000

Not exact arrangement 6 columns across

Alien Writing from book on Craft

CLASSIFICATION	(SECURITY INFORMATION when filled in)			

SUPPLEMENT TO AF FORM 112

ORIGINATING AGENCY	REPORT NO.			
100th Bomb Wing (M) SAC (DCOI)	100-1-61	PAGE 3	OF 3	PAGES

object. They continued on their trip and when they arrived in the vicinity of Ashland, N.H., about 30 miles from Lincoln, they again heard the "buzzing" sound of the "object"; however, they did not see it at this time.

Mrs Hill reported the flight pattern of the "object" to be erratic, changed directions rapidly, that during its flight it ascended and descended numerous times very rapidly. Its flight was described as jerky and not smooth.

Mr. Hill is a Civil Service employee in the Boston Post Office and doesn't possess any technical or scientific training. Neither does his wife.

During a later conversation with Mr. Hill, he volunteered the observation that he did not originally intend to report this incident but in as much as he & his wife did in fact see this occurence he decided to report it. He says that on looking back he feels that the whole thing is incredible and he feels somewhat foolish – he just can not believe that such a thing could or did happen. He says, on the other hand, that they both saw what they reported and this fact gives it some degree of reality.

Information contained herein was collected by means of telephone conversation between the observers and the preparing individual. The reliability of the observer cannot be judged and while his apparent honesty and seriousness appears to be valid it cannot be judged at this time.

PROJECT 10073 RECORD CARD — -8/12/70

Betty

	2. LOCATION	12. CONCLUSIONS
L	Lincoln, New Hampshire	☐ Was Balloon / ☐ Probably Balloon / ☐ Possibly Balloon
OUP -0100)1-0500Z	4. TYPE OF OBSERVATION	☐ Was Aircraft / ☐ Probably Aircraft / ☐ Possibly Aircraft
	X☒ Ground-Visual ☐ Ground-Radar	
	☐ Air-Visual ☒ Air-Intercept Radar	
*8	6. SOURCE	☐ Was Astronomical / ☐ Probably Astronomical / ☐ Possibly Astronomical
	Civilian	☒ Other Optical condition INSUFF
SERVATION	8. NUMBER OF OBJECTS	9. COURSE	☐ Insufficient Data for Evaluation / ☐ Unknown
	1	N	

OF SIGHTING Continuous band of lights at all times despite changes of .ngs seemed to appear fm main body. V shaped with red lights on tips; ppeared to extedn further. Appeared ried direction abruptly and dis- ...

COMMENTS: Both radar and visual sighting are probably due to conditions resulting fm strong inversion which prevaled in area on morning of sighting. Actual source of light viewed is not known but it has all characteristics of an advertising search light. Radar probably was looking at some ground target due to strong inversion No evidence indicating objts were due to other than natural causes.

IV 26 SEP 52) HILL CASE Folly hot cond.f Folls ...

:raft, Balloons, Airships, etc ———

er OBSERVATION DUE TO UNUSUAL OPTICAL IDITION RESULTING FROM ATMOSPHERIC CONDITIONS.

luation of Source Reliability PROBABLY GOOD.

lysis and Conclusions: BOTH THE RADAR AND VISUAL IGHTING ARE PROBABLY DUE TO CONDITIONS ESULTING FROM THE STRONG INVERSION WHICH REVAILED IN THE LINCOLN N.H. AREA IN THE MORNING OF THE SIGHTING. THE ACTUAL SOURCE OF LIGHT VIEWED BY THE WITNESSES WHO REPORTED THE VISUAL SIGHTING IS NOT KNOWN BUT IT ▬▬▬ HAS ALL OF THE CHARACTERISTICS OF AN ADVERTISING SEARCH LIGHT. THE RADAR PROBABLY WAS LOOKING AT SOME GROUND TARGET DUE TO THE STRONG INVERSION. THERE IS NO EVIDENCE WHICH ...... N INDICATE THAT THE OBJECTS

CLASSIFICATION

COUNTRY OF ACTIVITY REPORTING	REPORT NO. 100-1-61		(Leave blank)

AIR INTELLIGENCE INFORMATION REPORT

COUNTRY OR AREA REPORT CONCERNS	DATE OF INFORMATION		
United States	20 Sept 61		
ACTIVITY SUBMITTING REPORT	DATE OF COLLECTION	SRI STATUS (*If applicable*)	
100th Bomb Wing (M) SAC (DCOI) PEASE AFB, NEW HAMPSHIRE	21 Sept 61	SRI NO.	CANCELED/COMPLETE
PREPARING INDIVIDUAL	DATE OF REPORT	SRI NO.	
Major Paul W. Henderson	21 Sept 61		CANCELED/INCOMPLETE
NAME OR DESCRIPTION OF SOURCE	EVALUATION	SRI NO.	ACTIVE
Mr. & Mrs. Barney Hill 953 State St., Portsmouth, N.H.	F-6	ADDITIONAL INFORMATION ON (*Date*)	

REFERENCES (*BAIR Subject, previous reports, etc., as applicable*)
No previous reports.

SUBJECT (*Descriptive title. Use individual reports for separate subjects*)
Unidentified Flying Object

SUMMARY (*Give summary which highlights the salient factors of narrative report. Begin narrative text on AF Form 112a unless report can be fully stated on AF Form 112. List inclosures, including number of copies*)

On the night of 19-20 Sept between 20/0001 and 20/0100 Mr. & Mrs. Hill were traveling south on route 3 near Lincoln, N.H. when they observed, through the windshield of their car, a strange object in the sky. They noticed it because of its shape and the intensity of its lighting as compared to the stars in the sky. The weather and sky was clear at the time.

Report contained herein is IAW par. 15, AFR 200-2, dated 14 Sept 1959.

ADDITIONAL ITEM:

During a casual conversation on 22 Sept 61 between Major Gardiner B. Reynolds, 100th B W DCOI and Captain Robert O. Daughaday, Commander 1917-2 AACS DIT, Pease AFB, NH it was revealed that a strange incident occurred at 0214 local on 20 Sept. No importance was attached to the incident at the time. Subsequent interrogation failed to bring out any information in addition to the extract of the "Daily Report of Controller". Copy of this extract is attached.

It is not possible to determine any relationship between these two observations, as the radar observation provides no description. Time and distance between the events could hint of a possible relationship.

_____1_____ INCLS   2 cys

PAUL W HENDERSON
MAJOR   USAF
CHIEF COMBAT INTELLIGENCE

ORIGINATING AGENCY 100th Bomb Wing (M) SAC (DCCI)	REPORT NO. 100-1-61		PAGE 2 OF 3 PAGES

A. Description of Object
　1. Continious band of lights - cigar shaped at all times despite changes of direction.
　2. Size: When first observed it appeared to be about the size of a nickel at arms length. Later when it seemed to be a matter of hundreds of feet above the automobile it would be about the size of a dinner plate held at arms length.
　3. Color: Only color evident was that of the band of lights when was comparable to the intensity and color of a filament of an incandescent lamp. (See reference to "wing tip" lights.)
　4. Number: One
　5. Formation: None
　6. Features or details: See 1 above. During period of observation wings seemed to appear from the main body. Described as V shaped with red lights on tips. Later, wings appeared to extend further.
　7. Tail, trail or exhaust: None observed.
　8. Sound: None except as described in item.E.

B. Description of course of Object.
　1. First observed through windshield of car. Size and brightness of object compared to visible stars attracted observers' attention.
　2. Angle of elevation, first,observed: About 45°
　3. Angle of elevation at disappearance: Not determinable because of inability to observe its departure from the auto.
　4. Flight path & maneuvers: See item E.
　5. How object disappeared: See item E
　6. Length of observation: Approx 30 Min's.

C. Manner of Observation
　1. Ground -visual
　2. Binoculars used at times
　3. Sighting made from inside auto.while moving and stopped. Observed from within and outside auto.

E. Location and details: On the night of 19-20 September between 20/0001 and 20/0100 the observers were traveling by car in a southerly direction on Route 3 south of Lincoln, N.H. when they noticed a brightly lighted object ahead of their car at an angle of elevation of approximately 45°. It appeared strange to them because of its shape and the intensity of its lights compared to the stars in the sky. Weather and sky were clear. They continued to observe the object from their moving car for a few minutes then stopped. After stopping the car they used binoculars at times.
　They report that the object was traveling north very fast. They report it changed directions rather abruptly and then headed South. Shortly thereafter it stopped and hovered in the air. There was no sound evident up to this time. Both observers used the binoculars at this point. While hovering,objects began to appear from the body of the "object" which they describe as looking like wings which made a V shape when extended. The "wings" had red lights on the tips. At this point they observed it to appear to swoop down in the general direction of their auto. The object continued to descend until it appeared to be only a matter of "hundreds of feet" above their car.
　At this point they decided to get out of that area, and fast. Mr. Hill was driving and Mrs. Hill watched the object by sticking her head out the window. It departed in a generally North westerly direction but Mrs. Hill was prevented from observing its full departure by her position in the car.
　They report that while the object was above them after it had "swooped down" heard a series of short loud "buzzes" which they described as sounding like that they could feel these

HEADQUARTERS
817TH AIR DIVISION
United States Air Force
Pease Air Force Base, New Hampshire

REPLY TO
ATTN OF: 100DCOI

SUBJECT: Unidentified Flying Object (UFO)

29 SEP 1961

TO: ATIC
Wright-Patterson AFB
Ohio

Attached is AF Form 112, 100th Bomb Wing report number 100-1-61.
Non-availability of observers for early interrogation precluded
electrical transmission of report.

FOR THE COMMANDER:

E. B. LOBATO
CWO W2, USAF
Substitute or Administrative Service

1 Atch
AF Form 112 & 112a, 3 pgs, 1 cy ea,
w/1 Atch, Extract of Daily Report of
Controller, AACS Form 96, for the date
20 Sep 61, 2 cys

TRUE EXTRACT OF "DAILY REPORT OF CONTROLLER, AACS FORM 96, FOR THE DATE
OF 20 SEPTEMBER 1961.

* * *

0614Z OBSERVED UNIDENTIFIED A/C COME ON PAR 4 MILES OUT. A/C MADE APPROACH AND
PULLED UP AT 1/2 MILE. SHORTLY AFTER OBSERVED WEAK TARGET ON DOWNWIND, THEN
RADAR CTC LOST. TWR WAS ADVISED OF THE A/C WHEN IT WAS ON FINAL, THEN WHEN
IT MADE LOW APPROACH. TWR UNABLE TO SEE ANY A/C AT ANY TIME.....JC

* * *

CERTIFIED TRUE:

ROBERT O. DAUGHADAY
Captain, USAF
Commander

DATA PROCESSING DIVISION
CLIMATIC CENTER, USAF
Air Weather Service (MATS)
Asheville, North Carolina

REPLY TO
ATTN OF: CCDPD

SUBJECT: Copy of Selected Rawinsonde Observations   22 Nov 1961

   TO: Air Force Technical Intelligence Center
       Foreign Technology Division, TD-E
       Wright-Patterson Air Force Base, Ohio

       1. Reference: Your telephone call at 1415 EST 15 Nov 1961.

       2. We are sending copies of rawinsonde observations (WBAN 31 ABC)
       from Portland, Maine, for 17 through 22 Sep 1961.

       3. Lincoln, New Hampshire, does not take rawinsonde observations,
       and Portland, Maine, is the closest station.

   FOR THE DIRECTOR

   Pallas L. Tye
   PALLAS L. TYE, JR.   Atch
   Captain, USAF   Photocopies of Rawinsonde Obs
   Administrative Officer

Information on Barney Hill sighting, 20 September 1961, Lincoln, New Hampshire

    The Barney Hill sighting was investigated by officials from Pease AFB.
The case is carried as insufficient data in the Air Force Files. No direction
(azimuth) was reported and there are inconsistencies in the report. The sighting occurred about midnight and the object was observed for at least one hour.
No specific details on maneuverability were given. The planet Jupiter was in
the South West, at about 20 degrees elevation and would have set at the approximate time that the object disappeared. Without positional data the case could
not be evaluated as Jupiter. There was a strong inversion in the area. The
actual light source is not known. As no lateral or vertical movement was
noted, the object was in all probability Jupiter. No evidence was presented to

plan for
Ryschophysics Experiment

COMMUNICATION

. Today is _____ the _____ day of this year.

. In _____ more days go to _____ in New Hampshire

. Best science men are there.

. Show lights to science men.

. Come close to science men.

. All is safe.

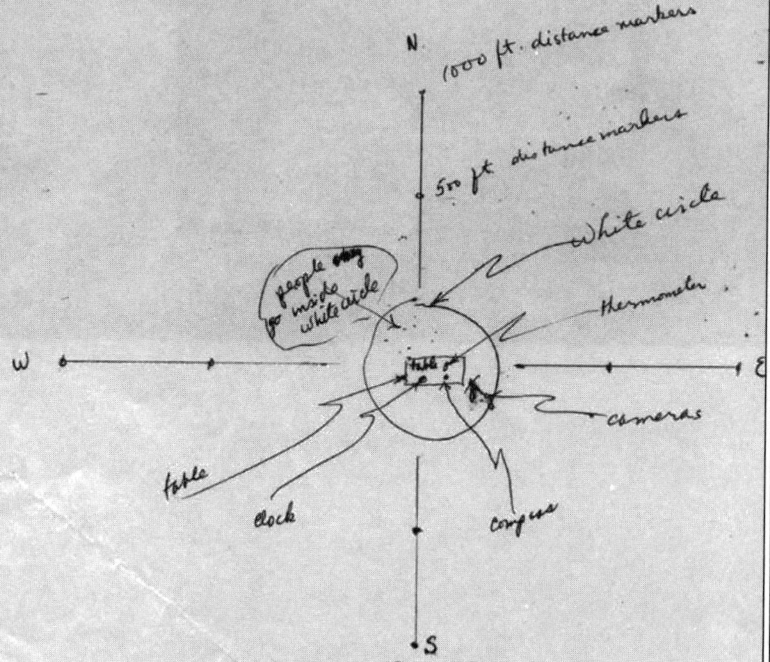

N.

1000 ft. distance markers

500 ft. distance markers

white circle

people may go inside white circle

thermometer

table

cameras

table

clock

compass

W — E

S

Ground Plan

The honor of your presence

is requested at the ceremonies

attending the Inauguration of the

President and Vice President

of the United States

January twentieth

Nineteen hundred sixty-five

B. Everett Jordan, *Chairman*
John Sparkman, Leverett Saltonstall,
John W. McCormack, Carl Albert,
Charles A. Halleck,
Committee on Arrangements.

*Please present the enclosed
card of admission.*

11:30 A.M.

Suncday:

Arrived in Washington, dinner with Carmen at the Dodge Hotel on Capitol
Hill

MONDAY:

Went to U. S. Senate Building to pay our respects to Sentor MacIntire;
Norris Cotton,   Pass to attend Senate from Tom
UnS. House of Representatives to visit Ollie Huot; met his sone David.
Mr. Niswander, administrative aid, and Carmen, Legislative Aide.
Went to a session of the Representatives with them
Lunch at the Represnentatives Dining Room
Tour of the Capital Building
Arlington National Gemetary to the Gravesite of Pres. Kennedy and the
    Tomb of the Unknown Soldier.
Dinner at Harveys - met Mayor of Lansing, Michigan; and Representative
from Pa.

TUESDAY:

Tour of the East Wing of the White House
Lunch at the International Inn with N. H. Peorple - Guv, Senator,
Congressman, their staffs, and N. H. People working in Washington,
Mr. Bill Dunfey, former N. H. National Committeeman
At 6 pm , Champagne party at the Senate Office Building with the
NH Society, organization of 300 N. H. people working in Washington.
    Met James Cleveland, U. S. Repeesantative, who on that day, was
attempting to prevent the seating of a Democratic representative from
N. Y. using the same methods as used by the N. H. Senate in thier
refusal to seat 2 Democratic senators.
Reception for Humphrey
Inaugural Concert with Pres. and vice-Pres. present.
    Others attended the Yound Yeocrats Reception and Dance where Linda
Bird attended, and V. Pres. visited

WEDNESDAY:

OfficInaugural Program
Official Inaugural Ceremony - standing room in the Sanate Section.
Parade - 3 hours.
Cocktail Party in Arlington Va. for all the NH people at Ollie Huot's
place.
Inaugural Ball -
Nightcap with Mayor of Youngstown, Ohio

633 Woodbury Avenue
Portsmouth, N. H.
July 9, 1965

Honorable Austin F. Quinney
Executive Councilor — Second District
148 Front Street
Exeter, New Hampshire

Dear Councilor Quinney:

I have been asked to forward the name of a prominent Negro leader of
Portsmouth for consideration by Governor King as a nominee to the
Human Rights Commission recently formed under a bill passed by the
Legislature and signed by Governor King. It would be of great help
if you could submit his name for the Governor's Consideration and the
approval of the Governor's Council.

Mr. Barney Hill, 394 State Street, Portsmouth, New Hampshire, a Postal
worker, is eminently qualified to serve on the Human Rights Commission
as a representative of the Negro Race.

Mr. Hill is an active member of the Portsmouth Chapter of NAACP now
serving as the Legal Redress Officer. He is presently on the Executive
Board of the New England Regional Chapter of NAACP.

Mr. Hill's sincere interest in human rights has been recognized on the
national level by being appointed to the New Hampshire Advisory Board
of the U.S. Civil Rights Commission.

On the local level Mr. Hill has been very active and effective in con-
vincing his people of the necessity of registering as voters and making
their voice heard by voting in all elections. He is convinced that the
Negroes will take their rightful place in society through the
educational process and steady and persistent pressure.

It is the consensus of the Democratic City Committee that Mr. Hill's
name and qualifications should be submitted to the Governor. We
respectfully request your assistance as Executive Councilor of our
District. We trust that you will concur with our recommendation.

Respectfully yours,

James P. Keenan
Democratic City Chairman

cc: Mr. Hill

Barney — Hope that this will convince the Governor that you will be an excellent choice. Good luck for the future in this work. Sincerely

UNITED STATES COMMISSION ON CIVIL RIGHTS
WASHINGTON, D.C. 20425

May 21, 1965

Mr. Barney Hill
953 State
Portsmouth, New Hampshire

Dear Mr. Hill:

It gives me great pleasure to advise you that the United States
Commission on Civil Rights, at a meeting held May 5, 1965, appointed
you a member of the New Hampshire State Advisory Committee for a term
ending December 31, 1966. I am certain that your participation on
the Committee with other representative citizens of the State will
be a rewarding experience. Please be assured that this office is
always available to assist you and the other members of the Committee in fulfilling your responsibilities.

For your information we are forwarding to you, under separate cover,
a roster of the current membership of the New Hampshire State Advisory
Committee, together with other information relating to the Commission
and Advisory Committee activities which may be of interest to you.

Mr. Louis A. Arnold, Acting Chairman of the New Hampshire Advisory Committee, has been informed of your appointment. He will be contacting
you regarding the time and place of the next Committee meeting. Also,
Mrs. Louise Lewisohn, the Commission's staff representative for your
State, will be in touch with you in the very near future.

With every good wish,

Sincerely yours,

Samuel J. Simmons
Director
Field Services Division

cc:
Mr. Louis A. Arnold
Hon. J. L. Blais, Secretary
Mrs. Louise Lewisohn

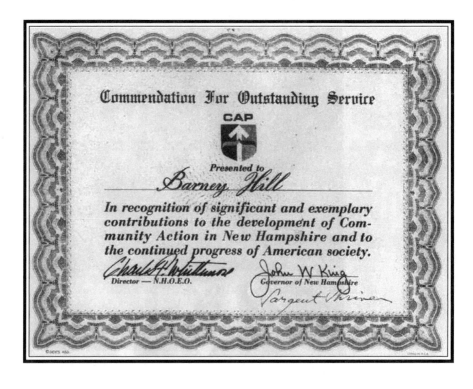

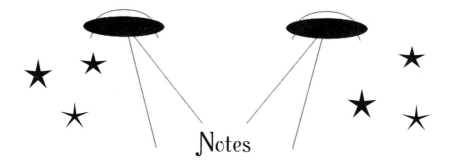

Notes

Chapter 1

1. For detailed information about the history of Pease Air Force Base see *www.globalsecurity.org/military /facility/pease.htm*.

2. Betty Hill's memoirs.

Chapter 2

1. Betty Hill's unpublished memoirs.

Chapter 3

1. Betty Hill's unpublished memoirs.

2. Brummett, p. 5. Also found at *www.cufon.org/afrstdy1.htm*.

3. Correspondence by coauthor with Tim Markle, Chief Meteorologist, MWO.

Chapter 4

1. Information received in personal correspondence with Walter Webb. Additional information taken from Editor Ronald D. Story, *The Encyclopedia of UFOs* (New York: Doubleday & CO., Inc., 1980), p. 391.

2. Notes from coauthor's phone conversation with Hohmann's widow.

Chapter 5

1. Hohmann and Jackson. *www.virtuallystrange.net/ufo/updates/1998/nov/m23-015.shtml*.

2. Sworn Testimony by Ben Swett, notarized certification: "I hereby certify that the foregoing document is a factual account of my interactions with Betty and Barney Hill of Portsmouth, New Hampshire, based on my personal knowledge and extensive notes taken at the time. I further certify that based on my own work with hypnosis and my thorough analysis of the contents of the audio tapes they made under hypnosis, I believe the Hill's experience was real. December 29, 2006. For a complete transcript see *http://bswett.com/1963-09BettyAndBarney.html*.

3. Dr. Stevens's obituary in Betty Hill's files.

4. Betty Hill's unpublished memoirs.

5. Letter from Betty's friend, Adele Fahey, dated November 28, 1966: "Steve Putnam asked if you were mad at him—and I said, 'yes'—that you didn't like him giving that tape to John Luttrell, etc." It has been reported that Putnam denied cooperating with Luttrell.

Chapter 6
1. Dr. Simon's obituary in Betty's files.

2. Ibid. Additional information derived from "Hypnosis in the Treatment of Military Neurosis," *Psychiatric Opinion,* Vol.4: No 5, October 1967, pp. 24–28.

3. Nash and Benham, pp. 48-49.

4. "Dissociative Amnesia." *www.merck.com/mmhe/print/sec07/ch106/ch106b.html.*

5. Hypnosis FAQ—Section 2, *www.Hypnosis.com/faq/faq2-3.html.*

6. "Bizarre Remembrances under Hypnosis," p. 14. *www.Hypnosis.com/faq/faq2-3.html.*

7. Nash and Benham, pp. 5–6.

8. Loftus.

9. Simon, pp. 27–28.

10. Fuller, p. xi.

11. Simon, pp. 27–28.

Chapter 7
1. Barrett.

2. *www.MacAleater.edu/-psych/whathap/UBNRP/nightmares.2005.*

Chapter 9
1. Fuller, Chapter 7.

2. Story, pp. 179–180.

3. Sheaffer.

4. For precise wording, see Chapter 7 in Fuller.

5. Hypnosis audiotape, March 7, 1964. Similar text in Fuller, p. 140.

6. Hypnosis audiotapes, January 29, 1964, and March 7, 1964. Similar text in Fuller, p. 80 and 140.

7. On page 81 in *The Interrupted Journey*, John Fuller quotes Barney's statement as, "And I feel—in the barren hostility of the wooded area...." His precise words were, "And I feel *less* in the barren hostility of the wooded area."

8. Hypnosis audiotape, January 22, 1964. Similar text in Fuller, p. 83.

9. Ibid., p. 90

10. Hypnosis audiotape, January 29, 1964. Similar text in Fuller, p. 90.

Chapter 10

1. Hypnosis audiotape, March 7, 1964. Similar text in Fuller, p.159.

2. Copied from Betty's original typed paper, November, 1961. For a full transcript of "Dreams or Reality?" see the Appendix in Fuller.

3. Hypnosis audiotape, February 29, 1964. Similar text in Fuller, p. 121.

Chapter 11

1. Hypnosis audiotape, February 29, 1964. Similar text in Fuller, pp. 122–123.

2. Hypnosis audiotape, March 7, 1964. Similar text in Fuller, p. 161.

3. Hypnosis audiotape, March 7, 1964. Complete account in Fuller, Chapter 7.

4. *www.Bookrags.com/Amniocentesis*.

5. For additional information, see: *www.Laparoscopyhospital.com, 2001*.

Chapter 12

1. Hypnosis audiotape, March 14, 1964. Similar text in Fuller, pp. 173–174.

2. Ibid., Chapter 8.

3. Ibid., p. 176.

4. Ibid., p. 177.

Chapter 13

1. Hypnosis audiotape, February 22, 1964. Similar text in Fuller, pp. 87–88.

2. "New Drawing of Hill Abductors." Text copied from original letter.

3. Dr. James Harder and Betty Hill, Hypnosis tape, January 19, 1976.

Chapter 14

1. Hypnosis audiotape, March 14, 1964. Similar text in Fuller, p. 178.

2. Hypnosis audiotape, February 29, 1964. Similar text in Fuller, p. 187.

3. Hypnosis audiotape, March 14, 1964.

4. Hypnosis audiotape, February 29, 1964. Similar text in Fuller, pp.124–126.

5. Hypnosis audiotape, March 14, 1964.

6. Hypnosis audiotape, March 21, 1964.

Chapter 15

1. Barney Hill, Post-Hypnosis interview with Dr. Simon.

2. Letter to Walter Webb, September 22, 1965.

Chapter 16
1. *www.ibiblio.org/hyperwar/USN/ships/dafs/APA/apa6.html.*
2. Office Memorandum. Also, *www.PresidentialUFO@Canada.com.*
3. Vallee, p. 123.
4. Keyhoe.
5. Smith, Wilbert B. "Memorandum."
6. Smith, Wilbert. "Sarbacher Interview."
7. Bray, pp. 336–337.
8. Zachary.
9. Smith, Wilbert B. "Memorandum."
10. Ibid.
11. Smith, Wilbert B. "Interim Report."
12. Smith, Wilbert B., "Memorandum." From material by Arthur Bray, David Haisell, and Greg Kanon.

Chapter 18
1. Letter from the Hills' attorney to Simon's attorney, February, 1966.

Chapter 20
1. Vallee, p. 273.

Chapter 22
1. Fish.

Chapter 23
1. *Project Bluebook Special Report Number 14.*
2. Menzel.
3. Condon.
4. McDonald.
5. Hall.
6. Klass, *UFO Abductions*, p. 11.
7. Randi.
8. Clancy, *Abducted*, pp. 19, 20, 26, 41, 51, 52, 95.

Chapter 24
1. Budinger.
2. "Examination of the Stain Area."

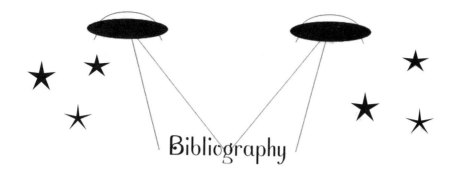

Bibliography

Barrett, D. *Trauma and Dreams.* Cambridge, Mass.: Harvard University Press, 1996. Also, *www.MacAleater.edu/-psych/whathap/UBNRP/nightmares*, November 2005.

Berlitz, Charles, and William Moore. *The Roswell Incident.* New York: Grosset & Dunlap, 1980.

Bickerton, Alexander W. "Presentation to the British Association for the Advancement of Science." 1926.

"Bizarre Remembrances Under Hypnosis." *Hypnosis.com/faq/faq2-3.html*, October 2005.

Bray, Arthur. *The Encyclopedia of UFOs.* Garden City, New York: Doubleday, 1980.

Brummett, Major William E., and Captain Ernest R. Zuick, Jr. "Should the USAF Reopen Project Blue Book?" Air Command and Staff College Research Study, Air University Report No. 0450-74. Alabama: Maxwell AFB, May 17, 1974.

Budinger, Phyllis. "Analysis of the Dress Worn by Betty Hill During the September 19, 1961 Abduction in New Hampshire." October 19, 2003.

Campbell, J.W. "Rocket Flight to the Moon." *Philosophical Magazine,* 7 (31), No. 204, January 1941, pp. 24–34.

Clancy, Susan. *Abducted: How People Come to Believe They Were Kidnapped by Aliens.* Cambridge, Mass.: Harvard University Press, 2005.

Clancy, Susan A., R.J. McNally, D.L. Schacter, M.F. Lenzenweeger, and R.J. Pitman. "Memory Distortion in People Reporting Abduction by Aliens." *Journal of Abnormal Psychology* 111 No. 3. 2002. pp. 455–61.

Collins, Robert, and Richard Doty. *Exempt from Disclosure.* Peregrine Communications, 2005.

Condon, Edward U. *Scientific Study of Unidentified Flying Objects.* Edited by Daniel S. Gillmor. New York: Bantam, 1969.

Dickinson, Terence. *The Zeta Reticuli Incident.* Astromedia. Full color from UFORI, POB 958, Houlton, Maine 04730-0958 $5, 32 pgs, 1974.

———. *Update on the Zeta Reticuli Incident.* UFORI, 1980.

"Dissociative Amnesia." *The Merck Manual.* Second Home Edition. Ch. 10. *http://www.merck.com.*

"Examination of the Stain Area on Betty Hill's 1961 'Abduction Dress.'" Pinelandia Biophysics Laboratory Research Report, January 4, 2002. *http://www.abduct.com/research/r15.htm,* March 2006.

Fowler, Raymond. *Allagash Abductions: Undeniable Evidence of Alien Intervention.* Tigard, Oregon: Wild Flower Press, 1993.

Fish, Marjorie. "Journey Into the Hill Star Map." MUFON UFO Symposium, 1974. *http://www.nicap.dabsol.co.uk/hillmap.html.*

Friedman, Stanton T. "A Scientific Approach to Flying Saucers Behavior." Presented at AIAA Symposium, Los Angeles, 1975. UFORI, POB 958, Houlton, Maine 04730-0958.

———. *Top Secret/Majic,* 2nd Edition. New York: Marlowe & Co., 2005.

Friedman, Stanton T, and B. Ann Slate. "UFO Star Bases Discovered" *SAGA Magazine,* July 1973.

Friedman, Stanton T, and Donald Berliner. *Crash at Corona, 2005 edition.* Paraview, 2nd Edition, Marlowe & Co, 1997.

Fuller, John G. *The Interrupted Journey.* New York: Dial Press, 1966.

Hall, Richard. *The UFO Evidence.* NICAP, 1962.

Henderson, Major Paul W. "Air Intelligence Information Report." 100th Bomb Wing (SAC), Pease Air Force Base, N.H., 1961.

Hendry, Allan. *UFO Handbook: A Guide to Investigating and Reporting UFO Sightings.* New York: Doubleday, 1979.

Hill, Betty. *A Common Sense Approach to UFOs.* Portsmouth, N.H., 1995.

Hohmann, Robert and C.D. Jackson. "An Historic Report on Life in Space." November 1962. *http://www.virtuallystrange.net/ufo/updates/1998/nov/m23-015,* March 2006.

Hopkins, Budd. *Intruders: The Incredible Visitation at Copley Woods.* New York: Ballantine Books, 1987.

———. *Witnessed.* New York: Pocket Books, 1997.

Hopkins, Budd, and Carol Rainey. *Sight Unseen: Science UFO Invisibility & Transgenic Beings.* New York: Atria Books, 2003.

"Hypnosis FAQ—Section 2." *http://www.hypnosis.com/faq/faq2-3.html,* June 2005.

Jacobs, David. *The Threat: Revealing the Secret Alien Agenda.* New York: Simon & Schuster, 1997.

———. Secret Life: *Firsthand Documented Accounts of UFO Abductions.* New York: Simon & Schuster, 1992.

———. *The UFO Controversy in America.* Bloomington, Ind.: Indiana University Press, 1975.

Keyhoe, Major Donald E. *Flying Saucers From Outer Space: The Canadian Project.* New York: Henry Holt, 1953. *http://ufojoe.tripod.com/gov/wbsebk.html,* April 2006.

Klass, Philip J. *UFO Abductions: A Dangerous Game.* Buffalo, N.Y.: Prometheus, 1989.

———. *UFOs Identified.* New York: Random House, 1968.

Kottmeyer, Martin. "Entirely Unpredisposed: The Cultural Background of UFO Abduction Reports." *http://www.debunker.com/texts/unpredis.html*, November 2005.

Loftus, Elizabeth. "Creating False Memories." *Scientific American*, 277(3): 70–75. Also, *http://faculty.washington.edu/eloftus/Articles/sciam.htm*, December 2005.

Lorenzen, C, and J. Lorenzen. *Encounters with UFO Occupants.* New York: Berkley Medallion Books, 1976.

Mack, John. *Abduction: Human Encounters with Aliens.* New York: Macmillan, 1995.

———. *Passport to the Cosmos: Human Transformation and Alien Encounters.* New York: Crown, 1999.

McDonald, James E. "Statement on UFOs." Congressional Hearings, July 29, 1968. From UFORI, POB 958, Houlton, Maine: 04730-0958, 71 pgs. $10.

McNally, R.J. and S.A. Clancy. "Sleep Paralysis, Sexual Abuse and Space Alien Abduction." *Transcultural Psychiatry.* 42(2005.): 113–22,

Menzel, Donald. *Physics Today.* June 1976.

Nash, Michael R, and Grant Benham. "The Truth and Hype of Hypnosis." – *Scientific American Mind*, 16(2), July 2005. 48- 49.

"New Drawing of Hill Abductors." *NICAP UFO Investigator.* Washington, D.C., April 1972 pp. 3–4.

Newcomb, Simon. "Flying Machine." Independent Vol. 55. October 22, 1903. pp. 2508–12

"Office Memorandum." United States Government, Director, FBI, 8/2/54 from SAC, WFO (62-0).

"Project Blue Book Special Report Number 14." UFORI, POB 958. Houlton, Maine: 04730-0958, October 1955.

Randi, James. *Flim Flam.* New York: Prometheus, 1980.

Randle, Kevin, and Donald Schmitt. *The Truth About the UFO Crash at Roswell.* New York: M. Evans and Co., 1994.

———. *UFO Crash at Roswell.* New York: Avon, 1991.

Recollections of Roswell. VHS Video. UFORI, POB 958, Houlton, Maine: 04730-0958, 105 minutes.

Sagan, Carl. *Cosmos.* TV Series. 1980.

———. *Other Worlds.* New York: Bantam Books, 1975.

———. "UFO Abductions." *Parade Magazine*, March 7, 1993.

Schwarz , Berthold Eric. "Talks with Betty Hill: 1-Aftermath of Encounter." *Flying Saucer Review* 23(2), 1977.

Schaefer, Annette. "Commuting Takes its Toll." *Scientific American Mind* 16(3): 2006. pp. 14–15.

Sheaffer, Robert. "The New Hampshire Abduction Explained." *Official UFO Magazine*, August, 1976, p. 43.

Simon, Benjamin. "Hypnosis in the Treatment of Military Neurosis." *Psychiatric Opinion* (4:5), October 1967. pp. 24–28.

Smith, Wilbert. "Sarbacher Interview." September 15, 1950. *http://presidential ufo.com/Sarbacher_interview.htm*, March 2006.

Smith, Wilbert B. "Interim Report on Project Magnet." June 25, 1952.

———."Memorandum to the Controller of Telecommunications." P. 4, November 21, 1950. *http://ufo-joe.tripod.com/gov/wbsebk.html*, March 2006. Reference to articles in *Ottawa Journal*, April 16, 1952; *Toronto Globe & Mail*, April 16, 1952; and *Ottawa Journal*, April 17, 1952.

Story, R.D., ed. *Encyclopedia of UFOs.* Garden City, New York: Doubleday Books, 1980.

Swett, Ben H. "Betty & Barney Hill." *http://bswett.com/1963-09BettyAndBarney.html*, March 2005.

UFOS Are Real. VHS, 93 minutes. UFORI, POB 958, Houlton, Maine: 04730-0958.

Vallee, Jacques. *Forbidden Science Journals 1957–1979*. Berkeley, Calif.: North Atlantic Books.

Walton, Travis. *Fire in the Sky: The Travis Walton Story.* New York: Marlowe & Co., 1997.

Webb, Walter. "A Dramatic UFO Encounter in the White Mountains, N.H." Confidential NICAP Report, October 26, 1961.

———. "A Dramatic Encounter in the White Mountains: The Hill Case." Final NICAP Report. August 30, 1965.

Zachary, G. Pascal. "Vannevar Bush Backs the Bomb." *1992 Bulletin of the Atomic Scientists*. December, 1992, 48(10), pp. 24–31.

Internet Resources

www.abduct.com/research/r15.htm, June 2005.

bswett.com/1963-09BettyAndBarney.html, March 2005.

www.Bookrags.com/sciences/sciencehistory/amniocentesis-woi.html, Amniocentesis/History, August 2005.

www.cufon.org/cufon/afrstdy1.htm, November 2005.

/www.debunker.com/texts/unpredis.html, February 2005.

faculty.washington.edu/eloftus/Articles/sciam.html, February 2005.

www.globalsecurity.org/military/facility/pease.htm, January 2005.

Hypnosis.com/faq/faq2-3.html, June 2005.

Hypnosis FAQ-Section 2, Hypnosis.com/faq/faq2-3.html, June 2005.

www.ibiblio.org/hyperwar/USN/ships/dafs/APA/apa6.html, November 2005.

www.MacAleater.edu/-psych/whathap/UBNRP/nightmares, November 2005.

www.madsci.org/posts/archives/1999-09/938402041.Es.r.html, April 2006.

www.merck.com/mmhe/print/sec07/ch106/ch106b.html, June 2005.

www.nicap.dabsol.co.uk/hillmap.htm, March 2006.

www.srh.noaa.gov/jetstream/remote/ua.htm, March 2006.

www.ua.nws.noaa.gov/factsheet.htm, March 2006.

ufo-joe.tripod.com/gov/wbsebk.html, March 2006 (from material by Arthur Bray, David Haisell, and Greg Kanon).

www.virtuallystrange.net/ufo/updates/1998/nov/m23-015, February 1999.

www.stantonfriedman.com, December 2005.

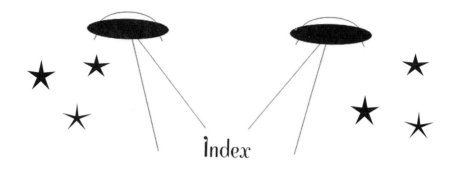

Index

About the Authors

Stanton T. Friedman

Nuclear physicist and lecturer Stanton T. Friedman grew up in Linden, New Jersey, spent two years at Rutgers University, and then received his B.S. and M.S. degrees in physics from the University of Chicago in 1955 and 1956. He was employed for 14 years as a nuclear physicist by such companies as GE, GM, Westinghouse, TRW Systems, Aerojet General Nucleonics, and McDonnell-Douglas, working in such highly advanced, classified, and eventually cancelled programs as nuclear aircraft, fission and fusion rockets, and various compact nuclear power plants for space applications.

He became interested in UFOs in 1958, and since 1967 has lectured about them at more than 600 colleges and 100 professional groups in 50 states, nine provinces, and 16 other countries, in addition to various consulting efforts. He has published more than 80 UFO papers and has appeared on hundreds of radio and TV programs. He is the original civilian investigator of the Roswell Incident and coauthored *Crash at Corona: The Definitive Study of the Roswell Incident. Top Secret/Majic*, his controversial book about the Majestic 12 group established in 1947 to deal with alien technology, was published in 1996 and went through six printings. A new edition was published in 2005. Stan was presented with a Lifetime UFO Achievement Award in Leeds, England, in 2002 by *UFO Magazine* of the UK.

He has provided written testimony to Congressional hearings, appeared twice at the UN, and been a pioneer in many aspects of ufology, including Roswell; Majestic 12; The Betty Hill-Marjorie Fish star map work; analysis of the Delphos, Kansas, physical trace case; crashed saucers; flying saucer technology; and challenges to the S.E.T.I. (Silly Effort To Investigate) cultists.

Stanton T. Friedman is a dual citizen of the United States and Canada, and may be contacted at:

79 Pembroke Crescent

Fredericton, NB, Canada E3B 2V1

(506) 457-0232

fsphys@rogers.com

www.stantonfriedman.com.

Kathleen Marden

Kathleen was trained as a social scientist and educator, and holds a B.A. degree from the University of New Hampshire. She participated in graduate studies in education at the University of Cincinnati and University of New Hampshire. During her 15 years as an educator, she innovated, designed, and implemented model educational programs. She also held a supervisory position, coordinating, training, and evaluating education staff. Additionally, she taught adult education classes on UFO and abduction history.

She was 13 years old on September 20, 1961, when Betty Hill phoned her nearby home to report that, the previous evening, she and Barney had encountered a flying saucer in New Hampshire's White Mountains. A primary witness to the evidence of the UFO encounter and the aftermath, Kathleen has intimate knowledge of the Hills' biographical histories, personalities, and the never-beforepublished historical data pertaining to their sensational story.

Because Kathy was so close to Betty Hill, especially over the last two decades of her life, she was able to review her extensive UFO files and have many long discussions with Betty to clear up puzzling questions pertaining to her UFO encounter. She recorded hours of taped interviews with Betty, and the two made several research trips through New Hampshire's White Mountains. Additionally, in 1996, Betty released to Kathy the audiotapes of the hypnosis sessions she and Barney participated in with renowned psychiatrist, Dr. Benjamin Simon. With Betty's approval, she transcribed the tapes and conducted a comparative analysis of the Hills' individual testimony.

For 10 years Kathy served on the MUFON board of directors as the director of field investigator training. In 2003, MUFON publicly recognized Kathy for her outstanding contribution of advancing the scientific study of the UFO phenomenon and demonstrating positive leadership. She has written articles for the *MUFON Journal* and the book *Best UFO Cases*, and published a professional paper on the use and misuse of hypnosis in UFO abduction investigations. Additionally, she has appeared individually and with Betty on local news programs, The History Channel, and The Discovery Channel.

Kathy, who resides in New Hampshire with her husband, Charles, can be contacted by writing to:

P.O.Box 93

East Kingston, N.H. 03827

Kmarden@aol.com.